THE SEAFARERS

The
SEAFARERS

A History of Maritime America 1620–1820

by Robert Carse

ILLUSTRATED BY RAY HOULIHAN

Bonanza Books • New York

LIBRARY OF CONGRESS CATALOG CARD NUMBER: 62-14523

This edition published by Bonanza Books,
a division of Crown Publishers, Inc.,
by arrangement with Harper & Row,
Publishers, Incorporated.
A   B   C   D   E   F   G   H

This for—

Bill Dobbs, and in memory
of the maiden voyage of the sloop Elena

4/14

CONTENTS

ACKNOWLEDGMENTS

This is to express my gratitude to the people who have so generously helped me with the preparation of the present book. They are: Mrs. Amy O. Bassford, Librarian of the Long Island Collection of the East Hampton Free Library, East Hampton, New York; Garry A. Stolzberg, Vice-President of the Commercial Bank of North America; Horace P. Beck, Middlebury College, Middlebury, Vermont; Charles A. Brooks, General Manager of the Mystic Seaport, Mystic, Connecticut; Carl Carmer, Irvington-on-Hudson, New York, for the loan of a number of volumes from his private library; Howard I. Chapelle, Curator of Division of Transportation, Smithsonian Institution, Washington, D.C., for his counsel; Mrs. Hester F. Cheney, Chief Librarian of the East Hampton Free Library, for her continued assistance; James Dugan, Philadelphia, Pennsylvania, for his counsel and the loan of books from his private library; Andrew Fiske, Shelter Island, New York, for the loan of various books, documents and memorabilia belonging to his family; Robert Keene, for his continued support of my work in any capacity demanded of him; Miss Alice McQuaid, Supervising Librarian of the Muhlenberg Branch of the New York Public Library, for her continued assistance; Donald H. Mugridge, Specialist in American History, the Library of Congress, Washington, D.C., for his counsel; Mrs. Arnold H. Rattray, East Hampton, New York, for her counsel; Edward Rattray, for the loan of volumes from his private library; Mrs. Alvah B. Small, Assistant Librarian, the Maine Historical Society, Portland, Maine; Edouard A. Stackpole, Curator of the Marine Historical Association, Mystic Seaport, Mystic, Connecticut; M. S. Wyeth, Jr., the editor of this book; and, last, my wife, whose help has been immeasurable.

Creek Cottage   R. C.
Shelter Island, New York

THE SEAFARERS

CHAPTER ONE

THE SEA AND THE FOREST

They were all made weary by the sea, and most of them, after two months aboard the overcrowded ship in gale weather, had come to fear and hate it. The land fascinated them. They stood close together against the rail of *Mayflower* as the ship shortened sail and moved slowly among the shoals off Cape Cod.* But this country that they were to call New England they found bitter, inhospitable and, in November, 1620, about to be gripped by winter.

The people were from the villages and farms of Middlesex, the county that contained the northwest part of London, and from London itself, and from Southampton, and from Leyden, in Holland, where a number of them had been forced to take refuge from the religious persecution that was sweeping England. Desire to worship in freedom, along with fear of the sea, formed their one common bond. Merchants, farmers and small artisans, the sea was as alien to them as the strange land they had now reached.

The beaches inshore bore a thin crust of ice. Frost had flecked the low, scrub growth, and sea birds, tern, gulls and a few ducks, which seemed to be the only inhabitants, cried flat-toned when the ship's longboat was put in the water and sent to explore what is

* For the sake of clarity all place names are modern.

1

today Provincetown harbor. The longboat came back without much to report. Darkness was close, and *Mayflower* anchored for the night.

Cooking fires were started in the sand-bottomed boxes in the waist of the ship. Salt beef was heated, and salt fish, and served along with bitter beer and biscuit riddled by worms. The women and the children returned to their crude little cabins at the foreside of the poop and the men to their quarters in the half deck, right above the main hold. They slept uncomfortably jammed together. Some of the men, because of lack of space, crawled into the ship's second boat, the shallop, which was stowed in the main hold.

Mayflower was heavily laden. She carried household furniture, domestic utensils, provisions in bulky hogsheads, 102 people and dogs, goats, pigs and chickens. She weighed only 180 tons, was stubby and high-sided, and there was no sanitary facility aboard her except wooden buckets. She had been in the wine trade between England and the Mediterranean ports before she was engaged for the New England voyage. When the longboat crew was downwind from her she gave them a fine, ripe reek.

There were Pilgrim prayers the next morning, although no more than forty-one of the people belonged to the sect. The rest were mainly Church of England, with a few from the Puritan wing. Five were hired men, and there were eighteen indentured servants. A good deal of grumbling went on among the latter; the Pilgrim leaders, John Carver, William Bradford, William Brewster, Edward Winslow and Thomas Weston, were openly determined to hold control of the colony. But they had no legal patent to any land along the coast here and very little knowledge of it.

Captain John Smith had sailed this coast in 1614, and a few years before him several other English shipmasters and the great French explorer-seaman, Samuel de Champlain, had cruised along it. The reports about the region were in the main still vague, though, and Thomas Weston, one of the principal negotiators in the procurement of the patent for the colony in Virginia, suspected the validity of the deed. So the leaders of the *Mayflower* people decided to make their New World home here and take care of patent matters when life ashore had been established.

They told those who opposed the choice that there was no time left to seek another site. Cape Cod was not Virginia. The leaders understood the fact quite clearly; the ship was well north of her intended course. But the threat of winter was severe. The people must leave the ship almost immediately and set up shelter for themselves somewhere close on the land.

The ship's carpenter took over the grumbling. He said so many people had slept hip to thigh in the shallop, stowed in three sections, that her frames were warped. She was lopsided, unseaworthy. It would take him days to put her in shape. He started at his work, and meanwhile the principal men aboard *Mayflower* gathered together in solemn meeting. They drew up a covenant, a document they called The Compact.

They were a strange group, lacking unity and common purpose. The Pilgrims, extremists in their religious views, had lived as exiles in Holland for ten years and had broken almost all ties with England. They had needed financial backing to be able to colonize the New World, and that had been supplied by London merchants, who had sent along the other people to fill out the complement of settlers. Still the entire group hoped to frame such "just and equall lawes" that the colony would live in peace and flourish. The covenant was carefully signed and John Carver, one of the most respected men among the Pilgrims, elected governor. He was given great authority, which he did not hesitate to use. But for the first ten days on the coast nobody went far from the ship.

Firewood was gathered on the beach. Fresh water was brought out in casks in the longboat. Women washed clothes and themselves and their children. Cargo stowage was changed so that stores and equipment could be put ashore quickly when the time came to establish the settlement. Though the land, this new continent, had become a compelling attraction, it was still just out of reach, and the longboat could only be used when the tide was high.

People became greatly impatient. A number of them waded ashore to the beach. They floundered through the mud flats and shallows, the women with their thick woolen skirts and many petticoats lifted around their knees, the men in their floppy breeches and knee-high boots heavily wallowing, splashing. The water was chill and the beach exposed; there was little shelter among the stunted trees beyond. Wet, shivering, they returned to the ship with the first of the germs that before the winter was over were to kill half of the company. They were already weakened by a poor diet, long confinement, dysentery and common colds. There was not much that Samuel Fuller, a Pilgrim doctor, or the ship's surgeon, Dr. Giles Heale, could do.

When the shallop was put in shape a scout party took her and sailed along the coast to the sandy bluffs at Truro. The men went ashore and dug into Indian corn hills, thoughtlessly opened graves, poked around abandoned wigwams. They were very lucky not to have been attacked by local Nauset braves. A snowstorm that lasted a day and a night blew while they were out, and they were gone from the ship four days, returning with a good description of the Pamet River and Indian ways of life.

Miles Standish led a large party from the ship on December 16, sailed alongshore with them in the shallop. They explored Wellfleet harbor, moved on westward, and on the next day, at present-day Eastham, were attacked by Indians. The fighting began with the rise of the dawn light in traditional Indian style, and all the arrows fired were wide of target, and the scout party proved themselves just as poor marksmen as the Nausets. Nobody was hurt on either side.

Miles Standish got his people back into the shallop, and sail was hoisted and she went with a stiffening breeze further along the coast. The excitement of the fight, the first sight of the natives in their soot-darkened buckskins and moccasins did not last long as the wind continued to freshen. Waves broke rough and hard here in the offshore shallows, and the day was very cold. The boat would soon take a dangerous sheath of ice.

First, though, the rudder carried away, and the men steered with the oars. Then a heavy gust of wind hit the loose-bottomed hemp sail. It swept billowing and slapping over the side and off to leeward. The shallop was about to enter the difficult channel into Plymouth harbor. Men must have stared at the shore and wondered if they would reach it. But the tide was on the rise and carried them through the entrance, and in the final dusk glimmer they were able to anchor in the protection of what was to be called Clark's Island.

Two days later they had explored the shore enough to know that this would be the site of Plymouth Plantation. Carver was in the scout party, and it was his decision, supported by Winslow and Standish. They went back to *Mayflower* the same day, under jury sail. She rode to her anchor with her usual broad-beamed roll, and they found her familiar and reassuring, surrounded by a circle of noisy gulls.

Mayflower brought her anchor up, spread canvas and moved to Plymouth harbor. It was December 26. She had been for five weeks off Cape Cod and outside Provincetown. Fourteen weeks ago she had left England.

The men began to build the settlement as fast as they could. The site for it was along a brook whose mouth gave them a good landing for their boats. Up the hill, where there had been Indian cornfields, they ran the line of their main street. This they called Leyden, in memory of the Pilgrims' stay in that city. Down at the foot of the street they built their Common House. They hoped to place in regular rows beside the length of the street their own dwellings, and they worked from dawn to dark cutting, hauling and trimming timber.

But in the cramped quarters aboard *Mayflower* people died one after another of grippe and pneumonia. The infections spread rapidly among the ship's company. The boats were put into use to bring the people ashore, save them from too close contact.

People died shoulder to shoulder on the pallets stretched over the floor of the Common House. Quite often, no more than seven or eight of the company were able to walk and tend to the dying or bury the dead. Men gazed bleakly out at the sea they had come to hate. It was the vast, cruel barrier between them and England; crossing it had weakened those who died of their needed strength.

The men turned from the sea. They went up the hill along Town Brook past the miserable little plank and sod huts. Snow stopped them beyond, and the forest. They gazed long at the forest. They knew that for them it was supposed to represent wealth.

Timber was to be taken from it, just as the Pilgrim leaders had once proposed, before the voyage, to take fish from the sea. But the forest was an endless and mysterious trap. Indians skulked at the edges of it. Hunting parties from the settlement that had dared go in among the immense stands of trees had met a formidable array of beasts.

Elk lurched through the forest shadows, grayish brown and seeming huge, the points of the wide-branched antlers as sharp as any spear. Moose of really enormous size had been seen at the rims of ponds and snow-clogged berry patches, the overhanging snouts atremble with excited breathing under the antler spread. Black bears had been roused from seasonal sleep beneath fallen trees by the unwary, who had fled for the village, and at night the scream of the panther was answered by the howling of wolves. The wolves seldom moved except in pairs or packs, and veteran soldiers like Miles Standish considered them a serious menace to the community.

Men who had known the English forests well were made timid by this one. The stands of trees were so high and strong that they would resist any attempt to fell them for generations to come. This forest was nearly impenetrable. No road could be cleared through it without incalculable cost. Settlements built inside it could expect attack from wild beasts and Indians. What timber Plymouth needed might be taken from the splendid oaks, pines, hemlocks and spruces at the edges.

The settlers looked out to sea again, and it reached gray, hard under the pale winter sun toward England. However, there was no possibility of return to England, even if easterly passage had been arranged aboard *Mayflower*. All chances of living in the home country were gone. Home was here, the New World, between the barriers of sea and forest.

Men who had farmed the land at home in England knelt down at Plymouth and groped beneath the snow. They dug loose bits of soil and examined them, crumbled the frost-stiff earth against their fingers. It was thin, poor loam, laced with gravel and sand. Nothing but miserable crops would be taken from it.

The Plymouth men who inspected the soil stood still on the hillside, no doubt, as the realization came to them. The sea in all likelihood became more immense in the east, and the forest appeared to fill the western sky. Total defeat was very close for them. But hope endured, and in the early spring the Indian warrior came to the settlement.

He came alone from the open sea in March, the month of great storms, paddling a canoe made of birch bark. The thick-shouldered Atlantic rollers pitched the craft until he was within the lee of the dunes on Long Beach. Then he steered his course steadily through the tortuous channel between the shoals and the grassy flats into Plymouth harbor.

Most of the men who were well enough to stand were in the Common House, called to a meeting to discuss plans for the military defense of the colony that had been proposed by Miles Standish. When lookouts reported the Indian the meeting broke up, and the members, amazed, hurried out into the street. They watched him beach his canoe at high-water mark on the beach and walk calmly up the street toward them.

"Welcome!" he called to the gaunt Englishmen outside the Common House.

His name was Samoset, he said. He was a Tarrantine sachem, from a tribe in central Maine, and was on the coast here to visit a friend, Massasoit, sachem of the Wampanoag tribe, who lived forty miles away at the mouth of the Taunton River on Narragansett Bay.

The Plymouth people had since their arrival seen no Indians except a few skulkers who circled the settlement at a distance. He was

the first warrior to walk among them and the first they had heard
speak even broken English.

Governor Carver, Miles Standish and the master of the *Mayflower,*
Christopher Jones, asked him how he knew their language and how
he dared venture into the village and sail in such a craft across the
March sea. Samoset answered that he had made friends with a
number of men in the crews aboard the English fishing boats that
cruised the Maine coast. It was they who had taught him bits of
their language. About the canoe, that was the only kind of craft
used by the Tarrantine tribes. He told the Englishmen that before
setting out on his visit to Massasoit he had fished offshore, and he
confirmed what was hard for them to believe. He had made the
voyage from Monhegan Island to Narragansett Bay by himself, hand-
lining for cod along the way. But now he was thirsty, he said. Might
he have some beer to drink?

Beer had run out of supply months ago in the Plymouth Colony.
There was, though, "strong water" that still remained, and Governor
Carver was quick to order it brought, and biscuit, butter, cheese
and a piece of mallard duck. Samoset wore only a breechclout and
moccasins, and across his back was his beautifully worked arrow
quiver; he carried with unconscious ease the five-and-a-half-foot
long bow.

Miles Standish and the master of the *Mayflower* gave him great
attention. They both knew that Monhegan Island was well over a
hundred miles away to the northward, off Boothbay on the Maine
coast. It would take a most extraordinarily skillful sailor to make the
voyage alone in a birchbark canoe. But there was no reason to doubt
Samoset. The muscles of the powerful shoulders and arms rippled
with the slightest exertion. The eyes within their crescents of yellow
paint were keen, narrowed by years of regard of danger and vast
sea distances. He wore three eagle feathers in his lank black hair,
his right as a sachem, and yet without them he would be unmistak-
ably chieftain of his tribe. Samoset rested quietly in the muddy,
rutted snow of the street. He was the calmest man there, at absolute ease.

When he was finished with the food and drink, he thanked Carver, and the governor bowed to him, offered him a coat to wear. Samoset accepted it and drew it about his shoulders. He must have sensed the extreme interest that some of these men had in his canoe, for right afterward he went with the group to the beach and showed them the craft.

John Clark, the pilot of the *Mayflower,* stood beside his captain. The other officers and the bosuns and the bosuns' mates and quartermasters joined him. Captain Jones had sailed for years in northern waters, but the pilot had more local experience. Clark had cruised this coast before, had been a settler in the Virginia colony, then was made a prisoner and held hostage by the Spaniards. It was Clark who asked Samoset most of the questions about the canoe.

Birchbark was the only material used for the hull covering. The pieces were fitted together cleverly, with a fir gum calk over the seams. Fir roots no bigger than a man's little finger served as a lacing that secured the covering to the gunwale poles. Those were of beech wood, and the horizontal slats that supported the frame were of cedar. The canoe was about eighteen feet in length, with a two-foot beam. The depth amidships brought the gunwales up to a man's armpits when he was seated in it.

A harpoon with a quartz head and a hickory haft were most likely in the canoe, and a spear that carried a point fashioned from deerhorn. The codlines were of hemp, coarse, loose stuff, and the hooks attached to them laboriously fashioned from various kinds of shell. But some of the gray, red-speckled fish lying frozen on the bottom slats weighed at least a hundred pounds. Samoset offered part of the catch as a gift before he said he must be on his way back to his friends at Narragansett Bay.

Mayflower sailors carried the canoe to the water's edge and launched it for him. He went aboard with casual grace, seated himself, lifted the paddle and in the late afternoon light, now almost dusk, started out from the dark shore. The canoe left a luminous, narrow wake, and the paddle dripped silver.

The Plymouth people stood silent. There was nobody among them, not even from the crew of the *Mayflower,* who could handle a craft like that. Samoset represented independence and freedom, a completely different life. He showed them that they need not fear the sea. It was not the vast and terrible barrier the settlers had believed it to be. He put out from Plymouth harbor in the same way a Middlesex farmer would walk the lane at home, and the significance of his feat was not lost on those who watched the departure.

Samoset was back in several days, this time striding from the forest with Indian companions. They brought beaver skins, fine, smooth pelts, and the Pilgrims were very content. Barter was made, and Samoset left to return again later with a local Indian. The man was a tragic and yet buoyant figure, a warrior named Tisquantum, called Squanto by the English.

Squanto was the last survivor of his tribe, the Patuxets, who had lived here at the site of Plymouth for centuries. There had been more than two hundred of them when young Captain Martin Pring came along the coast in June, 1603, and ventured ashore with some of his crew and two great mastiff dogs, Fool and Gallant. The dogs cavorted, leaping in the shallows, and the Indian folk stood in awe of them; they had never before seen such beasts. Soon, though, they became friendly with the English.

One of Pring's crew, luckily, was skilled at playing the gittern, and had brought the instrument ashore from the ship. Pring reported in his account of the voyage:

"We had a youth in our company that could play upon a gittern, in whose homely music they took great delight and would give him many things, as tobacco, tobacco-pipes, snakes' skins six foot long which they used for girdles, fawns' skins and suchlike. And danced twenty in a ring, and the gittern in the midst of them, using many savage gestures, singing Jo, Ja, Jo, Ja, Ja, Jo; him that first brake the ring the rest would knock and cry upon."

It must have been a remarkable scene, the sun-warmed beach, the nearly naked, tall Indian warriors leaping and gesticulating and crying out, the stocky English youth at the center of the ring with his crude form of guitar, the big mastiffs in random chase along the

sand, and Pring and the rest of his crew, a little anxious but more pleased and amused, close to the dancers. Squanto could not have forgotten that, even seventeen years later.

He very likely recalled also that Pring's men sampled the Indian gardens when the dancing was done and took some vegetables with them, including a large amount of sassafras and a canoe for which they bartered and which they called a wherry. The name of Pring's ship was *Discoverer*. She sailed with the ebb tide, on a slant of southwesterly wind.

Squanto remembered very clearly what happened years afterward, in 1614. Another English ship came into the harbor at Plymouth. But she had aboard no man like Martin Pring. Her master was Thomas Hunt, who was supposed to carry a cargo of fish from Monhegan Island to Europe for Captain John Smith. He proposed, however, to do a bit of business on his own account before he obeyed orders.

His crew, armed with cutlasses and muskets, gathered together twenty Patuxet warriors on the beach. The Indians were pitched into a boat, taken aboard the ship, put in irons and sent into the hold. Then the ship sailed and on her way outward-bound stopped again off Eastham, on Cape Cod. There the crew caught seven more warriors, and they were slung into the hold along with Squanto and the rest of the Patuxet people.

Hunt sold the lot at Málaga, made a deal with the Spaniards "for 20 £ to a Man." The Indians were separated, and Squanto came to know alone the hot, noisome cell of his prison at Málaga, then the terrible prison of the Casa de Contratación at Seville. But good luck was with him. Jesuit friars singled him out as a man to be redeemed and freed. English merchants lived in Seville, and he was entrusted to their mercy, sent by them in a ship to England.

Squanto lived then for several years in the home of John Slany, a merchant adventurer and an officer of the Newfoundland Company. He educated the warrior, and in turn Squanto gave him great information about his homeland. Slany let him go in 1618, got him passage aboard a ship bound for Newfoundland. A trading voyage to

New England was being prepared there, and Squanto's worth as a pilot was recognized. Captain Thomas Dermer took Squanto with him when he sailed south and carried the warrior home.

But Squanto returned to absolute desolation and disaster. His tribe was gone, wiped out by the mysterious disease which for three years, 1616 to 1619, had ravaged the Indian tribes all along the New England coast as far as northern Maine. No proof of its origin was known, although Europeans reported Indians with weltlike splotches on their faces and signs of fever before death, and while some of them slept in the same wigwams with Indians, none of them was infected.

Weeds grew in the Patuxet cornfields. Canoes rotted above high-water mark, abandoned and unclaimed. Fishweirs had been smashed by tidal drift ice. Further inshore, where the people had built their wigwams of saplings and bark slabs, a litter of bones lay among the ruins. There had been, toward the end, no attempt to bury the dead. Squanto turned his face away and went to stay with the Wampanoag survivors at Narragansett Bay.

No more than five thousand Indians were still alive in the area from Gloucester to New Bedford. There had originally been about a hundred thousand people there. For twenty miles inland the desolation spread, and the survivors could only blame the white man, who had brought with him his plague.

Still Squanto could not keep away from Plymouth. It was his home, and in his years of European exile he must have countless times thought of the bay gleaming in summer sunlight, the sea birds in busy flight over the salt marshes where the boys caught crabs, the sloping hillside fields beyond, the cluster of wigwams and the great, green forest that seemed to stretch forever toward the west. He had played football on this beach, run and blocked and kicked with the other young warriors, been in matches that lasted over into the next day. And here he had danced to the gittern plucked by the sailor from *Discoverer* and shouted himself hoarse. Englishmen had for the most part treated him well. He trusted them. He spoke their language with ease.

When Samoset returned to the settlement with Squanto he brought Massasoit, the Wampanoag sachem, for a ceremonial visit. Muskets were fired in salute, trumpets flourished, "a tucket of drums" was sounded, and many gifts were exchanged. Peace was established between red man and white. Massasoit and his warriors went back to Narragansett Bay, and Samoset returned home to Maine. It was Squanto's impulse, though, to stay on at Plymouth.

Squanto gave the settlers much of their knowledge about the forest, the crops that could be grown in the region, and the sea. He told them how to plant, with a codfish and a handful of kelp for each hill of corn and more kelp along the rows. With the progress of spring he took certain men to the edge of the forest. He pointed out to them the trees that were right for use as the hull of a dugout canoe. The best were oak, chestnut and pine.

Canoes would be needed soon, he explained, if the colonists wanted to make the alewife catch. The plump, round-bellied fish would appear along the coast in late spring and early summer in countless swarms to spawn. And with canoes, cod and mackerel and half a dozen other kinds of fish could be caught offshore.

The settlers sweated in the early spring sunlight as they felled the trees for their canoes. There was no birchbark here, such as Samoset's people used further north, so the work was considerably more difficult. It had been the fashion of the Patuxet tribe to fell the trees with a girdle of fire at the base, then hollow out the logs by applying hot stones to char the wood. That process had lasted at least ten days. But the Englishmen, with their saws and axes and mauls and chisels, performed the work in half the time.

They fashioned out broad, rather clumsy craft with knobby bow and stern ends, set thwarts along the length, chopped and whittled paddles. The Indian-derived word "canoe" was unfamiliar to them, so they called what they had built wherries, and they built them big enough to hold a dozen or fifteen men or a fine catch of fish.

The idea of the alewives seized the settlers' imagination. The farmers among them had made known to the others that the soil here would never yield large crops. The land was also under the control of a few men, the chief stockholders of the company, according to the terms of the charter, and now, with the arrival of spring, the fact was sharply realized. The poorer people, very much in the majority, had come to understand that unless a man owned a large share of land his one chance to make a living was to harvest the sea.

It was the one way to escape the trap in which he found himself. He could not yet penetrate the forest barrier and must go to the sea, learn to deal with her dangers. The alewife would provide food for the settlement and would bring a fair price in the market in England. A big catch would mean the ability to bargain for a place in a deep-water boat, to sail north for the prime sea haul of cod.

Weirs were built in preparation of the alewife run. They were tri-angular-shaped formations of saplings driven into the shallows of the shore along the bay, where, it was hoped, the alewife would blunder and stay until captured. Hand nets were made, and seine nets, and wicker baskets to hold the catch. Men practiced the use of their canoes. A lookout was kept as the time approached, and for several nights there was little sleep. The promise of a rich harvest right here in Plymouth harbor was almost unbelievable.

When the alewives arrived, they entered the bay and the creeks and backwaters by the millions. The canoes were soon filled to the gunwales, and the silver, thrashing cargo was heaped on the beach. Weirs strained with the weight of the trapped fish, and young indentured boys waded out at low tide and scooped them up with their hands. Women walked the creeks and backwaters waist-deep, flinging the fish into their aprons, skirts and petticoats.

People slipped on fish as they staggered in their haste along the shore. The village dogs were tired of snapping at the heaps, and lay exhausted. But the harvest was not complete. Men worked on through the night by the light of torches, hands raw from contact with the gills and fins, hungry, giddy, yet reluctant to stop.

The entire harvest took several days. Most of the fish were around fifteen inches in length and weighed about a pound when cleaned. The Plymouth people, working as fast as possible, could not save all that they brought ashore. But when the catch was cleaned, packed and finally sold the colony would realize a solid profit. For the first time in their lives many of the men sensed the power of money. They would be able to bargain and barter, and across their minds must have passed the memory of Samoset, alone on the sea, confident and unafraid.

The shallop from *Mayflower* was put in good condition. A complement of fishermen was chosen, some former farmers now without crops to till, some merchants with nothing to sell, both forced by necessity to learn a new and dangerous trade. The shallop was provisioned and equipped with lines, hooks and bait. The crew boarded her. She was cheered by those left behind, and then she set sail for the Grand Banks and cod.

CHAPTER TWO

THE SEA CALLS

For nearly a century now, since around 1500, Devon and East Anglia ports had sent as many as fifty craft a year to fish for cod along the Newfoundland coast. Their vessels had also sailed much more recently off the coast of Maine. Each weekday in any English coastwise town there was the sale on the quay of cod and mackerel, plaice, turbot, sole, skate, whiting and sturgeon. Tough Scottish seamen from Peterhead took their chances hunting whale off Greenland and came home with filled holds and casks.

They and the men from the English ports fought stubbornly with the hardy Dutch, French, Spanish and Portuguese fishermen. The others had controlled and worked for centuries the fishing grounds that reached from the North Cape of Norway all the way across the North Atlantic to Newfoundland and Nova Scotia and the cold, rich waters of the Labrador Current off Maine and Massachusetts.

Here were quite likely the finest sailors ever to go aboard a vessel. They lived on the Grand Banks for month after month, in chill, thick fog, among icebergs as high as mountains, set upon by gales, sleetstorms, hurricanes and squalls for which they had no warning except their own senses, and sleeping or working almost constantly wet, their food the half-rotten remains of salt meat, stale biscuit and beer carried with them from their home ports in Europe or England.

17

and decided to outfit more ships for the Maine trade. The same decision was reached in the West of England ports and even in fever-plagued Jamestown, in Virginia, where supplies were short.

English initiative represented by the Plymouth Company sent two vessels in May, 1607, to found a fishing colony on the Maine coast. One was a shallow-draft flyboat named *Gift of God,* the other a full ship named *Mary and John.* The crews from them went ashore at the mouth of the Kennebec, and on the west side, where the river almost forms an island, they built cabins, a church and storehouses and set up a stockade. They also built under the direction of their chief carpenter, a Londoner named Digby, "a pretty pinnace" of thirty tons which they christened *Virginia,* in hopes that she would enter the coastwise trade.

The rigors of the Maine winter and the menace of the primeval forest at their backs dispirited them, and in the spring they went home. No other large-scale attempt at settlement was made for some time on the coast, and only fishing stations were maintained. These were established on Monhegan Island, on Damariscove and at Pemaquid Point.

Stages were set up where the split fish lay white under the sun. The catch, as it was brought in from the fleet, was split, gutted, doused in the big salt boxes called kenches, then spread to dry. Salt and dried cod was the principal item of the European diet and in great, growing demand. The people who ran the fishing stations also traded with the Indians for furs and made a fine additional profit. During the early 1600's common sailors were often paid off in the West Coast ports of England with as much as fourteen pounds in wages when a voyage was finished, enough to support a family for a year.

The Plymouth men knew this when in 1621 they set out to join the fishing fleet on the northern grounds. They returned with a full cargo of cured fish which, after transfer to a regular trading vessel bound for England, eventually brought them a fair share of profit for their endeavor. They told each other that when a man had gathered together twenty-five pounds he could buy and outfit a vessel of his own and work independently here in the colony. Contact with the crews of other vessels met on the Banks had added to this conviction, and there was a great deal of talk about another voyage.

The colony had begun to take what it could from the sea. Trade conducted by small craft, some of them canoes, brought in furs from the coastal tribes. But the winter of 1621–22 was very hard, left the settlers sick and weak. In the spring of 1622 a meeting was called and a vote taken, and it was agreed that Edward Winslow receive command of the shallop and sail north to borrow food from the Grand Banks fishermen. The coastal trips, because of the condition of the men who made them, had not reached enough territory and failed of their purpose to get supplies.

Winslow had no trouble. In the summer, he met thirty vessels working the waters around Monhegan Island. The crews gladly gave him of their stocks of beer and biscuit, meat and fish, and the colony was able to pull through until the fall harvest was made. The fishermen were a carefree, openhanded lot whose morals did not at all agree with Pilgrim precepts. But the Pilgrims could not hold back their gratitude, although one of their number had been in Damariscove on the Maine coast that fall, and he had an unfavorable report to deliver about the fishermen.

His name was Phineas Prat, his presence at Damariscove at the end of the fishing season fully explained because of his work as a crew member aboard a vessel. He had seen, he said, some quite disturbing sights. The other men decorated and erected a maypole, then danced around it to music with various Indian maidens and squaws. Both maidens and squaws seemed to enjoy themselves greatly; so too did the men who had made the maypole. They were all, Phineas Prat said, "very merry."

Financial troubles in the colony caused by disputes with the London stockholders over disbursements and reduction of debts owed them kept the colony from making another venture to the Grand Banks until 1624. Then the Plymouth fishermen harvested enough cod for a cargo to be sent to England by trading vessel. The profit, if slow to be realized, was large, and with it two strong shallops were

built. The year of 1625 gave a very abundant corn crop, and remembering his former success, the settlers turned over some of it to
Edward Winslow and put him in command of one of the new vessels.

He went to a trading post on the Kennebec River in Maine, where
he bartered the corn for seven hundred pounds of beaver skins.
Then he went offshore to Monhegan Island, hearing that some trade
goods were to be sold at bargain rates. He secured cargo worth
£400, took it to the Kennebec post and made a deal for goods from
a French ship that had been wrecked on the coast.

The men Winslow dealt with were "truckers," reputedly a most ir-
religious and cunning lot. They were supposed to spend their time
debauching and cheating the Indians, selling the tribes cheap, tawdry
"truck goods," along with small amounts of powder and shot and
brandy and an occasional musket, for magnificent beaver, marten,
otter and lynx pelts. Still Winslow arranged to buy another £100
worth of furs, all the shallop would take. He battened down the
shallop's hatch, squared away and sailed home to Plymouth. A suave
and canny trader, Winslow had proven that the colony need not
concern itself with the land, and should in the future be almost
completely sea-minded.

During the year 1625, though, a far-reaching change had taken
place at Plymouth. Plagued by a majority of the English stockholders
of the company, who, broke and dispirited, wanted no more of any
New World venture, eight men among the settlers had chosen to
hold themselves responsible for the total debt. They were the new
governor, Bradford, and Standish, Winslow, Allerton, Brewster,
Howland, Alden and Prence. The annual sum that they contracted
to pay approximated $10,000 a year, a very considerable amount for
that time, and they were to make payments for nine years to come.

The group, in exchange for this obligation, was to have a complete monopoly of the trade of the colony and exclusive use of its
boats, now two pinnaces and a shallop. They would also have control
of the colony's stock of furs, skins, beads, hatchets and knives. Their
source of profit was to be the trade with the Indians for beaver,
otter, mink and other furs, the fishing rights for alewives, herring,

halibut, bass, salmon, trout, shad, cod and mackerel, and the right to raise and sell corn.

The group had assumed a galling, almost crippling debt, and yet if they succeeded and paid it, they would be personally wealthy. Meanwhile, and perhaps for some years, the rest of the settlers would, due to this financial arrangement, be just a little bit better than paupers. They would be working for the eventual profit of the group and not on their own account.

Anger flared. Old animosities that had started over unequal distribution of land were renewed. There were ugly words muttered in the dark as men who did not belong to the group met along the Town Brook. It was time, they said, that they got out of Plymouth.

The group had already, by way of the Manomet portage across Cape Cod, begun trade with the Indians of the Buzzards Bay region. They were dealing, too, with the Dutchmen at New Amsterdam, further south; and up north, as far as the Kennebec and Penobscot rivers, they bartered for furs with the natives. Some of their people had ventured inland along the Kennebec to the site of present-day Augusta and set up a trucking post there. Another was established for trade with the fishermen and Indians at Castine, on the easterly bank of the mouth of the Penobscot and at the head of the enormous bay.

The outsiders, those who did not belong to the group of eight, bitterly revised their private dreams. They were aware that the Reverend John White of Dorchester had sent out from England an expedition that was to make a permanent settlement on Cape Ann, across Massachusetts Bay. It was supposed to gather a store of venison and wild fowl during the winter, then plant crops and supply the fishing crews. But the rugged granite slopes and cranberry bogs of Cape Ann gave no favorable site for such a colony, and by 1626 the company had failed and most of the people had returned to England. The few who remained, stubborn, clannish Puritans, went to a place on the coast that the Indians called Naumkeag. They renamed it Salem before they built their huts and log wharf and started to fish.

That was the answer, the Plymouth outsiders told themselves. A

made train oil of it. The English named the uncleaned variety cod-fish and, along with the Dutch, continued to prefer their own method of curing.

What was known as dunfish was considered the best, and it was "made" by burying the largest cod in the ground and then drying them in the open air. The dunfish usually became ripe enough to please the palates of the European Catholics, who for the most part bought them. These were sold in France, Spain, Portugal, the Canary Islands and the Azores, and with them barrel staves and heads.

The second grade codfish, of middle size, was held for the home market and right from the beginning was considered a favorite New England dish. Salted, smoked and dried, it lasted through the winter, usually in a hogshead in a corner of the main room near the chimney. Stews were made from it, and it was served with loblolly gruel, maize johnny cake, peas and hoe cake. Other fish, mackerel and sturgeon, and sturgeon eggs served as caviar, were sometimes substituted. But the settlers were quite content with a trencher filled to the brim with simmering salt cod stew.

Fish continued to be the crop that made Plymouth prosperous, as well as the other towns that had begun to increase rapidly around the sweep of Massachusetts Bay. The original settlement was already in keen competition with Salem and with the new colony that in 1630 had been established by Puritans. The newcomers had taken as the site for their village a place called by them Backbay, behind a promontory with a three-pointed hill on it. They called their village Boston.

The Reverend White, who had been the principal figure in the Cape Ann colonization attempt that failed, was active in supporting both Salem and Boston. He sent from England highly skilled men, wheelwrights, carpenters and shipwrights, and they built in 1630 the first real shipyard in America, on the Mystic River at present Medford.

Another Puritan parson, Reverend Hugh Peter, was convinced that fish would be the major factor in the New England economy long after the fur and timber sources had diminished or were exhausted.

He appreciated this fully when in 1634 he came out as minister and took over the pulpit at Salem. He was an extremely gifted man, with a deep, fervent religious sense and great capability as an executive and a diplomat. Born of wealthy parents in England in 1599, he went to Cambridge and graduated in 1622, immediately taking holy orders. But his beliefs were looked upon as heretical by his superiors, and he was forced to flee the country and to serve the Puritan congregation in exile in Rotterdam before he left for Salem.

He found nearly all of the people of the colony living in log-walled houses that had thatched roofs and dirt floors. They still led a very primitive frontier existence, forming a link in the thin line of population that stretched to the borders of Massachusetts Bay and stopped there, held back by the forest. Heaps of shells littered the beach. Tarpots bubbled over driftwood fires where men calked the seams of smacks and shallops and patched their dugout canoes. But over on the Mystic River at Malden on July 4, 1631, a tidy 30-ton sloop named *Blessing of the Bay* and built of native locust had been launched. She was a busy vessel.

Freight rates between England and Massachusetts Bay were £3 a ton, and passengers paid £5 each; it cost £10 to ship a horse. English agents took a nice commission from their end of the deals, and Reverend Peter and a number of other canny Massachusetts Bay settlers calculated that without such cost a ship could pay for herself after a round voyage. The obvious answer was to build more ships in New England and do away entirely with the English agents—have the shipmasters deal directly on arrival in English ports.

Reverend Peter was able to raise money in the colony to help the fishing trade, and he wrote to England and got more. Over in Plymouth the General Court as the ruling body for that colony appointed six men to fish for "the general account." Alewives were for some time called common property. But as various men invested their effort and money in building fishweirs they were allowed to keep the catch, and restraints were put upon certain areas. John Clark was allowed to construct a weir, for instance, at Cambridge, though only on the condition that he would sell his fish to the inhabitants for bait alone. The price of alewives around 1640 was put at three shillings, sixpence per thousand. Another fisherman was hired by the community to bring home the alewives from a weir; "and he is to have XVId [sixteen pence] a thousand and load them himself for carriage; and to have the power to take any man to help him, he paying of him for his work."

The General Court, after urging by Reverend Peter, exempted in 1639 all fishing vessels from charges for seven years to come. Fishermen and ship carpenters were not forced to serve militia duty on training days. When fish were caught in the weirs the men who made fishing their trade were allowed to buy first, at a prearranged price. Land was set aside for fish-curing stages and pasture provided for cattle which fishermen owned "but could not attend while at sea."

Until as late as 1648 fishermen who came ashore to "make" their catch were allowed to use free of charge the property where they landed. They were permitted to cut timber and erect stages and drying frames. There must have been some strong dissent between property owners and the fishermen, because after 1648 prices were fixed for the use of timber and land. But in 1652 the demand was still so great that a law was passed by the General Court that provided "fish viewers" at "every fishing place." They were paid by the colony, and their main duty was to separate the cured fish into grades according to quality.

Salem people had made money from the trade since they began the venture, and by 1641 they were ready to build a three-hundred-ton vessel, a huge craft for her time. She was launched at Richard Hollingsworth's yard and at once loaded for sea. Reverend Peter went back to England soon afterward to act as ambassador for the colony, and Marblehead and Boston took over a great deal of her market for fish. But Salem kept on as an active port, particularly for small coastwise smacks and shallops that worked the Banks in the traditional way.

By 1700 Boston had come to dominate overseas shipping from the Massachusetts Bay region, and Plymouth found itself half-forgotten, the narrow and difficult approaches to her wharves little used.

Plymouth men again crossed the Bay and this time signed on in Boston. They sailed in vessels that took them on months-long transatlantic voyages.

The trade the shipmasters engaged in overseas was almost always in barter. Salt came from Cádiz, and Madeira and Canary wine from what the New Englanders called the Wine Islands. Grapes from Málaga and oranges from Valencia were exchanged for dunfish and taken aboard the ships for sale in both England and New England. The famous iron mines around Bilbao were the source of the ware that was still not being produced in any quantity in the New World, and also from Spain was drawn practically all of the coin used in the transactions, the carefully stamped and weighed pieces of eight.

Freight rates had begun to rise steadily and slowly from the £3 and £4 a ton of the first colonial ships. Crews drew much better wages than in any English ship, and were given in addition their share of what was known as the private venture. This meant that by law they were allowed a certain amount of stowage space for themselves aboard ship where they could carry cargo to be sold on their own account. A common sailor was paid an average of £2 10 s. a month. A mate made about £3 10 s. a month and the master of a vessel about £6 a month. All of them, though, often made more from the private venture than from their regular wages. A man had real incentive to go to sea.

CHAPTER THREE

OF WHALES AND MEN

Reporting to His Majesty Charles I in 1635, the Secretary to the Admiralty said that there were already forty ships regularly engaged in transatlantic trade with the New England colonies and that six of those were owned by settlers. The Stuart king was pleased. He looked forward to customs duties as a great part of his much-needed national income.

The next year a pair of Massachusetts Bay Colony men, Thomas Mayhew and John Winthrop, Jr., showed some of the sense of enterprise that was to make Boston famous—and wealthy. They started traffic with Bermuda. The lovely, cedar-clad group was at the time called the Summers Islands or the Somers Isles, both in honor of Sir George Somers, one of the founders of the settlement, whose ship had been lost there in a hurricane. The islands had been colonized since 1610, and produced crops which attracted the attention of the Massachusetts Bay partners.

They came carrying pork and corn in their vessel, went home with potatoes, oranges and lemons. That was very probably the first importation of the firm, smooth-skinned Bermuda potatoes to the mainland, and the citrus fruits found a good price in the New England market. Mayhew and Winthrop made a profit of "twenty od pounds" on the voyage.

30

Right in stride with them, an enterprising and early Maine resident named Winter built at Richmond Island a 30-ton shallop. He called her *Richmond* and loaded her with six thousand pipe staves that he thought he might sell to advantage in England. He cleared the coast, caught the prevailing westerly winds and made a nice run to England and a profit of slightly more than £25 on the staves.

Ventures such as this prompted a keen-witted Bristol shipmaster, Thomas Wiggin, to write home. "The English [he meant the New England colonists] numbering about two thousand, and generally most industrious, have done more in three years than others in seven times that space, and at a tenth of the expense."

Wiggin was also aware that the New Englanders took a splendid harvest from the whales that ranged the coast. These were mainly right whales, which came North into the cooler New England waters in the summer after their favorite diet of plankton. There were, too, what were known as drift whales, animals that suffered from pulmonary and other disorders and beached themselves in distress from Bermuda on north, and had been found by Dutch settlers in the upper reaches of the Hudson River near Poughkeepsie.

Men like Samoset, sea-wise Indians of the tribes around Massachusetts Bay, instructed the whites in the whale hunt. They took the settlers out in their canoes for the chase. The braves used harpoons tipped with bone or stone and short lengths of their loose hemp line that were attached to drogues. The drogues were a form of float fashioned from inflated animal bladders that stayed on the surface long after the wounded whale had dived and tried to free himself from the harpoons imbedded in his flesh.

The Indians lacked the iron-barbed weapons, both harpoon and lance, to kill the whale outright with a single thrust. Their method was to wound and weary the whale, harass him slowly in toward shore, surrounded by a flotilla of canoes. Then, in the shallows, the braves were joined by the women, the children, the old folks and the dogs. The whale was assaulted with every possible weapon, hacked at until, finally, he bled to death. For the braves, the slowness of the hunt did not count much; they had a great deal of time, and the blubber and meat from a sixty-foot right whale would be a main source of food supply for a tribe for all winter.

White men soon learned how to handle weapons, boats and whales and cruised steadily alongshore each season. But for quite a time, on into the 1700's, they enlisted Indians as harpooners. The braves through centuries of contact with the huge mammals had an almost instinctive skill in a whaleboat.

The pinnace, a boat of from eighteen to twenty-five feet in length, was the craft commonly used. She was clinker-built, and carried a lugsail on a short mast and an average of six men in her crew, among them the harpooner and boat steerer, the boat steerer in command. Local boatbuilders had already begun to get away from the round-bottomed design so long popular in England and Europe. They gave the whalers a craft with a fairly sharp bow that had a rake and flare to it, and from their designs developed the double-ended American whaleboat, which was to become the archetype of all other boats like it.

A whaleboat crew of Massachusetts Bay men in the middle 1600's very probably did not cruise beyond sight of land, even during fair summer weather. There were sudden line squalls to be met, and the coast was still badly charted. The whales, though, more often than not, swam close inshore, careless of any enemy.

The men would sail or row out beyond the long, snuff-yellow line of Nantasket Beach, past Allerton Point, Harding Ledge, Thieves Ledge and The Graves. The harpooner, in all probability an Indian, stood intent at the bow, his racked harpoons ready beside him, the lines that led from them carefully coiled in tubs. He studied the sea horizon mile after mile with an unbroken glance. It was the sparkling white double jet of spray, the invariable sign of the right whale, that informed him. He would speak softly to the boat steerer in the stern sheets, and the craft then headed around on an intercept course for the prize.

The boat sailed as close to the whale as the steerer could bring her. Then the long ash oars were used and, sometimes, when the whale seemed exceptionally nervous, paddles that made little sound, for the prey had very sensitive hearing. It was the customary manner of attack to put the harpooner right up on the whale, so close that he could drive the harpoon home with the first thrust, grievously wound the animal. A slanting course was steered that kept the boat abaft of the great, powerful fluke and the small and red, very watchful eye. With a last stroke of the oars, the harpooner was alongside, and reared back and drove the evilly sharp harpoon hard, the iron blade aimed to pierce a lung.

The beast shivered, reared. A cry came through the dark, curved baleen shield in the whale's mouth. The blunt head was high from the surface, and the clusters of barnacles around the blowholes and the white splotches along the fore part of the body shone in the sun. The whale was about to dive. It fell almost vertically back into the sea, the black body a plummet of immense force that often missed the whaleboat by inches, sometimes struck and crushed it.

But if the men remained safe, they paid out line just as fast and far as the whale dived. Then they snubbed it and began to fight the whale, wear the life from the beast. The whale swam on straight, furious courses, or in circles, and at last broached, came to the surface for air.

The harpooner delivered another thrust, perhaps two more, then relinquished his place to the boat steerer, who moved forward to try for the kill with a lance. He jabbed at the vitals until the whale lay dead or in a final paroxysm of agony parted all the lines that held it to the boat and escaped. But escape was rare. The Massachusetts Bay men had learned a great deal about the chase, and their Indian shipmates were master sea hunters.

One of them crawled up onto the dead beast's back from the boat and secured a line around the carcass. The line was brought aboard and belayed to a timber piece aft. Then the men braced themselves and started to row, painfully towing astern the prize.

But satisfaction must have lent the men strength as they came close to port. They did not haul here a drift whale for which the General Court could take for itself as much as one third of the value of the oil rendered. The prize would be divided with equal shares to all of them. And the beast had been killed according to law, which said that no whale when hunted at sea "shall be needlessly or fouellishly lanced behind ye vitall."

The demand for oil, whalebone and baleen took the crews into bigger vessels in the latter part of the seventeenth century. They cruised almost continuously offshore, and the share system changed. Harpooners and boat steerers asked for more and got it, along with the captains and the mates of the ships. This was the "lay" system that was to last, with various minor alterations, throughout all of American deepwater whaling. The new system meant that the captain got as his lay as much as one barrel of oil in seventeen to one in twenty-five. Mates received from one barrel in seventy-five taken, and so on down the list of hands aboard the ship, to the landsman at the bottom, who might get one barrel in two hundred.

Men were starting to acquire wealth in the towns that had sprung up around Massachusetts Bay. But in comparison with the fortunes of the great merchant adventurers in England, what they held was very little. By Massachusetts Bay standards, the sum of £4,000 was wealth. Money, in the actual sense of currency, was seldom exchanged. Ships were built, launched, rigged and sent loaded to sea with only the transferral of a few pound notes, sometimes less. Workmen were paid in goods that they needed. Neighbors working together shared in a vessel and her cargo. They traded timber, fish, cereals and furs to acquire iron and sails and cordage or paid off by giving the supplier of those articles a share in the ship and the profits of her intended voyage. Then the merchant who had outfitted the vessel traded in European ports, was paid off in cash there or brought home a cargo of commodities for further credit transferral and eventual cash profit.

The ship *Trial* made an early example that was widely followed. She was built in Boston in 1641, sailed for Fayal in the Azores the year after she was launched. A group of canny Salem people owned her, and they were in knowledge of the fact that in Fayal there were a number of days on the calendar when the Catholic population was not allowed to eat meat. So the cargo that *Trial* carried was salt cod and pipe staves. Fayal was noted for a very fine wine.

Captain Coytemore was in command of the ship. He found an excellent market at Fayal. The fish and staves were swapped for wine and sugar and other cargo, and Coytemore shoved off for St. Kitts in the West Indies.

He traded again at St. Kitts: wine for cotton and tobacco and some ironware that the local folks had taken from a ship wrecked on the coast. Ironware was an item in constant short supply in the New England towns. Captain Coytemore went out to inspect the wreck. Then he made a diving tub from some of his own Salem pipe staves, hung iron shackles on it to take it down and entered it stripped to his drawers.

He disregarded shark, barracuda, lung collapse and suffocation while he walked the decks of the wreck. Some of the crew from *Trial* waited anxiously on the beach, with a great part of the amazed and envious citizens of St. Kitts. The captain signaled his men and was hauled to the surface safely enough. He returned to the wreck and secured grapnels and lines to the ship's cannon. His men hoisted the cannon to the beach, and when Coytemore came to the surface once more, the pieces were loaded onto carts and taken to *Trial* and aboard her to Boston.

Trial later ran to Málaga and Bilbao and homeward-bound carried wine, fruit, iron and wool. Governor John Winthrop of the Bay Colony wrote of this, which, he said, "was of great advantage to the country and gave encouragement to trade." *Trial* was kept busy at sea and sent on voyages along the easterly coast of Canada to Acadia and in 1645 to London and ports in Holland, back home with English and Dutch commodities. She was still in service in 1659 and in her way an historic vessel.

Shipbuilding and commerce had become by the middle of the seventeenth century the leading activities of Boston, Charlestown, Dorchester and Salem. The Old Colony, Plymouth, because of its poor location and the rabid, narrow religious views of its leaders, had fallen far behind in the expansion of the region and would never recover. The exodus of her young men continued, and they left to join Boston ships or to apprentice themselves to shipwrights, carpenters and blockmakers and learn a trade not offered to them at home.

Ships as small as twelve tons, to be used as coasters, and as large as four hundred tons for transoceanic service were gradually transforming the life of the coastal towns. They were centers of a new wealth, a new prosperity. The days when the Massachusetts Bay Puritans had lived on the starvation diet of acorns, clams and Indian corn were gone. There was work for everybody, and the lower classes lived better than they ever had in England.

Most of the colonial fleet was still small, single-decked shallops, the usual rig for coasters, and lateen-rigged ketches, the rig favored by fishermen. These craft were of twenty to thirty tons burden and thirty-five to fifty feet long. A good number of them set topsails, and some, the bigger vessels, double topsails.

The first shipyard in the region had been established at Medford, on the Mystic River, in 1629, when the original contingent of Puritan settlers reached the Bay. Among them were many shipwrights and master carpenters and highly skilled artisans, and more followed from England the next year. The reputation for fine workmanship that they created was to last a long time, and "Medford-built" had real meaning both in the colonies and in England.

Other yards soon gained their own reputations, some for quite big ships. Benjamin Gillam at his yard near Copps Hill built the 300-ton *Welcome* at the order of a merchant named Valentine Hill, and the 400-ton *Seafort* was built in 1648 in a Boston yard. These vessels, though, were exceptionally large. The usual maximum size of a ship from the local Massachusetts Bay yards was about 90 feet in length, with a 23-foot beam and a 9- or 10-foot draft. Construction costs, around 1650, were at £3.5 a ton, and the ton, an arbitrary measurement, was worked out to represent forty cubic feet of space in a ship's hold.

The Massachusetts Bay shipbuilders were held to a very close operating margin, and in their original designs they discarded all of the fancy European ornamentation, gilt paint and scrollwork. Then they abolished the clumsy and outdated fore and after castles that for centuries had weakened hulls instead of strengthening them and made ships top-heavy and balky, hard to the helm because of their huge broadsides.

The square-sail rig was also not right, the designers discovered, where every point of sailing had to be used daily, alongshore, on the Banks and navigating the prevailing westerlies to Europe. A ship must be built to head to windward, steer any kind of course under all kinds of conditions. Less and less square sail was set up in the bay yards and much more of the spritsail and lugsail design. The ketch was already popular on the coast, and the schooner was about to come into existence. A great part of the men who built the Massachusetts Bay craft sailed in them, and were quick to find a defect, were constantly planning new and better designs. It was a coast now, too, where practically every man was a competent sailor, could rig, sew canvas, set up gear. Criticism was not spared the builders and was often correct.

Shallow harbors along the coast kept most of the local designs to shoal draft construction. This meant the craft were broad-beamed, with short masts and wide spars. They were fast sailers on the wind, though, and the fine oak timber that went into their hulls, the pine that went into their spars and the general qualities given them by their builders brought increasing trade to the yards.

English construction was badly crippled by corruption and graft. Cost was double that in the New England yards and as high as £8 a ton in some of the home yards. Timber was plentiful and easy to reach around Massachusetts Bay. The building of large ships on order or for speculation for the English market rapidly became a recognized industry.

The shipyards spread out beside the tidal rivers of the bay, and were very busy at Newbury, Ipswich, Gloucester, Salem and Boston. Ropewalks were set up, and hempen sailcloth was made on hand looms. Anchors and coarse ironware were forged from bog ore, and wooden trunnels (tree nails) were used to fasten planking to the ship frames. Spans of oxen hauled the massive balks of timber from the forest edge, and these were stacked to dry and season, then were given to the ax, the adze, the saw.

Men rose before dawn to go to work, came home in the dark. They were for the most part happy, though, and felt themselves adequately paid, with a bright future ahead of them. There was nothing to keep a man when he was ready from starting a ropewalk of his own or a yard where his sons would help him build and quite likely, later, take the vessels and their cargoes to sea. The old dreams that first had been formed in England could come true here on the new shore.

Sir Joshua Child, a foremost English shipping merchant, had come to understand fully the tremendous potential force behind the Massachusetts Bay growth. He wrote in his book on mercantilism a note of somber warning and prophecy. The book was published in England around 1650, but the warning was ignored. It was:

"Of all the American plantations His Majesty has none so apt for building of shipping as New England, nor any comparably so qualified for the breeding of seamen, not only by reason of the natural industry of that people, but principally by reason of their cod and mackerel fisheries." Then, in conclusion, he wrote: "And, in my poor opinion, there is nothing more prejudicial and in prospect more dangerous to any mother kingdom than the increase of shipping in her colonies."

CHAPTER FOUR

THE ISLANDS

The sea called strongly to the young men of the Massachusetts Bay towns despite the growing opportunities for advancement ashore. Each spring, as the ice broke and left the harbors, there were new recruits for crews. Several scores, along with them quite a number of teen-age boys, took their berths in a fo'c'sle for the first time. They had great incentive for shipping out; life at sea would settle many problems.

For the sons of the prosperous there were after 1636 the Boston Latin School and Harvard College. Strict and ferocious scholars were originally in charge of both. Ezekiel Cheever was at the head of Boston Latin School and was to rule that institution for thirty-eight years. He had studied at Emmanuel College, Cambridge University, and possessed formidable knowledge, a long white beard and a hawk's eyes. When he started to stroke the beard the boys in his classes knew that next would come a shrewdly applied thwack of the rod for any delinquent or dullard.

The first president of Harvard College was Nathaniel Eaton, who had the proper scholastic qualifications but also the habit of carrying a walnut club that was said to be heavy enough to kill a horse. It was alleged that his wife cheated on the amounts of beef, beer and bread issued the students, and Harvard started out in a miserable manner. Then Eaton almost beat his assistant to death, using the walnut club, and was discharged by the Board of Overseers. He left, taking his wife and a good deal of John Harvard's legacy to the college. Henry Dunster, who came after him in 1640, made a much better president, yet a lot of harm had already been done. Many young men formed the belief that if they were to be beaten and abused while they learned, they might as well do it at sea and be paid for it.

Most of the learning for the sons of the poor was confined to the crude one-room schoolhouses in the villages situated on the Bay. Only a very few of them ever got beyond the hornbook stage. The hornbook was a piece of wood, generally four to five inches long and about two inches wide, with a piece of printed paper placed upon it. The paper bore at the top the alphabet in capital and small letters and, below, simple syllables, such as *ab* and *eb,* and then the Lord's Prayer. A thin sheet of yellowish horn, much like a windowpane, covered the paper and was secured to the sides of the piece of wood by a metal strip tacked in place. A small wooden handle with a hole in it was at the bottom, in back. The hole was pierced for a piece of string, so that the "book" might be carried over the shoulder or around the neck.

During the winter and the long, cold falls and springs the school-houses were heated by clay-walled fireplaces or primitive stoves. The fathers of the students hauled the firewood to the schoolhouses and left it there. Older boys worked it up, and the younger ones lugged it inside. The first boy to arrive in the morning began the fire; he brought live coals from the house of the nearest neighbor. Girls once a week swept out the schoolhouse and occasionally, with the help of the boys, who fetched the water, scrubbed it, benches, desks, puncheon floor and all. But often, for weeks at a time, snow kept the children from school. The men teachers were in the main poorly equipped, some sadistic and mean-tempered, much too ready with the rod. Many of the boys who had grown strong and big doing the chores at home, rowing in the backwaters of the Bay or hunting along the perimeter of the forest, took their final satisfaction from the schoolmaster at the end of the spring term.

They waited for him outside the schoolhouse, caught him with a slingshot loaded with stones, or, in bitter anger, "wrastled" him or had a real stand-up fight that finished in bloody faces and broken bones. It was after encounters like that when the mates of seagoing ships, loaded and ready to shove off, picked up new fo'c'sle hands who had little to say about the wages to be paid them.

But more than the young people were oppressed by the way of life. A frightful pall of hatred and narrow, parochial dislike and distrust had entered the New England villages. Men and women were often accused of sexual or religious lapses, publicly flogged, ducked, put in the pillories and stocks. A hysteria of repression had begun that was to culminate in the ghastly Salem witch killings and the legalized murder of Quakers.

Whole families left such towns as Salem, went to Maine, Rhode Island, Connecticut, the Dutch colony of New Amsterdam or the West Indies. They thoroughly disliked an existence that had become more intolerant than anything they had known in England. The Puritans had brought back into practice the Assize at Arms of the Middle Ages. It had been out of use under English law for centuries, but here in New England it meant a strict form of universal military training.

Each boy when he became sixteen, unless he was a student at college, was forced to provide himself with a musket. This must be "not under three foote nine inches in length, nore above fower foote three inches." He was to see that his piece had a priming wire, a worm (cleaning brush) and scourer that fitted the bore. If the draftee believed that he would like to serve as a pikeman—the one bit of personal choice allowed him—he must have a six-foot-long pike, a "sufficient corselet, buffe coate, or quilted coate." From the age of ten boys were trained to handle half pikes and bows and arrows and muskets. Eight days each year were given to militia training, and not even indentured servants were exempt.

Back in England the trained bands had been called out about once every five years. Here in Massachusetts the militia companies went through monthly drill and an annual muster of the regiment from the four counties of Suffolk, Middlesex, Essex and Norfolk. The settlers were also forced to stand night guard, what was called "watching and warding," and they were liable for instant call-up for use in Indian warfare.

A great deal of the religious intolerance the men could excuse because of their backgrounds; they had come from a country where Catholic had fiercely opposed Protestant, and one splinter sect had shown no mercy to another. They could further accept the weary, time-consuming militia drills and musters. This was the frontier, and in their estimation the Indians were to be feared and exterminated just like the timber wolves that attacked the flocks of village sheep. But the additional restrictions, and the hour upon hour of Sabbath sermons which were quite incomprehensible and murky with involved religious logic, along with the actions of the tithing man, made life very trying ashore.

The tithing man was the most deeply hated official in early New England. He received the particular scorn of young men and boys in their teens. His usual duty was to supervise the lives of ten neighboring families. This he generally performed with great fervor. He enforced the learning of the catechism and visited the homes assigned to him to find if the children had memorized it. He questioned them closely, at length and with small mercy.

Then on Sunday he checked the same families. He discovered who went to church and who did not and whether they loitered on the way. It was within his power to arrest people who ran or rode too fast going to Sunday meeting and also for taking unnecessary rides on Sunday or otherwise breaking the Sunday laws. During divine service in the meeting house he maintained order.

He chased out the village dogs that sneaked through the door. Armed with a stick that had a knob on one end and a foxtail on the other, he walked up and down the aisles past the pews. He did not spare the use of the knob on the heads of unruly boys, and the foxtail was for the sleepers. He dangled that under their noses until they sneezed, twitched and awoke.

The tithing man in some Massachusetts Bay towns had additional duties. It was according to local regulation his duty to keep "boys and all persons from swimming in water." This, of course, brought him a distinct lack of popularity during hot July and August weather, and although there are no accounts left of tithing men being drowned by enraged groups of boys skinny-dipping in a forest brook or along a deserted beach, there must have been such attempts. The tithing man had also the responsibility of the inspection of taverns. He reported disorderly persons, and could forbid the sale of liquor to them. Further, he administered the "oath of fidelity" to new citizens and warned undesirables to leave town and saw that they obeyed him.

There were in these gloomy little towns many people who could remember a much happier life back in England. They recalled to themselves and to their children how in that other country the young had jigged and danced by firelight through the winter evenings. Dances were named—Leap Candle and the Cushion Dance—and descriptions given of games and singing rounds "Sellinger's Round," "John Come Kiss Me" and "Barley Break." Then stories were told of rush-bearing ceremonies, and the blessing of cornfields and of springs, the crowning of the May Queen, the roasting of geese at Michaelmas, and of suckling pigs at Lammas, the famous harvest festival held in August.

That was only a part of the jollity, though, that relieved life in England. Free beer was poured with abandon at Whitsun ales and harvest festivals, and boys dressed in wigs and petticoats and squawking like little girls bounced around on hobbyhorses and made everybody laugh. The City of London held Bartholomew's Fair in August, and that went on for nearly a fortnight. Allhallows was a great, gay time, too, and between Christmas and Twelfth Night general holiday was celebrated. Pipe, tabor and fiddle were played, and people danced, sang, cavorted, kissed, without benefit of the tithing man.

The teen-age New England lads must have sat very quietly as they listened to those stories out of the happy past. The world they knew was here, along this strip of coast, in these tight and miserable, fear-ridden towns. Take a sloop and with a fair day's sailing weather all of the coastal towns and villages of the Massachusetts Bay Colony could be seen. Two days' march inland and the last outpost house was reached, about forty miles from tidewater. The population of the colony, though, in 1640 was between fourteen and sixteen thousand people, most of them confined to the towns and none free from the rules, the regulations, the penalties and the punishments of the tithing man and his inflexible-minded superiors of the General Court.

The General Court in 1644 established regulations that prohibited the dumping of ballast by ships on the Sabbath and also any sailings on that day. Restrictions were put upon the actions of "incoming mariners and sailors," who had already made a considerable amount of trouble for the town fathers in the Massachusetts Bay region and in the Connecticut and New Haven colonies as well.

Keeping clear of the tithing man, the teen-age lads sought out the crews of the ships that had just made port. They talked with sailors, a mate or a good-natured captain. The sea for them was the world outside, all of it glistening, shimmering with the promise of freedom and wealth. The limits of it were not yet known; a great part of it was still to be explored. Drake had gone there, and Hawkins, and Raleigh, and the rest of them who had defeated the Spanish Armada. Let the timid, the weak, stay here on the Massachusetts shore. What really counted, a life of freedom and a chance to make a fortune, could only be found out beyond the sea horizon. The Puritan elders, the members of the General Court and the dour Pilgrim die-hards at Plymouth had not planned it this way. But the implacable rigidity of the moral and religious codes they enforced upon the people of the towns under their jurisdiction was an important factor in the creation of the seagoing tradition that was to dominate New England and the new nation for centuries.

The sea road for those who took it in the early colonial period led more often than not to the West Indies. "Merlasses" was already a great word around the bay towns, and so were sugar, rum and salt. The equivalents for them were cod, mackerel, pipe staves and corn.

Vessels carried an average crew of five men and a boy. They stood well offshore as soon as they could, picked up the trade wind and headed on their southing for Bermuda, St. Kitts, Jamaica and Barbados.

For a boy who had never been offshore before the first few days at sea were disappointing. If he shipped aboard a vessel that sailed in the wintertime, he was forced to keep on his heavy clothing, his cowhide boots and coonskin cap for several days. The vessel seemed cramped and small and the waves alongside enormous. He was not yet accustomed to the fo'c'sle smells and the slur and rap and rustle of the waves against the shipside just past his head as he stretched out in his narrow bunk. He suffered from claustrophobia, and from seasickness that brought him great shame and not much sympathy from his shipmates. When on watch he stumbled woefully around the deck and wished that he were home, where everything was familiar and secure, did not heave, spin and jerk.

But then, Bermuda-bound, the ship entered the Gulf Stream, crossed it and found her northeasterly wind. This was the trade wind of which the boy had heard so much, and he hurried with the rest of his watch to set topsails and a staysail, shake out an extra jib. The ship rode on a broad reach, pitching a bit and delicately rolling, the man at the tiller intent, poised, his glance lifted to the luff of the mainsail. Spume broke gold-flecked around the bow. The seaweed of the Gulf Stream was gone, and the wake lay like a vast blade, straight and shining, astern.

Along about sunset, after he had swabbed down fore and aft and built the supper fire in the half tub, the boy was called to the tiller. He was allowed to steer for a short while and instructed in the compass, the points, the half points, the sixteenths; and the stars that had begun to appear in the pale lavender sky above the still argent sea were identified for him. This was what he had sought, the boy suddenly realized. Here it was, the freedom, anyhow, and off past the bow somewhere must be the wealth.

His first landfall was to excite him even more than that first trick at the tiller. Bermuda came up out of the sea a blue, faint shadow under cumulus cloud. The boy was not sure until he heard the top-mast lookout hail the deck, "Land ho!" Then he stood lost in won-der, his work forgotten.

St. David's Head rested bold upon the sea. The boy could make out the slender curves of palm trees, and beaches that were unbe-lievably pink, houses and a church on a hillside that were prim white but owned red-tiled roofs. The boy may have thought that he could already smell the land and the tobacco that was grown as a crop here. But the mate certainly left him little time for thought once land was sighted.

Sail was being shortened. A sailor stood on the leeward side for-ward and heaved the sounding lead. There were coral reefs in these waters that took the bottom out of a ship with great ease, and Sir George Somers had lost *Sea-Venture* here in 1609 when she was hurled far off course by a hurricane. But the little New England trading vessel kept to her course, came neatly in past the headland, dipped her ensign to the fort and went to anchor in St. George's Harbor.

The boy worked hard now; he lacked the time to stare. He furled canvas, helped secure the anchor cable, took a line alongside for the use of His Majesty's Customs men in their cutter, yanked out hatch battens, rolled back tarpaulins, lifted hatch boards, and was surprised how much cargo the ship carried. The main hold, when exposed to the sunlight, looked like an immense cave. His Majesty's men were not impressed, though, and asked the mate sharply for the cargo manifest.

That night, very probably dressed in a pair of white duck pants borrowed from a shipmate, his hair clubbed and his neck clean, the boy went ashore. He saw much that excited and astonished him, and yet there was nothing like the moment when the lookout had sighted St. David's Head. This, somehow, was anticlimax, and al-though the boy did not know it, he had just become a sailor, would always love the sea instead of the land.

Bermuda in the early years of her settlement held promise for many people and surely seized the fancy of any young New Eng-

lander on his first voyage. Richard Moore had been sent out from Jamestown, Virginia, in 1612 in the ship *Plough* with "men, women and mariners" to occupy the island group. They found what Moore reported as huge "turkles," and an amazing variety of fish, fowl, fruit, palm trees, cedars, wild hogs in the woods, sperm whales cavorting off the beaches and three wholly unexpected settlers.

These were sailors, survivors of a shipwreck the year before. They lived in great comfort in a house they had built on high ground with a splendid view of the sea. Corn and other vegetables they had planted flourished in their garden, and they let the newcomers know that they had no intention of returning to sea or going anywhere. Life here, without neighbors, was exactly what they wanted. They had in their possession, though, a large piece of ambergris and some seed pearls they had discovered while they combed the beach. English law stated clearly that the King should get as much as 50 per cent of such property.

The sylvan peace was shattered. The trio of original settlers were in fine physical shape and obdurate men. They told those who represented the King that they proposed to keep the ambergris and the pearls. They cherished the ambergris in particular, because it would bring a very high price in Europe, where it was used in medicine, perfume and confectionery. But the King's men in their turn were obdurate, and the ambergris chunk was transferred back and forth among several people. A lot of it was wasted, and only £6,000 was eventually received for it.

The trio complained to the governor, Sir Thomas Smith, and got no satisfaction. They, like many other early pioneer people, were about to be battered away from their self-contained existence and overwhelmed by a highly organized society. Captain Daniel Tucker had succeeded Sir Thomas as governor, and his rule was quite merciless. Indentured servants, Negro and Arawak slaves, Scottish and Irish political prisoners and women, children, all were transported both from England and the Virginia colony.

For most of the men the daily task was the felling, cutting and trimming of timber and the clearing of land. Others worked as masons, sawed the coral that was easily quarried, built from it the houses that were then whitewashed and the sturdy red-tiled roofs added. The rest labored as field hands, planted, cultivated and harvested tobacco, corn, potatoes and a number of other crops. The overseers, with the lash, kept them at work, and a bitter, terrible flood of hatred filled their lives.

The same cruel laws that were in effect in Virginia were enforced here. A man who was to be hanged was whipped first, while he marched, or was dragged from the fort to the Georgetown gallows. Less guilty unfortunates were towed at the stern of a boat, instead of being ducked. They were put in the stocks or the pillory, laid in bolts, whipped at the whipping post, sometimes with a lash that had fishhooks attached to it. Then, quite often, whipcord was used, and a man was bound head to heels. This was called kissing the post, and he was whipped thoroughly while in that position.

Tucker had broken the land up into eight "tribes," or districts, of 1,250 acres apiece. Two burgesses were chosen to represent each tribe, and the total body met as the Assembly on August 1, 1620, in the new church at Georgetown. Tucker and his council proudly entered with them, and history was made. Since 1618, when the first stores ship, *Diana,* had arrived from England, vessels like her had spent regular periods of forty days in either Castle Harbor, St. George's Harbor or Nonsuch Bay. They came out from England and went home heavily loaded with cargo, most of it owed to the crown.

That debt paid to the crown increased the hatred by the Bermudian oppressed for those who ruled them. Whales were to be caught close offshore and in the sounds and bays around the island group. There was so much profit to be made from the hunt that a local company had been organized. The men who formed it called themselves "The Adventurers in the Whale-fishing Design," but they understood from the beginning that half of what they took in profit would go to King Charles, and as a result the people who handled their boats, harpoons, lances and try-pots for them would get little or nothing for their labor.

Island currency had become known as hog money because of the figure of a hog stamped on one side at the mint in England. But it was also of base metal, with very small value or buying power. The Bermudian workers regarded it with frustrated contempt, and were issued coarse food rations to keep them from starvation.

Reports of the beauty of Bermuda had reached England, and in part inspired Shakespeare to write *The Tempest*. The name of the main town had been changed after a few years from Georgetown to St. George, in direct homage to the great saint. But by 1660 the colony had become an uneasy, poor and overpopulated place. Strict orders had been passed to limit the use of timber. Trees could only be felled for boat construction, for roof thatching and for the making of hats. Tobacco fields were turned into grazing land. Tobacco as an island crop was finished.

People who could afford transportation left. They went to Antigua and Trinidad, Barbados and Tobago, St. Lucia and Jamaica, the Bahamas, the Carolinas and the New England colonies. It was part of the almost constant migration that was to continue back and forth through the Caribbean islands and along the Atlantic seaboard for another hundred years.

But there were many men who were too poor to leave Bermuda in legal fashion. Indenture held them, or debt. The sunny islands were for them a strange kind of prison. Yet the sea was all around, and just like the Plymouth men of an earlier generation they took to it. They built secretly, or bought or stole, cedar-planked craft that would bear them to the mainland. It was a dangerous gamble at best, for they went short-hauled, with little food and small amounts of water. But when Henry Morgan led his pirate army to the sack of Panama City in 1670, he had a number of former Bermudian settlers in the ranks. They had joined him freely; the pirate way of life could hold no more peril than what they had already known.

There were other men in Bermuda, though, who lacked the skill to navigate a boat alone. A good part of them during the middle 1600's stowed away aboard New England vessels about to leave port. The mainland beckoned to them, and once at sea, free from pursuit, capture and punishment, they sat enraptured on deck and asked lengthy questions about the northern country. Up there, they understood, a man would meet many hazards, and yet he could have land of his own. *Land* . . . The word was pronounced over and over, almost like a chant.

New England crews found very much the same conditions in all of the English-held islands of the Caribbean. The worst, without question, was Barbados. It was the hottest, lay the closest to the equator, and there the big landowners had driven out the smaller ones early and established a complete system of slavery. Indentured people, men, women and children, worked side by side in the cane fields with Negro slaves, the few native Arawaks who still sustained life on their own island and Scottish and Irish political prisoners sold by Cromwell's courtiers at auction into permanent enslavement. *Barbadoed* was a dread term in seventeenth-century England, containing just as much sense of brutal wrongdoing as the later term *shanghaied*. There was also a special term for the enslaved children, who were described as having been *trepanned*—knocked out—before they were sold as chattels, usually in the west coast port of Bristol, where a great deal of colonial shipping gathered.

But the New England merchants found these circumstances no deterrent to their trade with Barbados. John Winthrop established as early as 1627 the importance of traffic between the Massachusetts Bay area and the island. His family and his friends carefully fostered it and greatly profited by it. There was a regular postal service started in 1631 that handled letters sent from New England towns to London via Barbados. The island became the main depot for nearly all New England trade; goods were shipped from there on to South America or to other West Indian islands, and English finished goods and commodities were picked up for sale at home in New England.

The trade thrived, and the ties became closer each year despite Dutch and English competition. A large number of New England merchants, as they studied their account books and saw how their profits increased, bought plantations in the West Indies. They carried on trade with their own tobacco, sugar, indigo and cotton. John Winthrop wrote in his journal in October, 1642, "Two of our vessels . . . returned home with a good supply of cotton, and brought home letters with them from Barbados and other islands of those parts."

The Massachusetts Bay ship *Black Lyon* carried in August, 1659, a typical cargo to Barbados and returned home with a handsome profit. She met at the anchorage in Carlisle Bay offshore from Bridgetown ships that flew the Dutch, the French and Spanish flags and carried casks of meal and wine and even Russian flour taken aboard in Baltic ports. But *Black Lyon* had made a much shorter haul, and her cargo was in just as great demand. Her manifest read:

	£		
1,727 boards (37,216 ft.) @ 50 s. per 1,000 ft:	£ 93	12s.	0d.
1,890 pipe staves @ 14 10s. per 100:	7	1	9
630 hogshead staves and headings:	1	11	10
	£101	14s.	7d.

During the first three months of 1659 a firm of Salem merchants shipped out timber to Barbados and received in return 14,686 pounds of muscovado (raw, brown) sugar. The price for sugar at that time was a half pence per pound, and a good part of the sugar imported went to the rum distilleries that had begun to perfume the air along the Mystic River at Medford. The chief ports for the West Indian trade as it expanded were Boston, Salem and, to a lesser degree, Ipswich, Newport, New London, New Haven and Windsor.

A definite feeling of common purpose existed between the islanders and the New Englanders. But the men who worked the New England ships could never reconcile themselves to the treatment given the slaves and the indentured people on Barbados. They were already quite a hard-bitten and independent lot, the first of the breed that in a few years were going to man the privateer vessels that fought the French and then the English. Their own background was for the most part grim and bleak; their sympathy was for the underdog and not the wealthy, indolent landowner or his overseer who ruled by the lash and the pistol while the owner lived in London.

Barbados lacked the water that turned New England mill wheels.

So the island used windmills and, as the sugar trade expanded, New England-bred horses. Most of them came from Vermont stock and were shipped on deck to Barbados. They were small and spirited, full of vigor even while cooped up on deck in storm. The Barbadian overseers treated them badly, though, and they did not live long, and their number often had to be replenished. But the New England sailors were still convinced that the horses were given better treatment than the plantation field hands.

Proud Scottish officers who had been captured after the battles of Dunbar and Worcester were sold into servitude by Oliver Cromwell's direct command. An order had been passed in September, 1651, that no lieutenants or cornets of horse, or any above that rank, were to be shipped to the plantations. But it was generally ignored. A group of high-ranking officers was shipped out to Barbados in 1655, among them Colonel Gardiner and Major Thomas, who had already suffered imprisonment in the Tower of London. They were sold to various planters at public auction in Bridgetown and sent to the sugar fields to work under a sun that killed many of them in the space of a few years.

They met in the slave huts at night hundreds of former Irish officers and soldiers treated in the same way by Cromwell. The Irish had been taken after the failure of their uprising in 1649, sent into life servitude. Cromwell had stated in writing his sentiments about them and had described without waste of language the storming of Dhrogheda: "When they submitted, those officers were knocked on the head, and every tenth man of the soldiers killed, and the rest shipped for Barbados."

The Scots and the Irish shared the labor and the wretched, putrid food and foul quarters with felons whom Cromwell had shipped by the thousands. There were also in the plantation labor forces a number of pirates who had been caught on the high seas and held in jail at Dorchester and Plymouth. Then, in addition, there were the forlorn Arawak survivors, a simple and gentle people, and the strapping, lean-bodied Negroes from a dozen or more African tribes, new to this island, but able to take the sun.

When they talked at night in the darkness of their huts some of the Scots could not help recalling with irony the ancient Highland belief that told of *Tir Nan Og,* "The Islands of the Blest." It was there, in the ultimate West, beyond the furthest Hebrides, that eternal youth was to be found. Barbados was not *Tir Nan Og,* nor did any exist except in dream. Yet thought of it gave incentive to them who still had the strength to make an attempt at escape.

New England ships took a small number of escaped men North with them on the return voyages. But Barbados was carefully patrolled by dragoons and foot soldiers, and every overseer had his informers in the slave huts. The sailors did what they could, but it was not much. Some few escaped men were put down in the rugged country around St. Ann's Bay and Cagua in Jamaica. This northern part of the larger, more mountainous island was held by buccaneers, and inland, a sort of buffer between the buccaneers and the authorities, were former soldiers who made their living by hunting wild hogs. The government estimate was that the hog hunters brought in a thousand hundredweight of meat a month, so they were not disturbed, and neither were their neighbors, the buccaneers.

The remainder of the escaped men from Barbados were dropped off by the New England ships at the notorious buccaneer hangout of Tortuga, just past the northernmost headlands of Hispaniola, at the entrance to the Windward Passage. Here the Brothers of the Coast gathered, and men lived on the basis of share and share alike. The escaped people from Barbados were immediately accepted, and the New England crews sailed on home quite happy.

They knew that they were extraordinarily fortunate. Nothing except sheer chance kept them from slavery. They might very readily be under the lash in Bermuda or Barbados. Life back in New England was not the best that a man could contemplate, and yet it was better, much better than what those desperate, dying people suffered on the plantations.

England was supposed to have a more liberal government than any in Europe. That the French and Spanish and Dutch sailors admitted in the port taverns where the New England crews met them.

But a man did not need a Lord Protector like Cromwell, nor a king, either, to direct his life. He could do it for himself, and would.

There had not been a single colony of Englishmen in Asia, Africa or America in 1604 when the peace with Spain was signed. But before the end of the century there were twenty colonies along the Atlantic seaboard and in the West Indies. The people in them were chiefly of English stock, and their total number was close to 225,000. Still, of the lot the New Englanders were the first to decide that they must have their own independence and live wholly free.

CHAPTER FIVE

THE LONERS

Among the New England colonies it was Maine, then a province of Massachusetts, that drew the reckless, the independent-minded, the greatly ambitious and those who could no longer live within the law. Some of the men who came to the dark, rugged sweep of coast bore the cropped ears and the cheek brands of felons, and they had been expelled as unwelcome from the settlements. The others sought huge profit from trade with the Indian tribes or from land which in time might be the site of a settlement and, when cleared and sold, make a fortune.

They were usually a solitary lot, trusted nobody. If luck had been with them when they left the settlements, they sailed a small shallop, or a pinnace, and carried a collection of cheap truck goods for the Indians and a cask of rum. Any white man, the veteran Maine traders said, could outsmart the sharpest Indian if he gave the red-skin rum. After that it was a man's cunning and rapacity in barter that counted, and his ability to get away before the Indians became sober.

The first incident in the creation of the violent tradition of early life in Maine foretold disaster. As early as 1500, a Portuguese ad-venturer named Gaspar Corte-Real took a ship along the coast. He touched at Newfoundland, and he celebrated the fact by the capture of fifty-seven warriors of the Beothuk tribe. These he brought aboard, for sale in Europe as slaves. Corte-Real lacked imagination as well as any sense of humanity. He failed to see what would happen to the men who would come after him along the coast, although he wrote about the Beothuk people:

"There has been brought hence a piece of broken sword inlaid with gold which we can pronounce to have been made in Italy and one of the children had in his ears two pieces of silver which appear to have certainly been made in Venice—which induces me to believe that that country belongs to the continent."

The legacy of hatred left so carelessly by Corte-Real spread and increased. There were incidents of retaliation. Sailors were lured from their vessels, and never returned from shore. Members of the Sagadahoc colony while fishing off the beach were caught unarmed in their boats, killed, and the boats stolen. Then, on the central New England coast, near the Isle of Shoals, in May, 1602, the crew of the English ship *Concord* was made quite aware of what the Indians could do to repay old debts.

Bartholomew Gosnold was in command of *Concord,* and there was mist on the early morning sea, so he proceeded slowly and kept her offshore. Masthead lookouts reported what they believed to be a Basque fishing shallop and pointed her out in the mist. She came from inshore on a slant of wind past a large rock, pulled steadily alongside the English ship.

One of the company in *Concord* was a gentleman named Gabriel Archer. He later described what happened:

"From the said rock came towards us a Biscay shallop with sayle and oars having eight persons in it, whom we supposed at first to be Christians distressed. But approaching closer we perceived them to be savages— One that seemed to be the commander wore a waistcoat of black work, a pair of britches, cloth stockings, shoes, hat and band, one or two more had also things made by some Christians; these with a piece of chalk described the coasts thereabouts and could name Placentia of the Newfoundland."

There was in all probability a chill of fear that passed through the people of *Concord* as they realized what that description of the coasts meant. Placentia was far away to the northward, and certainly this well-equipped shallop had not been loaned or given away by its owners. The Indians who sailed it had very obviously seized it from the Basque crew and sailed it here, and if they so wished, would sail it back again. Gosnold was quick to bend on canvas aboard *Concord* and get to sea.

Then, in 1611, another English ship under the command of Captain Edward Harlowe came to the anchor at Monhegan Island on the Maine coast. Harlowe was of the same slaver persuasion as Corte-Real and tried to take by force five Indians from the beach for transportation to England. They fought the English, although three of them were finally captured. Their names were Epenow and Monopet and Pechmo, and Pechmo got away from his captors aboard by diving overside.

He swam ashore and roused the Indians on the island. They began an assault against the ship with arrows, spears and stones, and while it lasted one of the force swam out and cut the painter of the ship's longboat. She was a very valuable craft for pilotage work on this coast; Harlowe fought hard to get her back.

But the Indians had drawn her up on the beach, and they fought harder to keep her. Three Englishmen were hit and seriously wounded by arrows. The rest were driven off, without the longboat, and Harlowe decided to heave in anchor and stand clear of Monhegan. He went on to Cape Cod, where he seized more prisoners by treachery.

His actions were not forgotten. The next English ship to make landfall on the island was attacked by a flotilla of war canoes. The Indians were beaten away after a sharp fight and the use of cannon fire.

Greed brought the Englishmen again to the coast, and in 1614 a ship commanded by Captain Hobson appeared. She carried Epenow, one of the Indians taken from Monhegan, as interpreter. Epenow knew enough, though, to talk in such language with his people that twenty canoes came out and surrounded the ship. Then he dived overboard to freedom while his Penobscot tribesmen kept the English crew prone behind the bulwarks on deck, held down by showers of arrows.

There were further attacks when in 1616 a French ship was caught by storm and thrown ashore on Cape Cod. The local tribe had a keen memory of the past; they killed all but one of the crew, letting him, with odd compassion, marry a squaw, settle down and live among them. But the next year when a French ship put in to trade they boarded her with their knives hidden inside their bales of beaver pelts.

These were men of the Nauset tribe, and they turned upon the Frenchmen in great fury. They killed all of them and looted the ship at their leisure. She meant nothing to them, though, and the best they could do was burn her at the anchor while they danced in triumph on the beach.

Then, in 1618, and for two years afterward, disease scattered death through all of the coastal tribes, from Newfoundland to Long Island Sound. Thousands of Indians died from some mysterious white man's disease, probably smallpox. This was the plague that killed Squanto's tribe, the Patuxets, and left him a sole survivor at the site of Plymouth. The major result of the infliction was that strength left the remaining warriors all along the northern coast, and they no longer had the heart to fight the white men.

Peace came to the little Maine settlements and to the fishing stations on the offshore islands and to the region around Cape Cod. But the rapacious, the wholly unscrupulous, among the coastwise seagoing traders would not relent, and did not intend to change their ways. They continued to rob the Indians with whom they could still find barter. They courted death to make quick profit, and far from Maine, along the lovely Connecticut River in southern New England, they ignited sparks of hatred that were to cause a century and a half of intermittent, ghastly war that almost destroyed the colonies.

Maine continued to grow with amazing strength and tenacity during the early, extremely perilous years. There were fishing stations at Monhegan and Pemaquid and Damariscove, but the English colony at Sagadahoc had failed, and the French had been driven by the English from their settlement on Mount Desert Island, making no attempt to return. Until 1639 the only people in the territory were gathered at Kittery, at Richmond Island, and at Saco, between the Piscataqua River and Casco Bay. But a hardy Kentishman named Edward Godfrey had built a cabin above the tidal flats of the Agamenticus River in 1630, and around him a few more daring folks settled. They made their livelihood from farming rather than from timber or fish, and they decided to call the place Dover.

Sir Ferdinando Gorges, the West of England merchant adventurer who had spent huge sums trying to realize his dreams of colonial empire in Maine, was so enheartened by the success of the Dover settlement that he ordered more money spent. It went to build a manor house at Point Christian on the Agamenticus, and was for the use of his cousin, Thomas Gorges, who arrived from England in 1640 to serve as deputy governor of the colony.

For ten years, from 1628 to 1638, men from the Plymouth Colony had maintained a truck house at Cushnoc, the site of modern Augusta, on the Kennebec River. They later set up other trading stations at Castine, at the mouth of the Penobscot, and far North at Machias. The French had forced them from those, though, and they had left the Cushnoc station after taking great profit from it. The hazards were almost incalculable during the extremely long, severe winters.

The death toll among the men who spent a winter in garrison in Maine in the early seventeenth century was often as high as 50 per cent. Sooner or later, as the chill and cramped weeks passed, one of their number would come down with what was known as the winter scurvy. Then another got it, and another, and the corpses were piled until spring and a chance at burial. The survivors prayed and drank what so-called medicine that was handy and the rum and aqua vitae while those lasted.

The solitary trader came to the Maine coast in the summertime. He chose late June, or early July, when the tribes were down from their winter quarters inland where they hunted the moose and caribou and beaver. The trader probably kept well out to sea as he steered his Maine course. Vessels owned by the various colonies around Massachusetts Bay had the habit of sailing alongshore, and their armed crews might take him for a pirate. There were, too, actual pirates who had the very nasty trick of leaving their winter operation in the Caribbean to cruise the coast here in the summer, pick up a careless or defenseless fisherman and a trader and his cargo.

But after the high, surf-kicked cliffs of Monhegan Island were astern the trader raised Matinicus Island to the northward. It shone white in the summer sun, "like unto Dover cliffs." Here the trader hauled around on his southwesterly wind, went off on the port tack for the mainland. He could not spare any more time. He must close with the land and start to trade.

The Maine tribes had been on the coast since the ice was out of the rivers and they could navigate their canoes. They came for the alewife harvest and the salmon, the shad, the porpoise, the seal and the whale. Their camps were along the river mouths or on the shoreside islands in the vast, deeply indented bays. It was not hard to find them; they still had no abiding hatred of the white men, and they had brought with them from inland their bales of pelts, were ready to barter and sample the traders' rum.

These people were members of the Abenaki tribes and subtribes and clans. They came down all the great rivers of the region. The Norridgewocks were from the Kennebec; the Penobscots and Androscoggins were from the rivers of the same names; the Pennacooks had run the Merrimac; and the Pequawkets were from Saco. The trader found them busy with their fishing. The braves were offshore in birchbark canoes, sometimes with a small deerskin squaresail raised on a pole mast as they hand-lined for mackerel or cod. The old men and the women, the girls and younger boys, were on the beach, around the fires where the fish were dried and smoked. The bigger boys waded the shallows along the ledges, hardwood spears poised for lobsters.

It was the customary practice of the traders to anchor some distance from shore, at least a mile off. A number of men who had ventured too near the beach had been overcome by canoe-borne assailants or swimmers, their boats looted and afterward burned, their bodies tossed to the tide. So caution was necessary. A trader, when he had dropped jib and mainsail and put the anchor down, kept his primed blunderbuss unobtrusively by his knee in the cockpit as he signaled to the braves his willingness to trade.

There were times, though, when the tribes were not on the offshore islands or at the river mouths. A trader took the chance and followed them to their encampments beside the river banks. This was extremely dangerous; here ambush and assault were easy.

The boat, breasting the current with the offshore breeze, came on short tacks into the river. The trader must have stood very straight, very tense at the tiller. He stared around the foot of his brown, saggy mainsail at the shore. Behind him were sharp sunlight, the open sea and safety. He could still hear the squawking and the splash, the splatter of the great auks that lived on the offshore reefs. They stood almost three feet high, black-backed, white-breasted, in solemn rows, like beacons, and then dived into the surf after rock cod, their wings shunting them along through the water.

But the sounds of the auks and the other sea birds were suddenly gone. The trader entered a region of almost total silence, where the rasping of his mainsail hoops against the mast was loud. He heard the sibilance of the current over kelp-scummed boulders and, far off in the forest, the gobble of a turkey and the racket of a woodpecker. The forest smelled of death. Sunlight had never fully penetrated this immense vault. Fallen trees lay white, stark and skeletal among huge ferns, their trunks lumpy with weird fungoid growths. When a squirrel gnawed loose a pine cone and let it drop from a limb to the forest floor the repercussion was startling, and the trader jumped, his hand in instinctive fright on the blunderbuss.

Then he saw the Indians, or smelled them, heard their half-tame wolf dogs. He came about to his final tack, let go his sails, scrambled forward to the anchor. The bluff little craft swung to the current, backed on the anchor cable, took up slack and held. With the anchor right, the trader must have felt better. He no longer had to concern himself with the boat. His mind was ready for barter with the Indians. Braves were paddling canoes from the shore, tall, powerful and handsome men, their bear-greased bodies softly ashine in the faint sunlight on the river.

The trader brought out from the cabin his collection of truck goods, glass beads, mirrors and awls that the squaws adored for use in their buckskin work, a few yards of brightly dyed cloth, hatchets, knives, a kettle or two and a crude musket. Weapons like the musket were sold, outside the law, to the Indians for a usual price of twenty-five beaver pelts apiece. Twenty-five beaver pelts would buy ten muskets in Europe. The trader displayed the weapon carefully alongside the rum cask and the leather dram cup. Then he hailed the braves, but he let no more than half a dozen aboard at a time. A man could never be absolutely certain of the effects of rum on these people.

But the braves gazed in unrestrained anticipation at the rum cask right from the beginning of the barter. They seemed to forget almost completely the worth of the beautiful pelts they carried with them. And, with the second or third dram, they did forget. They stretched dull-eyed, about to become sick or enter stupor, and held out their hands for more rum.

The trader refused them. He bundled them over the side into their canoes, sometimes failing to pitch after them the goods they had brought. Then he invited aboard the next batch, and the next, until he was out of goods, or rum, and thought it was well that with the tidal ebb and before darkness he leave here. There were braves among the first batch who might be nearly sober by now, and it was possible that they resented what they had received in trade for a winter's work along the inland ponds and lakes and beaver meadows.

The trader hauled in his anchor, let the boat swerve with the tide. He did not bother to light a lantern in the dusk or raise more than the jib. The tidal pull would take him rapidly to sea, and he had made almost a 100 per cent profit on his cargo. He was also, of course, very lucky to be alive.

Men more careless of danger than the seagoing traders had settled on Richmond Island in Casco Bay as early as 1628. They were an extremely unsavory pair, one of them named Walter Bagnall and his partner known only as John P., for reasons that very likely had to do with violation of the law. Bagnall had in his time joined in the Merry Mount revels of the Providence Colony, danced around the maypole with the Indian girls "in their furr coats." His nickname, picked up along the way, was Great Walt, and he showed no sense of honesty whatsoever in his dealings with the Indians of the Casco Bay region.

He and John P. gave the island a very bad reputation, although Champlain during his exploration had called it Ile de Bacchus. The Spurwink River ran close to the island through both salt- and fresh-water marshes, and it was a favorite region for the Indians in the summer fishing season. Great Walt sorely cheated them in barter while John P. helped serve the rum, and the pair became so notorious for the flagrancy of their practices that Governor John Winthrop of the Massachusetts Bay Colony noted it in his journal.

Then, on the night of October 3, 1631, a local chief, Squidraset, and some of his braves who had been bilked by Great Walt paddled out to the island. They found Great Walt in his cabin and killed him there. No record remains of what happened to John P., but the Indians left the island after they had tended to the man they considered the major offender.

Nothing was done by the authorities for ten months. Maine was a territory, under the jurisdiction of the Massachusetts Bay Colony, and finally the General Court decided to act. A detachment of shipborne troops was sent to Richmond Island. They could not catch Squidraset or any of his braves. But they discovered on the island a wholly innocent Nahant Indian known as Black Will, and in August, 1632, they hanged him.

During the same year, the Bay Colony authorities were forced to act again on the Maine coast. A trader named Dixey Bull had been robbed of all he owned by Frenchmen, and as a consequence had turned pirate. He raided the newly built fort at Pemaquid and took what he pleased and fled to sea. The General Court, after long discussion of the case, moved to arrest him. It was recorded by the clerk of the court: "Pay'd Mr. Alcock for a fat hog to victual the pinnace for the taking of Dixey Bull."

Mr. Alcock missed his man, though, and Dixey Bull continued as a pirate for some time. Then his luck ran out. He was captured and taken to England, where he was convicted of his crimes and duly hanged in chains at Execution Dock above Thames tidewater.

The broad pattern of the lives and deaths of such men as Great Walt Bagnall and Dixey Bull had been established for over a century. From the earliest of recorded history, Maine knew violent crime, treachery, betrayal and piracy. A terrible tradition was created that was to last until after the Revolutionary War. The territory was the promised, fabulous land for many, but also the scene of almost incessant bloodshed. That was to have profound effect upon the final determination of what was to become famous as "Maine" character. The survivors of the events of the next century, and then their descendants, were exceptionally self-reliant, frightened by little, capable of a great deal.

CHAPTER SIX

RUM, FURS AND MASSACRE

In the 1630's the pressures of growth, ambition and restrictions in Massachusetts Bay and Plymouth caused some colonists there to look to western New England for settlement, just as earlier some had moved Down East. Governor Bradford and Edward Winslow of Plymouth tried unsuccessfully to interest Bay Colony leaders in a joint expedition to the Connecticut River in July of 1632. Nevertheless, in the fall of that year Winslow explored the Connecticut valley and commissioned Lieutenant Holmes to set up a trading post at Windsor, above Hartford. Not to be outdone, John Oldham brought a small party of settlers overland from the Bay Colony in the fall of 1633 and spent the winter at Wethersfield. There was further rivalry with the Dutch at New Amsterdam, who also claimed the territory and sent a ship up the river the same year and built a fort and trading post at Hartford. Restlessness in the Massachusetts coastal towns because of the shortage of grazing lands brought more settlers to the valley in 1635. This group settled in Windsor in defiance of the Plymouth claim there.

The situation was resolved when a wealthy group in London headed by Lord Saye and Sele decided to exercise their patent, assigned to them by the Council of New England in 1631, to settle the region. John Winthrop, son of the Bay Colony's governor, was authorized to take control of the river mouth in the winter of 1635–36. The man chosen to build and command the fort at Saybrook was a big, red-bearded professional soldier, an Englishman named Lion Gardiner. He was a tough veteran of the Lowland wars, where he had served as a senior noncommissioned officer, master engineer and fortress builder in Sir Edward Vere's company. Neither side took prisoners in the Lowland wars, and Gardiner was not worried by the prospect of what he might meet when he signed his contract for New World service. It was to run for four years, and he was given good terms and brought out from Holland with him his Dutch wife, Marichjen, her maid and his "workmaster" (foreman) William Job.

Gardiner sailed from Woerden, in Holland, in September, 1635, with a completed party of twelve people aboard a North Sea bark called *Batchelor*. She was only a twenty-five-ton vessel, and in London her Dutch captain, Jonathan Weber, had a very hard time recruiting a crew. Sailors did not like the idea of the "Western Ocean" in the winter gales, but she finally got her crew, and meanwhile Gardiner had loaded aboard fourteen pigs of stones, three barrels of pitch, two of tar and a large amount of miscellaneous gear among which were a wheelbarrow and pulleys, blocks, chains and hinges.

Batchelor took a pounding once she cleared Gravesend and was seabound for Boston. She came in past Castle Island in late November. Gardiner decided to spend the winter in Boston, go to the site of the new fort in the spring.

When he arrived he found work on the fort already started by a force of troops under the command of a lieutenant named Gibbons. The lieutenant was glad to be relieved, and Gardiner took over from him at once. The fort was built on a very small point of land on the west bank. It was set upon a hillock and constructed of square-hewn timber hauled from the splendid stands of trees in the nearby forest. Gardiner designed it in the classical European style: a stockade, a moat, a drawbridge, the bridge operated by the iron fittings he had brought from England in *Batchelor*.

His immediate impression was that he liked the place. The river bore all sorts of fish and seafood. Wild fowl flew thick over the marshes. Deer and other big game were easy targets in the forest. But Gardiner was pleased most of all by the fact that the local Pequots were friendly, came without hesitation to the fort.

He began to learn their language and their way of life, and yet he could not bring himself to put complete trust in them. There was too much against friendship. These Indians were forced to hate white men. They were being cheated and betrayed constantly, and not only by the traders who sailed the river. In 1633 eight rum-and-rob traders had been killed by Pequot braves on the Connecticut. Gardiner's orders were to inspect, check and control the passage of every kind of craft in and out of the river or the Sound. He was soon able to realize that the Indians had begun to plan outright, massed attack, and he repeatedly warned the people in the Massachusetts Bay region. The Pequots, Gardiner realized, recognized that they were no longer masters of the beautiful river valley. They knew, too, that at his trading post on Narragansett Bay an Englishman named Richard Smith cheated braves of their pelts when they had drunk his rum. The same thing was true at the Dutch post at Narragansett, and in the deep forest, along the far trails, were the Dutch *boschlopers* and the English pack traders.

The *boschlopers* were itinerant peddlers who took their name from running the woodland trails in the summertime and their profit from Indian furs in exchange for cheap alcohol and cheaper trinkets. Even the Mohawks, who were the great traders among the inland tribes, complained that the *boschlopers* and their English competitors never gave them anything that resembled fair barter.

Lion Gardiner came to understand that the Pequots and their neighbors, the Narragansetts, felt an ever-increasing fear of the future. They would soon have no inshore land left to them as the river settlements expanded, and the white men had already taken away great parts of the coast and their use of the sea. There was one answer, one alone—war.

It came very much as Gardiner had anticipated. Narragansett braves from Block Island boarded a pinnace that lay close offshore in the Sound. The craft belonged to a rascally character named John

Oldham, who had been thrown out of the Bay Colony for his disgraceful actions and since made his base at Watertown. The braves, who had been cheated in the past by Oldham, split his head open and hacked his arms and legs.

This happened in broad daylight on July 20, 1636. The pinnace was sighted by a Boston trader, John Gallop, who was cruising to the eastward from Saybrook Fort with two men and two boys in his crew. He sailed his boat alongside, saw the braves armed with English muskets and suspected what had been given Oldham in final payment.

He fired buckshot at the braves, made six of them jump over the side, and they sank and drowned. Then he came about on another tack and rammed the pinnace bow-on. The maneuver frightened the Indians who remained, and Gallop and his crew boarded the craft. He accepted the surrender of the pair who were on deck, although he heaved one of them over the side to drown. Oldham's body was underneath an old sail, still warm.

Gallop kept the other brave on deck as a prisoner, and also two more who had hidden themselves in the hold, cutlasses in hand. He towed the pinnace until nightfall, when he cast off and proceeded for Boston with all of the sail he could crowd on his own craft. He wanted to report to the authorities; John Oldham's split skull should be enough to make them think about war and greatly increased protection for traders.

Sir Henry Vane was the new governor at Boston and of a warlike disposition after he had listened to Gallop. He mustered an expeditionary force of ninety men and gave command of it to John Endecott of Salem. They were to sail to Block Island and put to death every brave they found there, but spare the squaws and children.

Lion Gardiner heard that news and realized it meant the end of peace for very probably a long time to come. He prepared the fort against Indian attack, but it had been a poor summer for the garrison. The group of titled Puritans who directed the affairs of the Connecticut Company in London had run short of money. The garrison had been without bread and beer and other food supplies all summer long, and were reduced to the dismal diet of pease porridge.

Gardiner did not have much enthusiasm for the expeditionary force when Endecott brought the men over from Block Island. They had killed, burned and destroyed, and felt the flush of victory. Endecott suggested that the Saybrook Fort garrison join his force and go and raid the Pequot villages. A storm had begun to blow that lasted four days, and during it Gardiner was able to convince Endecott of the worth of an alternate plan.

He foresaw a long and hard winter of siege, with reduced rations. This was the harvest season. The Pequot corn lay ripe in the fields along the river. With his men added to those Endecott commanded the corn could be quickly gathered. But, Gardiner warned, the force must divide into three equal groups. Two of those would cover the third while it gathered the corn in the Indian fields, filled the sacks and brought them down to the vessels that were to be held ready at the river bank.

A Dutch trader had just reached the fort from an upstream settlement. Gardiner rented his shallop and hired the Dutchman, too, as pilot. He put twelve men from the garrison in her, and Endecott put the Bay Colony men aboard their own craft. They sailed early in the day with Endecott in command.

But Endecott failed to keep to Gardiner's plan. The Pequots knew what had happened on Block Island, and they did not want an open fight with the English. They deserted their village. They hid in the woods behind it, along the mouth of the Pequot River, and the braves only shot a few arrows at the force to show their resistance.

Endecott was delighted. He marched his men into the village and ordered them to set fire to it and to the cornfields. When the bark-slab wigwams were burning brightly in the clear September air, he marched his men back aboard and left the Saybrook Fort detachment to get away alone.

The Saybrook Fort men had gone ashore to gather corn. They were exposed out in the suddenly blazing field, and two of them were wounded by arrows before they could return to the Dutchman's shallop. The Dutchman was extremely worried about his scalp and his boat. He shoved off as fast as he could, raised sail and headed for the fort. But there was no pursuit. The Pequot braves chose to wait.

A war party attacked the fort two days later. They dragged off singly seven men who worked outside. The captured struggled until they were beaten unconscious. Their fate was certain; they were to be flayed at the stake, then burned slowly to death.

Gardiner went out from the fort afterward, though, and harvested corn in the fields that the garrison had planted near it. He needed the crop to survive the winter. Frost was already on the forest. Game would become scarce and impossible to hunt with Pequots on the warpath. Ice would soon fill the river, and then no vessel could move up or down, carry in supplies.

Gardiner lost more men to the Pequots. Still he kept the survivors at the harvest work. They would starve otherwise, he warned them.

His old ship, *Batchelor,* had been sent to Bermuda for a load of potatoes, and when he learned of it he wrote Governor Winthrop and asked for a portion of the cargo. But he was refused. And he did not have the money to buy corn and rye offered him by the captain of a Dutch smack who came past the fort. Then, desperate, he decided to build a craft of his own if it became necessary for him to abandon the place.

A Dutch shipwright and a Dutch tailor who had left the upriver settlements because of the Indian danger came to seek refuge from him. He turned to the shipwright on the construction of a 30-ton smack with a 3½-foot draft, conscripted the tailor also and set the man to sewing sails. But before the craft was finished a New Amsterdam smack pushed her way through the new-formed ice and reached the fort from the Sound.

Gardiner got a hundred bushels of corn from her, and with his own harvest it was enough to keep his people for the winter. The garrison recouped. Gardiner worked to strengthen the fort, prepare for the major assault that he was sure the Pequots would deliver.

Many of the fort's cows and sheep had been stolen or killed by

Pequot skulkers from the edge of the forest. Braves were seen daily around the land sides, and Gardiner knew he must open up a space for a zone of fire for the two small cannon and his musketeers. He led out a work party on February 22, 1638, and as soon as the men began to burn reeds and grass along the slope below the fort, they were attacked.

The Pequot braves sprang from the forest, used their bows in a rapid volley, then their tomahawks, war clubs and knives. Gardiner was wounded in the thigh. Several of his men were killed beside him while they fired their clumsy muskets point-blank.

Gardiner led the rest back into the fort. They crossed the moat over the little plank drawbridge, and it was raised and they were safe. But out on the slope, beyond range, the braves stripped the dead. Yelling taunts, they strutted the blood-splashed snow in buff coats, corselets and helmets.

Gardiner must have watched with glum concentration. It would not be long now, he knew, before the next of the bloodletting began. But he kept the fort from further loss until spring, and when the ice broke and the channel cleared he set up a boldly lettered sign over the main gate. It could be seen and read from the river, and the language was plain. It ordered every vessel that passed to stop for inspection and warned captains not to stop afterward bound upstream until they had reached Wethersfield. Gardiner anticipated Pequot ambush along the river, and he was right.

With fair weather a trader named John Tilly came in from Boston and tied up his boat at the fort wharf. He had left trade goods in the warehouse in Gardiner's care, and he put them aboard, got ready to sail. Tilly was something of a peculiar character; he had been given the nickname of Sergeant Kettle because of the fact that in any engagement with the Indians he wore a brass pot on his head instead of a helmet. He did not think much of Gardiner's talk about taking precaution, told the veteran so and left the fort. Gardiner could not keep him without the use of physical force. Tilly and the man who served as crew aboard Tilly's boat cast off, hoisted sail and set a course upriver.

The trader stopped and anchored some miles above the fort. The spot was known later as Tilly's Folly. He and the other man rowed ashore from the vessel. They had time to fire a single shot before the Pequots took them prisoner, and Tilly was not wearing the brass pot as a helmet.

Gardiner was given the chance to see Tilly again when the trader was brought past the fort in a Pequot canoe. Tilly sat bareheaded, bound, motionless. He was on his way to awful torture and death at the stake.

Gardiner could do nothing but send an armed party upstream in an attempt to find Tilly's boat. She lay quietly, unharmed, at the anchor. The party sailed her back to the fort, and the cargo was moved out of her, stowed once more in the warehouse. The man who had served Tilly remained missing. It was believed at the fort that he had been killed instantly by the Pequots, his body dumped in the river.

The garrison waited tensely through the soft spring days. All of them knew that once the Pequots had lifted the tomahawk it was not easily put down. Gardiner had sent warning by a Dutch trader to Wethersfield right after Tilly's capture. He was extremely worried about the possibility of a raid upon the settlement. Then the trader returned in his boat and reported.

Two hundred Pequot raiders had struck the village on the night of April 23 and without mercy. Seven men had been killed, and a woman and a child. A pair of teen-age girls, the daughters of Abraham Swain, had been carried off as captives.

Gardiner kept a close watch on the river. Two days after he had received the Wethersfield news, a fleet of Pequot canoes passed, pointed downstream. The braves paddled through the salt creek in the marshland below the fort, and the poles which they held up like masts carried smocks and white shirts in imitation of sails. Gardiner saw that the Swain girls were seated amidships in the lead canoe.

He talked with his carpenter, who also served the fort as gunner. The man told Gardiner that he would do his best, and trained one of the snub-nosed little cannon on the lead canoe, fired. His aim was excellent. The six-pounder shot knocked the bow cleanly out of the craft, spilled the Swain girls and their captors into the water.

But braves in the canoes astern picked them up, and the fleet kept on, outside the gunner's range. Gardiner considered what might happen to the sisters. He gave some time to careful talk with a group of Dutchmen who had arrived at the fort. The Dutchmen were traders who liked the sight of money, and Gardiner bribed them with a ten-pound note. They took a boat and went over to the Pequot village and joined in powwow with Saccasus, the sachem. He agreed to release the girls, and they were brought to the fort, and although they were half-naked and greatly frightened, Mrs. Gardiner found them to be "unharmed."

News of the Wethersfield massacre had been sent along swiftly by Gardiner to the Bay Colony. The governor and the members of the General Court were furious, proposed terrible retribution. A force of veteran troops was raised and sent almost at once to Connecticut. They were able to surround in the middle of the night the huge, stockaded Pequot fort at the mouth of the Mystic River. Within the fort, the Pequots drummed, danced and celebrated the Wethersfield victory. More than a thousand of them were killed right there, either by the soldiers or the fires the soldiers started among the summer-dry bark wigwams. When they started forth they were driven back, inside the stockade, to the flames.

Some few Indians escaped. They hid in the forest until hunger drove them down to the sea to dig oysters. Soldiers caught them, and were allowed to keep the young squaws and girls. The warriors were held for sale as slaves in the West Indies islands.

That was the end of the so-called Pequot War, and the tribe had been effectively crushed. But Gardiner felt no particular elation. He wanted little to do with men whose actions were as cruel as those of the savages they fought. His contract with the Connecticut Company was about to expire, too, and he did not seek to renew it, although he had been raised to the rank of lieutenant, was recognized officially as the commander of the fort.

George Fenwick, one of the aristocratic Puritans who was a chief proprietor in the company, had just come to Saybrook with his wife, his two aunts and many servants. The party arrived from England in July, 1639, and took up residence in the great hall of the fort. Gardiner was no longer at his ease in the place, and with Fenwick present, not the commander.

During the intervals of peace since he had been at the fort Gardiner had made a very good friend of Wyandanch, a senior warrior of the Montauk tribe. Wyandanch was soon to become the principal sachem of all the eastern Long Island tribes, and he assured Gardiner that he and his family would be safe if he left the protection of the fort and went to live across the Sound.

Gardiner placed full trust in Wyandanch. He and the Montauk cruised the easterly waters of the Sound to find a suitable home site. Gardiner chose a magnificent star-shaped island called Manchonack by the Indians and only a few miles away from Saybrook. He renamed it Isle of Wight, secured the rights to it both from the Montauks and the Earl of Sterling, who had been given immense land grants in the area by King Charles.

The veteran moved his family to the island and lived there for fourteen years in peace and understanding with the Montauks and the other neighbor tribes. His only trouble came from marauding bands of Narragansett braves who landed on the island beaches in the long, winter-heavy nights. But he built his house with a stout stockade of oak logs around it, and Wyandanch remained his trusted friend, respected him so much that upon his death he left his possessions to the old soldier.

The Gardiner family lived for many generations on Manchonack after Lion Gardiner's death, and its name was eventually changed to Gardiner's Island. They sold its produce of marsh salt, dried fish, corn and whale oil to the colonies that began to spring up on the marshland across Long Island Sound, and because of their location they were frequently visited by the crews of many ships. Their dependence on the sea was total, even more so than the mainland settlements, but none of them could exist without it.

CHAPTER SEVEN

TRADE AND WAR

During the peaceful years that followed the Pequot slaughter more settlements began to appear on the New England coast. New Haven was founded in June, 1636, by a religious group from England under the leadership of the Reverend John Davenport, and in the next eight years was joined by Stamford, Guilford and Milford. Roger Williams, an exile from Massachusetts Bay, founded Providence in June, 1636, and two years later was joined by another group of exiles from Boston who went on to settle Newport.

Sir Ferdinando Gorges and an ambitious settler named John Mason had shared between them since 1629 the New Hampshire land that flanked the Piscataqua River. The land north of it was taken by Sir Ferdinando, and that to the south was held by Mason. The two men also shared a trading grant that extended over an immense area that stretched to Lake Champlain and the St. Lawrence. Settlements had been set up at what was to be called Portsmouth and at South Berwick. The town of Portsmouth was growing fast, and had come to gather quite a reputation for the skill of its shipwrights.

New Amsterdam was flourishing under the Dutch. It was an active port that attracted a lot of shipping. But the Dutchmen's chief concentration was upon furs, and most of their traders and colonists moved up the Hudson River, then from it over into the Mohawk Valley. They paid hardly any attention to eastern Long Island, although down at the other end, around Gravesend and Sheepshead bays and in Brooklyn, they maintained fine farms, the houses built of dressed stone and gabled in the old-country style, the barns broad and strong, the windmills exactly like those in Holland.

Philadelphia and the rest of the settlements on the broad-sweeping Delaware were prosperous under William Penn, with a great deal of ship traffic on the river during the months that it was free from ice. The Maryland colony, founded by the Catholic second Lord Baltimore, grew steadily beyond it on the Chesapeake, although its southern boundary, at the Potomac River, conflicted with claims made by Virginia.

Virginia had some years back lost position as foremost among the mainland colonies. New England dominated increasingly both politics and commerce. Rhode Island had grown to the stature of a colony in 1663, and in 1668, the "Province of Maine" was taken over by the Massachusetts Bay Colony. The Hampshire Grant had been absorbed by the Bay Colony in 1641 as her merchants reached out further alongshore, and Boston was firmly established as the center of shipping for all of New England.

The colonies had become a massive force during their first fifty years of existence. Still their potential strength was recognized by only a few of the New World leaders and all but rejected if not ignored in England. The various parts of this huge structure gathered power in an almost inexorable fashion as their populations and then their wealth gradually enlarged. England considered them a source of income, little more, and their own people had as yet no clear thought of independence.

The mother country was still relatively poor. Her merchants were determined to share in the New World wealth and control trade there. Holland was her great competitor at home and overseas, and the merchants knew that the Dutchmen, keen traders and fine sailors, might well defeat them. Dutch ships moved a great part of the West

Indies cargoes; Dutch merchants offered prices considerably lower than the English in Barbados and Jamaica and St. Kitts and for goods that were equally as good.

So representations were made to King Charles II, and a board was established, by odd historical circumstance, on July 4, 1660, to govern closely all colonial trade. It was under the direct supervision of the "Lords Commissioners of the Council of Trade and Plantations." The main responsibility of the members of the board was to examine every transaction that had anything to do with the colonies, check upon each phase of policy and practice, then report in detail their findings to His Majesty.

Parliament had passed an act in 1651 that protected English ship-owners and merchants. It restricted the importation of American, Asian or African cargoes. They could only be moved in ships owned, commanded and manned for the most part by English seamen. Now, in 1660, a further act was passed that continued to bar foreigners from English trade. It named also various articles, such as cotton and tobacco, which could be shipped only from the colonies to the mother country and goods consigned to European ports. This made reshipment necessary and provided more profit for English merchants. But the Lords Commissioners were not yet content, and in 1663 passed another act. It demanded that all foreign goods shipped to America must clear from English ports. The act also forebade one colony from trading with another.

The Lords Commissioners had no idea of how much the passage of the Navigation Acts affected the temper of the people in the colonies. They were not interested. Their concern was profits, and taxes paid into the Royal Treasury. If the colonials were hurt by strict trade barriers, that was regrettable, no more.

Freedom of trade simply could not be allowed. It was a form of treason to deal with foreigners, and the same sort of crime as trade with an enemy in war. Let the Massachusetts folk, and the Virginians and the rest of them, respect the home government and be proud of the fact that they were under English rule, belonged to the glorious realm.

But the people who made their lives in the colonies along the Atlantic coast were not ready to accept the Navigation Acts. They understood that the acts were by deliberate design unfair to them. It was their immediate, inescapable reaction to disobey what Parliament had so carefully created.

They refused in reality any sort of strict control from overseas. Thousands of them had come out from the home country in painful and difficult circumstances to get away from religious persecution. Many more had arrived as indentured servants, worked bitter years to gain freedom. Now they were eager to satisfy their private ambitions and live as they wished, without much restraint from any source.

This conviction held throughout the colonies from Maine on down to New York, New Jersey, Pennsylvania, Maryland and Virginia. All classes, from the prosperous shipowner in Salem to the New York merchant, just freed of Dutch rule in 1664, to the farmer with a frontier homesite back on the Patuxent River off the Chesapeake—all shared a violent dislike of the Navagation Acts. They began to smuggle just as soon as the regulations were passed.

It was in New England that the acts were absolutely flouted. The New Englanders had been in a fierce, lengthy struggle with the sea, the forest and the Indians. Their sense of independence could not be shaken. When they had come to these shores they had decided among themselves who should rule, how and by what set of laws. They were now wholly unwilling to give up their rights, or be deflected from full use of them. Puritanism and their intense desire to get ahead in the world—in their own fashion—brought about a phrase that expressed their feelings. They were compelled, they said, by "the higher law" to reject the Navigation Acts. What they meant, simply, was that the higher law suited their particular interests, had nothing to do with the demands of the Lords Commissioners or His Majesty, King Charles II.

Smuggling in violation of the acts became a very popular form of endeavor. Reports from various royal governors and agents informed King Charles that in the year 1664 alone, when the New

Amsterdam colony was still in Dutch hands, £10,000 worth of
tobacco was smuggled to Manhattan Island. This was so flagrant
that the King was forced to take notice of it. He complained officially in 1665, and the General Court of the Massachusetts Bay
Colony was told to enforce the law. The members of the court took
care with their reply. They answered that they were not aware of
having "greatly violated" any laws.

The Lords Commissioners, along with their friends and associates,
the London, Bristol and Plymouth merchants, had legitimate cause
for complaint to the King. Colonial merchants were merrily under-
selling them in the international market, and with forthright disobedi-
ence brought cargoes directly to European ports. But it was also true
that the Boston merchants could not find suitable cargoes for the
English trade.

Massachusetts lacked such a staple product as tobacco. The Mercantile Theory, which was supposed to support the English economy
and meant that raw materials should be shipped to England to be
manufactured there for further export, did not work for the Bay
Colony. Along its bays and rivers, where watermills and windmills
and forges had been set up, small operations had begun that produced
ironware and textiles and leather goods for the local market without
dependence on England.

The best market for New England fish was not England, but the
Continental countries. That was also true for timber and ships' spars
and masts, and corn and pork, and iron and wool. The West Indian
colonies that did not belong to England were a fine market for
Rhode Island horses, and butter and cheese, and flour and dried
peas. Cargoes that New England ships brought back from West
Indian trade found a brisk sale in Boston. French brandies, Canary
wines, Spanish fruit, olive oil, silk, linen and lace were in constant
demand. So were sugar and molasses and indigo and cotton and log-
wood and silver, along with salt taken from the sea by a crude bucket
system in the Dry Tortugas.

Records kept in Boston showed that by 1688 there were 154 vessels that entered or left the port in the first six-month period. About

eighty-five of these were on West Indian voyages; about thirty-five more were in traffic with other mainland American colonies. But only seven were bound for England, and only two of them arrived from there. There were eighteen bound out for European ports, and seven which entered from them.

The cries of the English merchants reached an almost hysterical pitch. Petitioners to the King warned him of impending collapse of a great part of the economic system. The Lords of Trade had succeeded the Lords Commissioners in 1675, and took over the colonial problem. But they had done little with it. Edward Randolph, a man of resolution and firm will, was chosen after royal approval and sent out several times to Boston to make sure the acts were enforced.

He had no more success than the Lords of Trade. He was forced to report to the King in 1676 that Governor Leverett insisted that laws made by Parliament did not apply to Massachusetts; the Bay Colony, through the General Court, made its own and accepted none other. The outcry was again tremendous when Leverett's report was given to the English merchants. But the best Massachusetts would do in the way of compromise was to reinstate a public oath of allegiance to the King.

The weird and tacit, nonviolent war between home country and colonies was interrupted by a conflict far more grave and terrible for New England. The destruction of the Pequot tribe had never been forgotten by the northern Indian tribes. Word had been carried to each tribe, subtribe and clan from Connecticut on into Canada. The massacre at Mystic was an ugly, galling and open wound for them.

The pressures on the Indians had grown with the establishment of every new settlement, and was particularly severe on the Wampanoags, Narragansetts, Mohegans, Podunks and Nipmucs. Philip, son of the friendly chief Massasoit, was chief of the Wampanoags in 1675, when the situation came to a head over the murder of a settler and the execution of three braves accused of the deed. Philip organized a force and struck at Swansea in June and followed this with many attacks throughout Massachusetts in the next few months. The New England Confederation quickly mobilized and declared war, seizing and destroying Indian villages in Rhode Island and Massachusetts, killing and capturing many Indian women and children. By May of 1676 the Indians had been driven out of the coastal areas, and with their supplies gone and their severe losses they began to surrender in large numbers. Philip himself was discovered and shot in August, his wife and nine-year-old child sold into slavery in the West Indies.

But the war carried on for two more years in the isolated Maine region, where the settlers were the most vulnerable and were subjected to the worst of the horrors.

Death was a close, constant threat for the isolated Maine settlers during the seventeenth and eighteenth centuries. Yet men took their wives and their children alongshore in any sort of craft that would sail, or that they could afford to buy in the last settlement, in a search for freedom and opportunity.

Cruising along the coast, when the fog lifted with the summer sun the husband would leave his family in the boat, his wife probably seated aft, the youngest child on her lap; the spare musket was within reach of her hand. He would take the wherry and row into some cove or slip around a headland on the tide into a small river mouth. Alone, musket gripped chest-high, he searched the undergrowth beyond the beach, inspected for timber, reckoned where he would put his wharf and fishweirs and the mooring for the boat, counted the trees to be felled for cabin space and garden.

He and his wife learned to listen to the sea, but even more to the forest, because from it, surely in time, Indians would come. The forest meant menace and destruction. The sea was hope, escape.

The wife learned to know each sound in the clearing. She could tell when the tide began to change out past the headland and the breeze brought the cries of the herring gulls. She identified the hop of rabbits in her scraggly garden, the waddle and scurry of a woodchuck, the rasp of bees at the top of the clay-and-stick chimney, the thud of her husband's ax against a tall spruce at the edge of the field.

She heard the dog that her husband kept with him and the heifer tethered outside the shed, the chickens scratching for worms in the warm August dirt. The breeze came in the trees, and a fish hawk let go a thin, quick whistle, very high. Ducks flapped in the marsh water. Fire crackled on the hearth under the stewpot. Her youngest child sucked a thumb happily in the cradle, and within the dooryard sunlight the other two played with their pet raccoon.

Her temptation was to sing. Singing was a great habit among frontier women. It walled away the loneliness. But the Maine woman kept silent. There were other sounds, which she heard only in imagination. The war whoop cut like a lash across the nerves. Her husband's musket answered, and the barking of the dog, the lowing of the heifer, for even animals knew the smell, the sound, of Indians. It was then she must move fast and get to the door and see if her husband still lived.

The wife moved to the door, compelled by the keenness of her imagination, living in anticipation the real scene. The path down to the wharf was rough. There were boulders in it, and stumps, old pine roots which the frost had brought up last spring. She would have to run spry as could be and still with care. She had the young ones to think about and the musket to keep.

It was about a hundred yards to the wharf, and then the canoe flopped off it, the young ones chucked in, and herself. Even if she lost the paddle, she could still get going with her hands. And if the braves were too near, she could give one the load from the musket. The boy might reload for her before they were aboard the shallop.

Slip the mooring was what her husband had told her. There was no bother with casting off wharf lines, and time lost. Just that single mooring line to slip. Head for the point and open water. Braves weren't too ready to chase far out to sea. Then, for her and the children, there were the settlements to the westward and a lee at Orr's Island, and Bailey's or Ragged. Folks would come and give her help.

The wife must have stood times without count in the cabin doorway while held by the dream. It was often a stark, terrible fact on the coast. All that was found after a raid was the column of smoke from the burning cabin, and for those who went there to look, a few bones gnawed by the foxes, a child's toy and maybe a bit of London ribbon a brave had dropped.

The sea remained the only road to and from safety for the early settlers. The people who lived along the great, forbidding headlands, the tide-bedeviled bays and the swift rivers became superlative sailors. They perfected their seamanly skill so that they might stay alive and took from the forest rim timber that they made into craft that would withstand anything except the severest winter gales or the pressure of tons of ice.

But by 1675 and the outbreak of King Philip's War the Indians of the northeastern tribes also used the sea. They had learned the white men's sailing methods, and they understood amphibious attack. During September of that year they crossed the river at Saco in a fleet of pulling boats of English design, went into the settlement with the torch, the musket, the tomahawk and the knife. They were finally driven off, and the attack was only in part successful. Still they were able to stave in their boat bottoms, make sure the hulks floated downstream before they entered the forest.

A war party hit two months later at New Dartmouth. The target this time was a new shallop just completed by an ambitious pair of settlers, Thomas Tucker and George Hiskett. She was launched in the water alongside her dock and being rigged when the Abenakis jumped her crew. The white men fought hard, but the Indians drove them out of the boat and took her. Indian riggers finished the work that was needed, and she was sailed to sea.

No record is left of what the Abenakis did with her. But there is an account of how she was recaptured some time later. She met His Majesty's sloop-of-war *Mary* at sea off the coast. The Abenakis engaged *Mary* in a cruel, stiff fight with muskets and cutlasses before the English sailors seized her.

Almost every settlement on the coast, either built by white men or Indian wigwam villages, was set ablaze in the following year of terror, 1676. The fires reared weird beacons alongshore at night, and Indian sea raiders set courses by them in their captured craft. The

Indians had an admiral now, a leader who directed the raids and had a detailed plan of action that included a final, major assault upon Boston.

This was a man whom the English called Rogue Mugg, in terms of hatred, and from the fragmentary reports about him he was an Abenaki sachem, a man of great bravery, sea cunning and sense of strategy. He made raid after raid during 1676, increased his fleet of small craft and trained their crews to handle canvas and cannon. Then, in September, he took a large amphibious force against Jewel's Island, in Casco Bay, and against the Sagadahoc colony.

The braves were divided into two groups. Those who went to Jewel's Island landed and raced up the beach and killed every person in the settlement. Rogue Mugg was in command of the group that made the landing at Sagadahoc. He left as soon as he had secured the place. Prisoners had told him that a shallop and a ketch were at Damariscove, in the Kennebec.

He sailed over with a picked crew of warriors, boarded and captured the shallop. But the men in the ketch were a tougher lot. Two of them were killed and yet the rest pulled the craft clear into the river, got away after a running fight.

Rogue Mugg had gathered the basis of a solid fleet of coastal craft. By the end of 1676 he held a thirty-ton ketch, a shallop that could carry eighty men and another, smaller shallop. There were in addition to these, whaleboats, wherries, skiffs and canoes, all of the common types to be picked up around a settlement and all of them valuable when a raiding party was to be put ashore.

Francis Card, a local settler taken prisoner at the time, was able to talk at length with Rogue Mugg in the lapses in the fighting. The Abenaki did not have the usual, implacable Indian hatred of all white men, and Card learned from him Mugg's ideas for future operations. Card wrote afterward about them. He said that Mugg intended to "take vessels and go to all the fishing islands and soe drive the country before him in the spring."

The plan had great validity. The so-called fishing islands, Matinicus and Monhegan, held the major portion of the white population in eastern Maine. Once Mugg had cut them off, he could stop the coastal trade, and without them the other settlements must soon starve or surrender to the Indians.

With the vessels he had seized Mugg could move on to the Massachusetts Bay region. He would assault from the sea the various islands in the bay, blockade or directly attack Boston. A prominent objective in the plan, Card reported, was "to burn Boston." If Mugg took and burned the place, the condition of the English in the New World became at once very precarious. The victory could easily set off other massive Indian attacks as far south as Virginia, sweep also up into Nova Scotia.

Mugg was the leader of perhaps as many as a thousand braves, a very considerable force for the period. They owned every reason to hate the English. Survivors of the defeated tribes that had taken part in King Philip's War came North and described how Philip had died and why. Bands of Mohawks from the Hudson River valley, lasting friends of the English because the French had once fired on them with muskets, marched overland to the Penobscot and wantonly pillaged and burned Penobscot tribal villages. English traders working along the river used rum as a lure, trapped, bound and kept aboard their boats a number of braves whom they later sold as slaves. The established price for an Indian scalp, paid readily on Monhegan Island, was five pounds.

So Saco went up in flame, and Brunswick, New Meadows, Scarboro. The Indians raided by land and sea. Whites were forced to retreat to their garrison "strong houses" and the fortified, stockaded villages, abandon any outlying settlements. The killing continued, although some of the eastern tribes of the Abenaki still did not seek open war. Woolwich was burned, and Arrowsic, Pemaquid, Damariscove, New Harbor; Monhegan was filled with refugees.

Behind Rogue Mugg appeared two men who might well have aided him in his grand plan of attack. One was Madockawando, the sagamore of the Penobscot tribe, a man of decided authority and ability who had done his best to maintain peace, then furiously entered the war, ashore and afloat. The other was a most remarkable French nobleman, Baron Jean Vincent l'Abadie St. Castin.

St. Castin had been born in the town of Béarn, at the foot of the Pyrenees, and joined the French Army as an ensign while still in his teens. He served with distinction against the Turks and in his early twenties came out to Canada. The concept of life in the vast wilds of the continent fascinated him, and he left the narrow, high-walled French towns in the North, moved along gradually to Penobscot Bay.

He chose for his homesite the finest promontory on the east side of the immense, rugged body of water. He built as Lion Gardiner had done in Long Island Sound, but the baron went much further. Conditions were different here.

St. Castin built a log fort to protect his trading post. He emplaced cannon, equipped his personal force of Penobscot braves with muskets, pikes and cutlasses. Then, as his fur trade with the tribes prospered, he sent vessels back to Quebec. He ordered from France splendid, fragile furniture and rugs, tapestries and glassware to hold homeland brandies and wines. Madockawando became his close friend, and St. Castin formally married the sagamore's eldest daughter, although he had at the time a number of other wives taken from Abenaki stock.

St. Castin was much more of a landed proprietor than he could have ever become at home. He fulfilled and surpassed the hopes of such men as Sir Ferdinando Gorges and the Puritan aristocrats who had clung to the belief that here in the New World they could maintain an existence of idyllic splendor. They had been defeated; Sir Ferdinando had lost several fortunes in attempts at colonization, and his cousin, and the members of the other merchant adventurer groups had soon given up, admitted failure, gone home to England.

The French baron thrived. His nature was satisfied here. He was a man in his middle forties, with an estimated fortune in furs of 300,000 crowns and at least a score of half-caste children, when King Philip's War was fought and the worst of the Maine raids began. He wanted no part of them. Peace was to his fashion, not war. Yet it is quite probable that he had reason to fear the English, who openly coveted his trade with the Indians, and he was in many ways allied with the Abenaki people. He could have privately advised Rogue Mugg and Madockawando, pointed out to them how they might wage war.

Still it is equally probable that as a veteran European officer he could recognize the small chance of Mugg's eventual success. The Indian sea leader had enough braves to form crews for the captured vessels, but they had been trained in canoes. They knew nothing about sail handling, steering offshore courses, long-range night pursuit and gunnery. The Indian flotilla had an even more serious problem. Rogue Mugg lacked powder for his ordnance, and the source of supply was in French Canada, hard to reach and maintain. Then, with each ship arrival from England, the white forces were being strengthened, and steadily, in their fierce raids, Mugg and Madockawando lost braves they could not replace.

The warfare continued, sporadic, sometimes halted for intervals of uneasy truce, then renewed with savage ferocity by both sides. Word was brought to Salem on July 16, 1677, that thirteen locally owned ketches and their crews had been captured to the eastward. A group of fourteen principal citizens immediately offered a petition to the General Court that asked for punitive measures against the Indian sea raiders. Money was spent quite liberally, a "man of war Ketch" equipped, a crew of forty men found for her and her command given to Captain Manning. Then a fast day was proclaimed, and people of the town scrupulously attended church meeting after the ketch had sailed for the coast of Maine.

Captain Manning returned a few weeks later with some of the captured vessels and nineteen wounded men from their crews. Salem considered itself lucky. There was widespread rejoicing in the primly whitewashed little town. There was a rumor that Rogue Mugg had been killed in a violent attack upon Black Point, May 16, 1677, yet no positive identification had been made, and Mugg's name as an Indian leader was to persist for another fifty years of New England history.

Peace came after almost incredible destruction and periods of truce that were often broken by a sudden, bloody raid. The treaty was signed at Brunswick, Maine, just below Merrymeeting Bay, on April 12, 1678. All told, the four New England colonies had lost approximately six hundred men and a great number of women and children. Ten per cent of the available fighting force in New England was gone. Thirteen settlements were gutted to the ground, and approximately 1,200 houses and barns. There was also a vast loss of seagoing vessels, canoes and wherries. Livestock had been slain wholesale. For two years straight no crops had been harvested. The war cost Plymouth the estimated sum of £100,000 and the Massachusetts Bay Colony much more than that.

The tribes had suffered tragic, irremediable losses. Three thousand of them were dead, killed in combat, caught by a new outbreak of a white man's epidemic for which they held no immunity or dead from hunger and exposure. The white men as they had raided in the back and forth surge of war had destroyed the tribal villages, the plantings, the fishweirs and the canoes.

A few "neutral" bands remained near the coast, and a sorry lot known as "praying Indians," who mainly for want of food had been converted by missionaries. The rest, a temporarily broken people, retreated into Canada and Nova Scotia and gathered strength for another assault, their hatred of the whites greater than ever.

CHAPTER EIGHT

AN INDIAN NAVY

The indomitable spirit of the Maine settlers was shown by the group that chose to settle on Casco Bay after King Philip's War. Thirteen Salem men who had served as militia soldiers in the region were given a five-mile-square grant "at the bottom of Casco Bay on a river called Swegustagoe." Three years after the ghastly slaughter here they moved from Salem with their families, prepared to risk their lives in the attempt to stay, sustained by an amazing courage that must have had at its base the absolute conviction that this country belonged naturally and irrevocably to the white man.

They had nine years of peace; then, in 1690, fighting was renewed. This time joint colonial action was taken against the French, whose cruisers from Port Royal, Nova Scotia, had been harassing the Grand Banks fleet and the coastwise and West Indian trades and whose agents had been inciting the Indians against Maine trading posts. So the first colonial amphibious task force was mustered at Boston and command of it given to a Maine-born man.

He was Sir William Phips, whose reputation was just as fantastic as that of Baron Castin. But, unlike the chateau-born baron, Phips was raised in a dirt-floored cabin in the frontier settlement of Wool-wich on the East bank of the Kennebec. His father was a gunsmith from Bristol, and both his parents were of the Puritan faith. They

91

reared between them twenty-six children, of whom twenty-one were sons, and William, the last, was born in 1650.

The rest had left home and Woolwich by the time he was able to earn a living. His father was dead and his mother in want, and William worked as soon as he could heft an ax. But he was big, heavy-shouldered, and there was a lot of work in the Kennebec shipyards. He made a living as apprentice and then shipwright and finally went to sea as a carpenter in one of the vessels built by the yard where he worked.

He was forty-two by the time he had taught himself to read, but that was not uncommon in the period, and he had already married a wealthy widow, made a fortune, found a title along with sunken treasure and been appointed by Charles II to be High Sheriff of the Massachusetts Bay Colony. Then, of course, for his task force duties he was known as Admiral and later as Royal Governor of Sagadahoc.

The story of the sunken treasure and what was called "Phips's luck" was well-known in every New England seaport tavern. Phips had heard about the trove during a voyage. A Spanish galleon was supposed to have grounded, broken her back and sunk on a reef in the Bahamas, with $1,500,000 in gold and silver ingot in her holds. Phips verified the story as much as possible and then managed to get royal backing in London. His Majesty, Charles II, lent him the frigate *Algier Rose,* and Phips took her to the Caribbean in 1687 and sent down local Indian divers who raised the treasure. Phips was knighted for that and given a small share of the treasure, $75,000, but along with it the High Sheriff office in the Bay Colony. It seemed to many who knew him that perhaps he was not the best potential admiral in the colonies. Still he was liked by His Majesty, and this would be a royal force he commanded.

Phips brought together a very mixed fleet of eight small ships. They carried almost eight hundred soldiers, mainly Massachusetts militiamen, and he took them to sea April 28, 1690, from Nantasket Roads, outside Boston. It was a fair weather voyage, and the motley collection of vessels kept reasonably good station, arrived off Port

Royal together. The commandant of the French garrison knew better than to fight against a force that outnumbered his ten to one, and on May 11 he surrendered. The brawny, ship-weary Massachusettsers went ashore and thoroughly plundered the place, expressing their Puritan devotion by very complete demolition of the Catholic chapel.

Phips sailed back to Boston with a greatly increased belief in his abilities as an admiral. But the campaign had achieved two purposes, the first of which was to show the colonies that it was well worth the effort to fight together against the common enemy. The second purpose was to prove the extraordinary worth of the most mobile part of Phips's force, the whaleboat-borne Cape Cod infantry companies.

The whaleboat fleet, fifty craft at maximum strength, was commanded by Lieutenant Colonel John Gorham, an excellent soldier and the son of a locally famous Indian fighter. Gorham was a Barnstable man, and so was Captain Ben Church, who had actual command of the men. Church wrote the Royal Governor, Dummer, and described the fleet. He said he had called for forty or fifty "good whaleboats, well-equipped, with good oars and twelve to fifteen paddles to every boat. And upon the wale [gunwale] of each boat, five pieces of strong leather to be fastened to each side to slip five small ash bars through, so that, whenever they land, the men may step overboard and slip in said bars across, and take up said boat that she may not be hurt against the rocks."

Captain Church estimated that under maximum conditions a force of as many as five hundred men could be carried by a fleet of fifty boats. These craft were of the magnificent, slender-hulled design that had long since become so popular along the stormy shores of Cape Cod. They were generally of 28-foot length, with about 4-foot beam and quite shallow draft, so they were particularly useful in river and bay work for reconnaissance. The men who handled them were from Barnstable and Eastham and Yarmouth and Sandwich and Provincetown; for any distance over a mile they would much rather row than walk.

The boats they took to war used the regular lugsail, and all of the

men's equipment and provisions were carried in them. When Colonel Gorham gave the command to halt at night and pitch camp the boats were brought ashore with the ash bars through the gunwale loops, careened on the beaches and then made to serve as shelters that were much more substantial than any tent. It was quite logical that a great amount of pride was generated by the sea-borne companies, and one of their boasts was that they had in their ranks many Indians, men born and reared alongside each other on Cape Cod.

But, while Phips had scored what was regarded a real victory at Port Royal, the French recaptured the port the next year, and the unity of action of the colonies did not last long. Commissioners from Massachusetts, Plymouth, Connecticut and New York had met at New York to plan a general, massive attack against Canada. A land force was to go up the Hudson River from New York, then overland along the traditional route to Montreal. Contingents of troops from Maryland and the four northern colonies were to be in it. They

would march while a fleet sailed from Boston and navigated the St. Lawrence and attacked Quebec.

The plan was grandiose and existed mainly on paper. New York could only send 150 men, although she had promised 400 as her share. Massachusetts recalled 160 of her troops after Casco was sacked, burned. Plymouth failed to send a man, and Connecticut was well below her quota. Indian volunteers who alleged to hate the French and love all English settlers were too glib to be fully believed, and they began to desert, and then various militiamen.

The rest of the expedition blundered through the woods past Albany, somehow missed ambush and reached Wood Creek, where they camped. This was near the southern end of Lake Champlain, and the conviction of both officers and men was that it would be foolhardy if not outright unhealthy to go any further toward Canada. Some hostile Indians finally appeared, and some Frenchmen. Small skirmishes were fought; then the colonial force went home, unhindered.

Phips was in command of the amphibious force, though, and he had sailed from Boston on August 9, 1690, with the firmly declared promise that he would take Quebec. He again led a very mixed fleet of thirty-four vessels, brigs, schooners, ketches, shallops and pinkies, and into them were crammed about 2,200 men. The whaleboat companies were with the fleet, often sailed ahead of it and scouted the coast. They found the scattered and sparse French garrisons unwilling to fight; still the fleet took nine weeks from Nantasket Roads to Quebec.

Phips lacked a pilot to negotiate the last few dangerous miles of rapid river below the citadel. He broke out a signal for the fleet to anchor, and for three weeks the vessels remained there. It was a strange experience for the high-strung, badly disciplined men of the militia outfits. They wanted to go ashore and fight, and over yonder on the bank were the hated Frenchies in their gaudy white uniforms and along with the Frenchies the even more hated "Tawnies," the Frenchmen's Indian allies.

Phips made several tentative sorties, tried to put men ashore, and was met by intensive French fire. He released his feeling of frustration by extended cannon fire from the fleet. When his powder stores were exhausted he realized that he must sail for home and could not take Quebec.

He reached Boston in November in his flagship, and the other vessels straggled astern of her. Some did not make port at Boston until February, and others were never reported after they had cleared from the St. Lawrence. It is likely that Indian sea raiders accounted for several in the wide, foggy reaches of the Gulf of St. Lawrence, in Passamaquoddy Bay, off Grand Manan Island and along the snowbound and bitter winter coast of Maine.

The colonies had suffered enormous disaster as a consequence of Phips's stupidity as a commander. There had been a dire lack of medicine, blankets, uniforms, boots and food. Pneumonia joined with smallpox in the evil, dank holds that were called troop quarters in the transports, and a thousand men, almost half of the force, died of disease. Those who survived staggered ashore and found they were to receive no pay for their service.

Promises were made by the various colonial treasuries, but all of them were broken, and there had been nothing like loot in Canada. The veterans raised their voices in rage, and finally a form of paper money was issued to quiet them. It was politely called Indented Notes, and £4,000 of it was distributed and afterward discounted at from 30 to 50 per cent. Phips himself died in 1695.

In 1703, as a result of Queen Anne's War in Europe, also known as the War of the Spanish Succession, fighting broke out again in the New England colonies, and the Maine settlers once more bore the brunt of it. Governor Dudley had brought together a number of Indian chiefs at Casco in June of that year. They stood solemnly under a tent and heard him promise lasting peace and replied with the presentation of a wampum belt as a sign of their good intentions. Some of Dudley's officers, though, examined the muskets the warriors carried and discovered that they were loaded with shot, primed, ready to be fired. Six weeks later, every unprotected house in Maine was aflame or had already been burnt. The war was to continue for ten straight years.

During that decade of terror many of the leading men of the northern colonies came to realize that Canada must be conquered before the Indian raids would stop. After two unsuccessful expeditions against Port Royal in 1704 and 1707, once again an important French and Indian base, a man named Samuel Vetch, a Scot and a former officer in the British Army, became convinced that a concerted attack should be mounted. Vetch had come out to New York and met and married the daughter of Robert Livingstone, a wealthy merchant, and then gone into the fur trade and moved to Boston.

He often left Boston in a small craft loaded with truck goods and sailed north as far as the St. Lawrence and the French settlements there. He learned a lot from the Indians with whom he traded and after several voyages established the fact that the French-held territory was very poorly protected. He told men in Boston and New York that he knew more about eastern Canada than the French, and aware of his record, his listeners agreed.

The colonial authorities sent him to London in 1708 to represent them. Queen Anne received him at court and accepted every request he put forward, promised to make him governor of Port Royal if he took the place from the French. It had become the base for French privateer activity, and menaced all English shipping on the coast. He returned filled with ardor and was met by the same two-pronged attack theory which had been used at the time of the abortive attack by Phips on Quebec.

Vetch could only agree to it, and then waited through the winter of 1709 while the land operation dragged and stopped. British regular infantry and Royal Marines and Royal Navy ships had been promised Vetch, and they at last were ready in Boston harbor, along with a strong force of colonial militia, among them Cape Cod whaleboat men.

A dinner was given at the Green Dragon Inn on the evening of September 18 by Sir Charles Hobby, the commander-in-chief of the expedition. Then, the next day, with the wind and tide right, the force sailed. It was made up of 400 Royal Marines and about 1,500 colonials divided into four battalions. The ships were the Royal Navy fourth-rate frigates *Dragon, Chester* and *Falmouth* and two fifth-rates, *Lowestoffe* and *Faversham*. There were also the quite famous colonial Indian-fighting shallop *Province Galley,* which had been commanded by Captain Cyprian Southack in a number of engagements, and a bomb ketch, twenty-four small transports, two or three hospital ships, a tender and several coasters that were loaded with timber to make beds for the cannon and mortars.

Vetch served as chief pilot and second in command and brought the force in good style into Port Royal harbor on September 24. But the tide boiled through the narrow harbor entrance with mill-rip speed, and one of the leading vessels was slung out of control, hit the rocks, cracked herself wide and sank with the loss of twenty-six men.

Vetch moved the rest ahead safely, put them to the anchor above Goat Island and in unobstructed sight of the French garrison.

The whaleboat men discharged the transports the next day. Vetch had been given command of two battalions and took them to the northern side of the fort, and Colonel Francis Nicholson landed with the other two and occupied the southern flank. French cannon and musket fire became sharp the day after as Nicholson's men hacked through underbrush toward the outerworks of the fort.

Offshore, the bomb ketch had already begun to fling her slow-tumbling missiles into the fort, and siege guns and mortars were hauled to the beach. The heavy pieces were set in position, and the Marines in their bright red coats and the colonials in their greasy buckskins were within four hundred yards of the ramparts.

The French commander, Subercase, was a veteran. He sent out emissaries under a white flag. There were in the fort ladies who should not be subjected to the British cannon fire. But Sir Charles Hobby wanted complete surrender and not parley. Subercase surrendered.

It was all performed with extreme ceremony. The British officers gave a breakfast party for the French ladies in the fort, although none of them could be called at all fluent in their guests' language. Then Vetch took over as governor. He had as a garrison force 200 Royal Marines and 250 colonial militiamen who had volunteered for the duty.

The name of the place was changed to Annapolis Royal. Signals were made aboard the fleet. Salutes were exchanged between the fleet and the fort, and the fleet sailed for Boston before ice began to enter the bay. This had been a real victory.

There was afterward for some few years a troubled, never wholly realized peace. Fishermen working the Banks alone in summer fog were suddenly surprised by braves who silently paddled bark canoes. Settlers who stooped for a moment too long over their fishweirs beside a river bank looked up at red-daubed faces, musket muzzles and death. Crews back from Caribbean voyages reported being met at sea by craft that Indians sailed. Some of those Indian vessels carried swivel guns, and the braves were eager to close with the white men, use their pistols and cutlasses.

The *Boston News Letter* of Thursday, February 20, 1724, contained a proclamation by Governor Dummer. He asked for a general fast to be held for relief from Indians and pirates. But the main result of the penance was hunger. No more Indian sea rovers were caught, and Dummer conceived the idea of decoys. He inveigled various Cape Cod "tame" Indians to go to sea and trick into capture the sea rovers. The Cape Cod braves failed him, though, and happily enough went back to work ashore.

By the middle of June the Indian sea fighters had taken eleven fishing vessels, with a total complement of forty-five men. Twenty-two of the lot were killed in combat and twenty-three made prisoner, of whom several were wounded. Ships and men were held for ransom, and the Indians stated their terms: £50 apiece for the vessels, and £30 each for the men. The Indians also put a time limit on the transaction; the exchange must be made within three weeks.

The news excited intense fury in Boston. Two ships were fitted out at once for punitive action and given crews of twenty-five men each. Then they were sent to the eastward on an Indian hunt and were to make rendezvous with two other strongly armed ships from New Hampshire. The New Hampshire ships carried crews of twenty men apiece, and it was the hope of the authorities that the combined squadron could meet and overcome the Indians, free the captives.

But then on July 13 there was news that an Indian-manned schooner had seized a shallop and possibly other vessels. Boston fishermen talked of pursuit of the schooner, yet did not leave the harbor. The House of Representatives was told on July 16 that the crews of two schooners, fourteen men in each, lacked any desire to sail to the eastward. The crews offered a petition to the government. They wanted "their friends and relations" ransomed from the Indians and the captured vessels returned to their rightful owners.

Samuel Hicks of Piscatua, in Maine, offered to give his ship and the services of a thoroughly armed crew to go after "the heavily armed Indian Pyrat who goes in a Marblehead Sconer [schooner] with a Great Gun that chases Everything and has taken Many and has driven the Fishermen from the sea."

The *Boston News Letter* carried a story that came from New Hampshire. Indians had just seized a pair of shallops that belonged to settlers who lived on the Isle of Shoals. This seizure prompted the Lieutenant Governor to send two armed shallops to sea with crews of twenty men apiece. They were to make a rendezvous up the coast with a pair of Maine shipmasters, Dr. George Jackson, who sailed a schooner, and Sylvester Lakeman, in command of a shallop. The Maine vessels were manned by seasoned crews of twenty sailors, and they eagerly sought the "Marblehead Sconer."

Then, on the same day that the *Boston News Letter* printed its story, word came in from Ipswich. Indians during the preceding week had taken several fishing vessels owned by townsfolk and killed four men. The Lieutenant Governor issued another proclamation in Boston. The watch turned out, the drum was beaten through the main streets and before all the taverns, and volunteers asked for immediate sea duty. Fifty men responded and boarded two vessels, one of which carried six swivel guns. The crews were cheered as they left port.

Word of the force was received July 30. The message said that Dr. Jackson and Captain Lakeman had made port in New Hampshire on July 24, following action at sea. They had been cruising further north, off the mouth of the Penobscot, when they met a big Indian schooner. She was armed with two swivel guns and did not attempt evasive tactics of any sort. She hauled in toward the enemy vessels.

Dr. Jackson sailed the bigger and faster of the colonial ships. He trimmed canvas aboard the schooner and pointed her on an intercept course that should allow his gunners to rake the Indians broadside. But the Indians changed tack for tack with him and held the fire of their guns. Lakeman in the slower shallop fell astern, and the action would be fought at first by the schooners alone.

Then the Indian commander hauled his wind. He came around on another tack, braced his square topsails hard and ran across Jackson's bow at close range. It was the classical battle maneuver and flawlessly executed. While the former Marblehead craft leaned to the wind and sprays slapped the deck, her redskinned gunners in their breechclouts and gaudy war paint thrust the slow-match embers against the touch holes of the swivel guns.

The round shot took the mainsheet and the shrouds out of Jackson's schooner. Her mainmast shivered and almost snapped, and Jackson shouted to the helmsman to take her off the wind, release the pressure on the spar. Then Indian musketeers raked them with a volley of swan shot. Jackson and two of his sailors were wounded by it. An Indian sharpshooter with exceptional aim then struck the mate with a musket ball. Well past the foundering schooner, the Indian commander rounded up and went on an inshore course. The Indian vessel was last seen as she sailed swiftly into the upper reaches of Penobscot Bay.

But Captain Lakeman in the shallop did not chase. He knew better than to go after gunners and sharpshooters like that in the confines of the bay. His duty was to stand alongside the crippled Jackson schooner, and he put men aboard to help set up jury rigging. Then, with Jackson's mainmast secured, Lakeman moved ahead and gave the doctor a towline. Weather held fair, and he was able to tow the schooner into Portsmouth.

The news of what was really a dismal defeat caused further fury in Boston, and protestations of the superiority of white seamanship. Command of another search squadron was given to Lieutenant Chambers, who must have been emphatic about his needs. He was assigned two schooners and a shallop, a crew of forty men in each.

The Lieutenant had no success, though, despite the size of his command. A Salem man named Marjory was commissioned on August 10 to take the sloop *Lark* and a whaleboat out after "Indian pirates." It meant that the colony had at sea a fleet of at least fifteen vessels carrying a force of between four and five hundred men.

Time still served the side of the colonists, and by the next year the Indian leaders must have been aware that they could not win.

Norridgewock, a large Abenaki village on the Kennebec, had been surprised in August, 1725, and the inhabitants massacred. They were Christian converts and had built in the village a fine church for their preceptor, the famous French missionary priest, Father Sébastien Râle. He had been killed while he stood in the doorway of his cabin, and it was burned along with the entire village.

Indian settlements the length of the northern coast were heaps of ashes. Brush grew across the cornfields. Braves did not dare go ashore and take fish from the river weirs; they would be ambushed while they worked. The last dream of the tribes was that they might be able to live at sea.

A settler named Westbrook wrote to Royal Governor Dummer and told him, "Saccaristis affirms that 2 of the [Indian] sconers are to go fishing . . . and they have taken seals at Grand Manan and St. Johns." Another man, named Giles, reported that Indians "were sealing on Matinicus." There were further similar messages, and Dummer became worried. A sloop was sent from Boston to Barnstable to recruit Cape Cod Indians to go and fight against their northern cousins. The Nauset braves accepted the pay and went to sea, but with no great willingness, and achieved little. They were allowed to return home and go back to fishing.

The Abenaki, the Micmac and Beothuk braves who with their families had made the sea their final refuge fought to the end. A fisherman named James Marsh gave word that on July 6, 1725, the fishing fleet was attacked while off Cape Negro, Nova Scotia. There were one hundred warriors in the canoe assault, and they took five ships, imprisoned the crews. Then they manned one of their prizes and pursued Marsh. He escaped them only because of the headstart they allowed him when they transferred to the new vessel and the fact that he had a fast-sailing vessel under his feet.

There were other attacks and violent victories. They diminished, though, and the white men were able to defend themselves, keep clear. The Indians did not have a home port where they might careen and repair their ship hulls. There were for them no shipyards, no ropewalks, no sail lofts. When a spar was shot away in action it was renewed only with vast difficulty and the replacement taken from another vessel. Blocks wore out or were smashed; rope frayed, was spliced, respliced and spliced again; anchors were needed, and cable and tar, pitch and paint; gunners spoke about the shortage of powder and slow matches and the danger when a cannon with a worn-thin bore was overheated and exploded.

The braves at last accepted defeat. They had lost the sea, as well as the land. Nothing was left to them except the distant inland regions of northern Canada. They left their ships and retreated to it, all hope gone.

CHAPTER NINE

TAXES AND REBELS

Even while the bitter years of Indian warfare lasted, the New England colonists continued their increasing, undeclared conflict with England. It was based on the same old issue of the freedom to trade without undue restriction and taxation enforced by the home country. When England remained obdurate the outcome could only be revolution in search of independence.

Beneath the surface calm that was still maintained during the last decades of the seventeenth century the surge of sharpened resistance could be felt. The more intelligent of the King's counselors were seriously worried. They gave intense thought to a possible solution. There were, they discovered, a number of men of a moderate disposition who were prominent leaders in colonial affairs and who wished to hold onto the ties with the home country just as much as the King's people.

The strange and religiously lopsided government of the Massachusetts Bay Colony was changed in 1686 without much trouble. The validity of the colony's charter had been challenged because of violations of the Navigation Acts and persecution of Quakers, who, after all, were English subjects. A man named Joseph Dudley, the son of a famous early governor, was sent out from Boston to protect the charter. But after it was annulled by the Court of

Chancery, dominion status was established instead, and Dudley was appointed by the King to rule as governor of Massachusetts, Maine and New Hampshire.

When Charles II died in 1685, a professional, fire-breathing soldier was chosen by the Lords of Trade and the Duke of York to supplant Dudley. Sir Edmund Andros, who had already served briefly as governor of New York, was given sweeping powers over what was to be known as the Dominion of New England, all of the territory from Maine to New York and later, in 1688, New Jersey. His orders were to crush the irascible, independent Yankee spirit and keep the bustling and ambitious pack of colonials firmly in line.

He began by going after Baron St. Castin's small domain in Maine. A Royal Navy frigate, H.M.S. *Rose,* had been stationed at Boston, and Andros sent her to wipe out the log-walled French trading post on Penobscot Bay.

H.M.S. *Rose* opened fire from offshore, then dispatched a landing party. The defenders disappeared into the forest before the Royal Navy men landed, and the place was looted and burned. The baron had left for France several years before, but the post was occupied by his half-caste son and a group of Abenaki warriors. It was quite understandable that young St. Castin became thereafter a violent enemy of the English and kept the Abenaki tomahawks lifted against them.

Andros went on and annexed Maine in the name of King James II. He spent large sums in bribes and barter goods, made friends with the Five Nations, the Indian tribes who held great power through western New York State. He built forts at harbor mouths and where rivers met the sea. He reorganized the militia units and greatly tightened their discipline. Under his rule King James was to be respected and things done right, just so and fully according to English law.

The colonists, though, did not share his patriotic fervor. And they had no liking at all for his imposition of quitrents, a property tax they had never paid to the crown. They resented the fact that Andros had forced himself into Old South Church in Boston and insisted that a Church of England service be held.

Then in 1689 there was revolution in England. William of Orange took the throne, and the Massachusetts people started their own rebellion. A detachment of mutinous troops had just returned to Boston from duty along the frontier, and were threatened with disciplinary action. Armed bands of civilians went into the streets to keep them from arrest. The Town House was seized, and a very unpopular character, Edward Randolph, still employed by the Lords of Trade as a customs collector, was captured, along with a number of the King's officers.

Governor Andros had fled to the protection of the fort on Fort Hill. Twenty companies of rebels took up positions around it. They mounted cannon and got ready to attack. Andros surrendered rather than risk bloodshed, and a Committee of Safety was formed by the colonists.

Cotton and Increase Mather had been leaders of the rebellion, and were active in the formation of a convention that brought back the charter form of government. Other colonies that were part of the dominion followed the Massachusetts action and declared themselves free. William of Orange had a difficult choice and finally overlooked the rebellion and called it a manifestation of respect for his new dynasty. Andros, Randolph and the rest of the King's men were allowed to take ship for England.

But the colonists had no great enthusiasm for King William despite his gesture of peace. They knew that in time he, too, would begin to tax them. This was a change of rulers only; the system was just the same.

Another Navigation Act was passed in 1696, and this one contained a registration clause of extreme importance to the colonists. It stated that all decked vessels engaged in ocean-going commerce should be registered. Bonds were to be posted by the owners of the craft, and would be claimed by His Majesty's government upon failure to comply. Even canoes were included in the clause, and permits were issued for them. But undecked vessels doing trade within "plantation waters" were not required to register.

Colonial dislike of the home government turned to hatred. Shipowners and shipmasters, fishermen and merchants who dealt with them entered the offices of the customs collectors in the various ports to ask some very embarrassing questions. They said that navigation inside Chesapeake or Delaware Bay, and coastwise, which under the law included voyages to the Bahamas, the Leeward Island group in the West Indies, and fishing off New England and Nova Scotia and Newfoundland, was almost as dangerous as any transatlantic passage. In very simple language the so-called coastwise vessels needed the same seaworthy qualities as those engaged in overseas trade. Why, then, were the decked vessels taxed and not the undecked? And why bother with canoes at all?

The customs collectors, remembering what had happened in Boston, were quite polite and vague with their answers. They placed the blame upon the Lords of Trade and said that they must write London for further instructions. But in 1697 a far more serious blow was struck at colonial independence. Vice-admiralty courts were established in the major ports, and Royal Navy officers were shipped out as staff for them and to serve as customs collectors and inspectors.

It was the beginning of the final, irreparable rift between the mother country and the colonial community along the Atlantic seaboard. A grievous mistake had been made by the Lords of Trade, by Parliament and the King. None of them had appreciated the fact that the entire foundation of life in the colonies was sea-borne trade. Without it, and without free use of it, colonial America could not exist.

William Wood, an early visitor to Salem, had written as far back as 1634 in his book *New England's Prospect* about the common need for canoes. He described them as "made of whole pine trees, being about two and a half feet over and twenty feet long. There be more canoes in this town than in the whole Patent; every household having a water-horse or two."

Men went to work in canoes and came home that way at night. There were thousands of them in use in the great, deep Maine bays, in Massachusetts and along the Hudson and the other waterways to the South. When Captain John Smith went to explore upriver from Jamestown in the Virginia Colony he rode a "water-horse" and watched the local Potomac Indians while they killed deer from the same sort of craft. The animals had been flushed out from the forest by a hunting party that set fire to the underbrush. They were frightened and in panic as they entered the river; the waiting warriors in the canoes killed them with ease at short arrow shot.

Smith learned to hunt in the Potomac fashion and taught other Jamestown settlers. But canoes were used for all kinds of purposes, hauling corn and fish and oysters and bales of furs and the first bales of tobacco. People who had need for larger craft propelled by sail generally bought or built shallops and ketches. They cherished the vessels, maintained them in the best possible condition.

Families who had ventured away from the settlements and taken up homesites out in the wilderness appeared regularly for Sabbath meeting aboard their boats. Father held the tiller, and his wife was beside him on the stern seat. The eldest boy handled the sheets and the docklines with his younger brothers. Everything was done smartly, with a great deal of style. This was a seagoing community, and the parson watched the landing along with the rest of the village folks.

Road conditions were still miserable in all of the colonies. It was not until 1722 that a team of horses was driven for the first time from Connecticut to Rhode Island. During one week in September of 1725 there were twenty bears killed within a radius of two miles of Boston. Land travel was not only hard along the so-called King's Roads; it was highly dangerous. People kept to the water whenever they could and built their homes and towns and livings along it.

Manhattan Island merchants moved Hudson River scows with

cargoes of wheat that cost them twopence a bushel for a hundred-mile haul. But inland, over in Pennsylvania, to make the same haul it cost a shilling a bushel, or six times as much. Forty wagons and 160 horses and 80 teamsters were needed to haul the goods that could go as cargo aboard a scow with a crew of two or three men.

The colonies had constructed and put in use a really amazingly complex fleet. There were the well-known canoes, often called piraguas, and the sloops, shallops and ketches. Then there were wherries, and pinnaces, and scows, and wood boats, and flatboats, and lighters and ferryboats. There were also special types like the double-hulled catamaran rig used for spear fishing and the Chebacco, which had a sharp, "pink" stern and was built in what was known later as Essex, Massachusetts, and put in service for inshore fishing.

The moses boat was built for a special purpose in the West Indian trade. She was an open craft used to haul hogsheads of sugar and molasses from shore to ship. Oars moved her, and she was broad and flat-bottomed, shaped a good deal like a walnut shell. Her hull was of lapstrake construction, about eight feet long, and generally one man handled her and carried a single hogshead as load. Young Massachusettsers making their first trips to sea became very familiar with moses boats and pulled them back and forth under the West Indian sun until they were dizzy.

The whaleboat had been refined in hull design and construction until it was one of the most beautiful and seaworthy crafts ever to be launched. The gundalow was not very much like the sleek Venetian passenger carrier from which her name was taken. She was really a coastwise sailing barge with a roughhewn log hull, a stump mast and a big, single hold sometimes sixty feet in length, where loads of marsh hay were stowed, or timber or brick or almost anything.

For offshore work there were brigs and snows and barks. But none of them was much bigger than *Mayflower,* and they were kept mainly within the two-hundred-foot over-all length. Designers still held to the theory that a ship should be no longer than three times the width of her beam. Colonial ships were less ornate, better built

SLOOP

GUNDALOW

PINNACE

SHALLOP

CHEBACCO

PINKY

double-end MOSES BOAT

"BALTICK"
an 18th Century SCHOONER

WHALEBOAT

"SPARROW HAWK" 17th Century KETCH

Penobscot WHERRY

and faster sailers than the vessels that came from English yards, though they looked boxlike and in a heavy seaway rolled their beam-ends under.

The new men among the Royal Navy officers assigned to the colonies soon became familiar with the various elements of the American merchant fleet. They also found strong, continuing opposition to the Navigation Acts. This was particularly true in New England.

A very large part of the population of the New England towns was engaged in shipbuilding. The farms of the region were of necessity all within horse-and-wagon range of navigable water. Excess farm crops that could not be sold locally went by ship to some other colony or to Europe. It was quite ordinary for a farmer to help load such cargo. When winter closed in, too, many farmers left the land.

They had learned young how to reef sail and how to hand and steer. So they shipped out for a coastwise run and for the West Indies and Europe and England. The memory of their parents' great voyage from England to settle here was a powerful influence in their lives. They were moved by tradition and a deep curiosity about the world offshore.

There was, though, no unified effort in the colonies to bring about repeal of the Navigation Acts and no immediate sign of rebellion against the crown like that at Boston. An almost fatal weakness was in the colonists' dislike and distrust of each other. They were much further apart mentally than they were from any physical separation. People rarely went from one colony to another, and only a few leaders or men on pressing business took the trouble to travel.

People spoke of their neighbors in the next colony as "strangers." They sometimes called the land beyond their own borders "foreign," and to go there was to go "abroad," and that was dangerous and costly. All of the old religious and political differences were remembered, and the broken promises about help in time of Indian trouble. Life was much different in Maine than in Massachusetts and again more so in the Carolinas and Virginia.

The Royal Navy officers were able to take over gradually and at least set up customs control and systems of registration, inspection and taxation. Some form of control had already been established, because in theory the governors of the colonies were assigned to those duties. Delegation of naval officer authority had been given in Massachusetts to the secretary of the colony, and the same was true in Pennsylvania.

There were so many creeks and rivers and bays and tidal backwaters in Virginia and Maryland, and as a result no fixed ports of entry, that the first naval officers were forced to cover more than one county. This was obviously a physical impossibility if the crown was to expect anything like efficient service. So the staffs were increased, and became finally six for each colony. The officers, though, often held several jobs at the same time; they were members of the colonial councils also and even justices of the peace. Many of them, on into the early part of the eighteenth century, were appointed by the royal governors. Then this method, clogged thick with graft, was abolished. The naval officers served by His Majesty's warrant and commission, and the graft was just as great as ever, only paid in London instead of the colonial capitals.

Between 1675 and 1715 customs offices were opened in forty-nine different ports. The staff included more than ninety surveyors general, surveyors, riding surveyors, collectors, comptrollers, searchers, preventive officers, landwaiters and tidewaiters. There were in addition clerks, accountants attached to some of the offices, watermen and boatmen on stand-by call at the waterside.

Their number grew as further offices were declared necessary and pressure was brought upon the customs service and the royal treasury to recruit new men and prevent smuggling and the running of contraband goods. It became quite common for the same man to serve as collector, surveyor, seacher, naval officer and comptroller. Great friction was built up between surveyors general and collectors and between collectors and royal governors. The barrage of charges of bribery, negligence, connivance and joining in illegal trade was constant, and there was a swirl of involved stories about imperfect and erroneous accounts.

Corruption had of course spread like dry rot for generations through the Royal Navy and all English maritime life. Officers paid for their appointments to various ships; victualers supplied bribes along with rotten beef and biscuit for the fleet. Contractors paid inspectors to overlook slovenly work, and shipwrights and carpenters and riggers paid the contractors to be hired to do it. So the customs service was by no means exempt.

All kinds of men were attracted as recruits. Some came because their fathers had been in the service in England. There were others who were transferred from duty in England and Ireland. Families, friends and relatives recommended a further number. Then there was a bigger than usual collection of people looking for easy work, and ordinary hangers-on.

The head of the American service held the title of surveyor general, and the first was a man named William Dyer. He was sent out in 1683 to check the work of the collectors and to "endeavour to reduce all his Majesty's officers in the colonys to one uniform method and practice in the execution of their respective dutyes." But Dyer never got very far, and it was Edward Randolph, as surveyor, collector and searcher while stationed at Boston in 1678, who was given the most severe blasts of colonial hatred.

The colonist had been offered right along all sorts of inducements to violate the Navigation Acts. It was unlawful to haul tobacco from the colonies direct to a foreign port. But a man could export fish and barrel staves. Salt was permitted as an import, but not Spanish iron. Spanish iron, the law said, must be bought in England, and this was at a time when it was in keen demand for shipbuilding use. Restrictions on tobacco added to the cost or reduced the profit for the weed in the colonies, while the price of iron climbed. Sail a ship with a tobacco cargo straight into a Spanish port and come home laden with iron, and there was a lot of profit. It was easy arithmetic to prove the homeward-bound cargo would bring in more, too, if the revenue charges, the dues and port fees weren't paid.

The naval officers were paid by the fees they collected and in some cases by a percentage of the cargo values. They did their utmost, unless dissuaded by violence or a bribe, to catch any ship that tried to slip into port duty-free. It was their duty to grant certificates of entrance and clearance, which were valid only when signed by the collector; and also to take the oaths of the master or the bosun of each vessel leaving port that she cleared legally; and to examine all certificates and clearance records and navigation bonds brought in by the masters of arriving vessels. These last documents, after they had been proven authentic, were stamped by the naval officer's own seal. He was directly responsible to the governor, and was often called the governor's man. The ship lists were turned over to the governor for examination by him or his secretary and were then sent on to London and the Lords of Trade.

There were further duties for the naval officers. They reported the exact details of each ship that entered or cleared port. This demanded a description of the vessel: her kind of rig, her tonnage, where and when she was registered, the master's name, the owner's name, the number and caliber of the guns aboard, a crew list and a copy of the cargo manifest. The Lords of Trade, who at last received such data, had become sharply interested in exact knowledge of colonial shipping.

England was almost steadily engaged in warfare with her European neighbors. It was quite important to have accurate information about the armament carried aboard her merchant ships. The Lords of Trade learned for example that thirty-three ships given clearance to sail from Maryland and Virginia in the month of January, 1690, carried an average of sixteen cannon apiece. They were also informed of the calibers, the amounts of powder and shot.

But with all the exactions of their duties the naval officers were paid, in legal terms, very little. A most extraordinary man who holds a weird, unclear corner in history and who owned the name of Richard Coote, Earl of Bellomont, had a great deal to do with the colonial customs service. He was royal governor of New York in the 1690's and later of Massachusetts. The tax collection problem galled him severely, and he sent many lengthy complaints to the Lords of Trade.

He stated in one report written in 1700 that the New York Assembly had reduced naval officers' pay so low that " 'tis worth no man's acceptance." Then he wrote further that in Massachusetts the Assembly had reduced such wages until "they are not sufficient for the true subsistence of an honest man."

Officers in some of the colonies were paid by fees alone. There were others who received a percentage of the values of the cargoes they inspected. Neither form of payment was enough; yet appointments to the customs service were eagerly sought, if only because a member of it was often in the governor's confidence and had both political influence and an inside, often financially worth-while knowledge of ship movements.

When the collection system was fully established in a port such as Boston around 1700 it was found that a collector was needed, and a comptroller, also a surveyor, a searcher, a tide surveyor and four port waiters. Two of these port waiters served as weighers and gaugers, and there were also on the Boston staff eight "able-bodied" men who served as tidesmen and boatmen when vessels with dutiable cargo were expected to reach port. The tide surveyor and tidewaiter stayed aboard an incoming ship until she was completely unloaded. A landwaiter or a waterman boarded a ship when she was tied up at her wharf. He notified either the collector or the comptroller of how the cargo discharge was handled and further helped the searcher in the supervision of the landing and disposal of the ship's goods.

There was at first a quite wide range of payment for the officers who worked on a percentage basis. They took from one eighth to three fourths of all customs receipts. The rest of the money, sooner or later, reached the King's hands. Then, in 1696, after the Lords of Trade had decided to reorganize the service, all officials above the rank of tidesman, except the surveyor general, were made a part of the home country establishment.

This meant that, like the surveyor general, who all along had been paid directly from England, they were given the same rights and powers, and were subjected to the same penalties, as the officials at home. Their pay came out of the English exchequer, but the fact did not stop or in any way slow down the flow of graft. Smuggling still flourished; dutiable cargo items were not listed, and went from ship to shore at night, and sometimes, if the market demanded, in broad daylight.

When the ship *Fortune* came into the port of New York under the command of Captain Thomas Moston, a very disreputable character, it was known that her cargo had been bought from Madagascar pirates and was worth at least £20,000. Bellomont in his capacity as governor ordered Chidley Brooks, the collector of customs, to seize the ship. He told Brooks that Captain Moston was an admitted pirate and made no secret about where the cargo was. Brooks replied to Bellomont, "It was none of his business, but belonged to a Man of Warr."

Brooks delayed for four more days after that before he took any action. Meantime, Moston was busy moving and selling cargo. He got rid of all but a thousand pounds' worth before the customs service people told him he should pay duty.

There was just as much trouble for Bellomont outside New York. He wrote the Lords of Trade that the four closest ports on Long Island openly defied the King's right to taxation of goods. The people there received lawless cargo from "ships and sloops" every day. They were "so lawless and desperate" that Bellomont could not get anybody who was willing to try to collect the royal revenue from them.

Further north, in the Boston area, the citizens worked against him in flagrant contempt of the law, and he felt beleaguered. He informed the Lords of Trade, "When ships come in the masters swear to their manifests; that is, they swear to the number of parcels they bring, but the contents unknown; then the merchant comes and produces an invoice, and whether true or false it is left to his ingenuity." This was not all, and Bellomont hurried to make known:

"If the merchants of Boston be minded to run their goods, there's nothing to hinder them. Mr. Brenton, the Collector is absent and has been these two years; his deputy is a merchant; the two waiters keep public houses, and besides that coast is naturall shap'd and cut out to favour unlawful trade."

A great many inward-bound ships put their cargo ashore on Cape Ann. Then, without any particular attempt at concealment, the goods were brought to Boston in "wood boats," a thin layer of kindling pieces stacked on top. There were merchants, though, who did not believe in this form of subterfuge. They ran the ships that carried their cargoes right into Boston harbor.

It was economical, and it gave quicker service to the consumer. Boston had sixty-three wharves where a ship could tie up and discharge. There were another fourteen in Charlestown. None of them was guarded.

Lord Bellomont, who had become involved in the strange and never satisfactorily explained affair of Captain William Kidd, the alleged pirate, was the target of outright derision on the part of the Boston merchants. During his rule as royal governor shipmasters went regularly to Newfoundland and Canadian ports. They put their vessels alongside French, Spanish and Dutch ships and bartered various cargo items. Then they returned to Boston, and the goods they had picked up were sorted out for distribution in the West Indies, in Paramaribo, and along the Brazilian coast.

Bellomont once more wearily made his plea for help to the Lords of Trade. This was in 1700 and from New York. He wrote to admit that he was "quite dispirited from want of orders" from England. His superiors gave him an answer that contained small satisfaction. His letters, they said, were so long and so confused that it was difficult to reply to them. He was advised to confine himself to discussion of just one subject at a time.

What had happened, much more than Bellomont or any of his superiors realized, was that the entire system of the King's government had fallen into very serious disrepute in the American colonies. Men flaunted the regulations and then went further; they doubted the ability of the royal officers to enforce what was called law in London. Smuggling, as such, was a small share of the feeling of lawlessness. Only about 5 per cent of the population engaged in it.

There was a great deal of work and a considerable amount of danger connected with landing contraband cargo at night in some fast-flowing Maine river or on the broad, sandy beaches of Long Island and the tidal flats of Currituck or Pasquotank Inlets, the backwaters of Port Royal Sound, the Delaware, the Chesapeake. A man could do better aboard a privateer, and if that did not give enough, he could go "on the account" and join the Madagascar lot as a pirate.

The vice-admiralty courts were a constant source of irritation for the colonists. They resented them and their judgments, did everything possible to block enforcement of the verdicts. Then there were the collectors and receivers of the King's casual revenues to stir up hatred of the regime. These officers were appointed directly by the crown, were under no authority in the colonies and right from the beginning caused trouble.

Their duty was to collect the casual revenues that came from royal licenses and from escheats—confiscations in the name of the King. They gathered in waifs, strays, wild cattle, horses, hogs, treasure trove and goods that had belonged to felons and suicides. They exacted the fines issued in vice-admiralty court, and the King's thirds from ships seized for illegal trading, and from whales and from deodands. A deodand was anything that moved, either animate or inanimate, and was a cause of death. It could be a falling tree or a sawmill blade or a log that rolled along a skidway. It could also be a weapon or an animal or a ferryboat that capsized. The law said, too, that a ship that entered fresh water was considered to be deodand. If she should careen and kill people working aboard her, the ship's owner was liable to prosecution.

The law held other stipulations to outrage the colonist. Vice-admiralty courts took it upon themselves to pass down decisions that had to do with the rights and ownership of whales and the many, constant disputes that arose on the whaling grounds. The officers of the crown contended that by royal grant "whales, dolphins, sturgeon, porpoises, grampuses, and in general all fish whatever remarkable for their largeness and fatness" belonged to the Admiralty. They should be handed over, with a tenth of all train oil and whalebone.

When the colonists strenuously objected, the vice-admiralty courts divided the decision into two parts. The judges claimed entirely for the crown drift whales, those which because of illness cast themselves up onto beaches and died there. They went on, despite repeated objections, to the second part of the ruling. This had to do with whales that had been struck by a harpoon while being pursued, had escaped and then later died of their wounds.

The court's decision was made in favor of the man—or boat crew —that had struck the first blow. It was usual for the judges to award five eighths of the value of the prize to the plaintiff and the remaining three eighths to the defendant. This, though, was ancient and unwritten fishermen's law, and the colonists were vexed that they had to go to court to establish a verdict.

More and more, the feeling along all of the coast had become one of rejection of England's ways, her laws, her authority. Still the independent-minded men of influence who would be needed to lead a successful rebellion of any sort held themselves from action. They were too busy making a living and starting their family fortunes.

The Massachusetts Bay shipowners, a very powerful group in the colonies, prospered. They grumbled, mocked people like Bellomont, refused to pay exorbitant taxes and let it go at that. Despite the losses of vessels in the Indian wars and the restrictions of the Lords of Trade and the menace of piracy, shipbuilding had greatly increased around Boston.

Governor Hutchinson had reported in 1676 that there were thirty vessels of between one hundred and two hundred tons in the vicinity of the bay. Later, at the end of the century, Boston officials said there were almost 200 seagoing vessels sailing out of that port, whereas in New York only 124 similar ships were registered. New York sailors were already accustomed to the twanging, cocky verse they had heard often overseas and come to dislike. It was:

> *Wide-awake Down-Easters,*
> *No-mistake Down-Easters,*
> *Old Massachusetts will carry the day.*

CHAPTER TEN

PIRATES AND PROFITS

The contempt for English law that the shore population felt was gradually sharpened to a fine edge by the men who went to sea in colonial ships. They had learned early that their ships could outsail most of the Royal Navy vessels, and they were certain they were better sailors than the impressed English crews. Their gunnery was just as good if not better, and their officers could lay off a course, bring a vessel along to hold the weather gauge faster than His Majesty's supposed finest in their tight white pants, lobsterback coats and fancy wigs.

Colonial vessels had been equipped with cannon almost since the first of them was launched and put in service. The legacy of piracy that for centuries had plagued honest seamen who sailed the waters around the British Isles had been transferred and vastly expanded in the New World. Right at the heart of all piratical venture was the enormous wealth owned by the colonial Spanish and so clumsily moved from the Caribbean on annual voyages to Spain. It was a tremendous temptation for a ship's crew to follow the wallowing, slow-sailing *flota* and cut out one of the vessels that was sure to lose station and fall astern, expose herself to capture. A flat, rough bar of Inca gold, or a hatful of pieces of eight was all a man would need to buy a couple of hundred tidewater acres at home.

Religious intolerance was another factor in the increase in piracy. Englishman hated Spaniard as a heretical unbeliever, and the other way around, and no mercy was shown by either. An English or colonial seaman captured by a Spanish crew could at best expect quick death from a bullet or a cutlass blade; if he were really unlucky, he would be held for the Inquisition torturers at Cartagena, in South America, or be shipped back in irons to Spain to be burned publicly at the stake in the main square of Seville.

Young seagoing New Englanders of Puritan and Pilgrim stock solemnly swore to each other that they would never be taken alive by the Spaniards. While their ships were in doldrums during a slow watch they practiced cutlass handystrokes by the hour, went furiously through attack and parry. They snapped their pistols at imaginary targets, even hurled them butt first across the hatches into piles of old sails as a secondary use of the weapon. Those were supposed to fetch up against some Spanish captain's jaw.

Many of the New England shipowners encouraged this form of belligerency among their crews. The more rapacious instructed the shipmasters to practice gunnery at regular intervals at sea. What represented a fully legal letter of marque vessel was most difficult to prove offshore, and the difference between privateer and pirate had always been in doubt. A Spanish vessel was of course a fair prize at all times, and the government in London was forever getting into wars with Holland and France. Those ships could also be attacked—if they were not too fast and heavily armed. If they were, the order was to haul around, change course at once and run.

New England ships were not usually supplied with heavy armament. They had been built as cargo carriers, and that was still their primary function. Their guns were mainly culverins, which weighed about two and a half tons apiece and could throw an eighteen-pound iron ball approximately a half mile with fair accuracy. The ships might also mount as battery weapons in broadside position a couple of sakers. These weighed around fifteen hundred pounds, and their projectile was a six-pound ball.

It was customary to put into most ships swivel guns that were called petereros, or "murdering pieces." They were light, of small caliber, long in the barrel and with a bulbous muzzle, fired at point-blank range a charge of shrapnel made of old iron, broken bottles and glassware. They were mounted on the ships' bulwarks and more feared than the long-range, powerful weapons.

For over a century, from late in the 1550's until after the sack of Cartagena in 1697, many of the colonial crews found their favorite port of call at Tortuga. They picked up there all sorts of information about naval gunnery, ship combat and boarding tactics. They came away with amazingly low-priced cargo items, loot taken from Spanish *flota* ships. Back home they told long, strange stories about the place.

Tortuga was a small and hilly island a short sail beyond the sweep of Cap Haitien on the northernmost coast of Hispaniola. The great island stretched to the south and formed with Cuba, over the horizon to the west, the Windward Passage. Here nearly all of the important Caribbean traffic passed and must pass. Tortuga, which meant "turtle" in Spanish, held an extremely strategic position, and on the beach above the shallow anchorage and further, on top of the highest hill, were the huts of the headquarters settlement of the only completely free society ever to exist in the New World.

It had been started by Frenchmen, a group of Huguenots who with their leader, Pierre d'Esnambuc, came out in search of religious liberty to St. Kitts. But they fought with the English already settled there and went to Tortuga. A few Englishmen of a different kind were on the smaller island; they were deserters from ships, castaways, and runaway indentured men who had been helped to escape by the crews of various vessels in the colonial trade. Huguenot French and outlawed English joined together in almost instant understanding. They were the men, about a hundred originally, who called themselves Brothers of the Coast, and were to be known later as filibusters, buccaneers and freebooters.

With some of the original English as pilots, they crossed the strait between Tortuga and Hispaniola, secured their boats on the smooth yellow sand at Cape Haitien and struggled through the sea grape up from the beach. They filed through cactus, wild cane brakes, bamboo and head-high ferns, past groves of palms bent by the Trade Wind. Then they entered the beautiful northern plain and the narrow, rain-cut valleys that led from it into the mountains of the Massif du Nord.

This was country that Columbus had first explored. The Frenchmen found that cattle he had put ashore were in great abundance in the mountain pastures. They were excellent shots and armed with well-made French muskets that had a good carry. A number of them decided to stay on Hispaniola as hunters of cattle, made an agreement with the other Brothers to bring in basic supplies from Tortuga and to sell their hides to homeward-bound Dutch ships.

The men who stayed were called *chasseurs;* those who supplied them with shot, powder, salt and rum were called *freiboteros* in the weird polyglot language the Brothers talked. The *freiboteros*—or freebooters—were named after the lugsail craft they sailed. The third group remained on Tortuga and did some primitive farming along with barter and the sale of the *chasseur* hides and were known as *habitans*. But no matter which part of the organization a man had chosen, they all shared equally in everything. There was no personal profit; they were truly brothers.

For a time they worked and lived in perfect peace. This, though, could not last, they knew. So they accepted a Frenchman named Bertrand d'Ogeron as governor and made a loose working agreement with the French West Indies Company for supplies and military assistance in the case of Spanish attack.

It was the Spanish they feared, nobody else. The *chasseurs* living in the wild highlands of the Massif du Nord on Hispaniola had at first hunted in pairs and then with young apprentices called *valets* to help them skin and peg and stretch and lug the green hides. But Spanish garrisons were in central Hispaniola, and their officers were acutely aware of the Brothers of the Coast.

Word about the organization had spread across the Spanish Main, from Cartagena to Cuba and the Bahamas. Men came steadily to join it. They were of half a dozen nations, but none of them Spanish, and they shared two things in common, love of freedom and hatred of all Spaniards.

Detachments from the Hispaniola garrisons were sent against the hunters in the mountains. Men were surprised in their sleep, or as they stalked the cattle through the guinea grass of some savannah or crouched at dusk over a fire pit and roasted meat for supper. They were systematically destroyed by the detachments until they took to hunting in groups of ten and twenty. Their method of roasting meat and drying the cattle hides in Arawak Indian style over a fire pit called a *boucan* got them the name of buccaneers, and their ability to fight back brought further Spanish attacks.

The Brothers were driven from the mountains. The idyllic life was finished, although for some time they refused to admit it. Many of the men had married former streetwalkers shipped out from Paris, settled down as farmers along the northern plain. They were also mercilessly slaughtered by the Spaniards, and Tortuga was attacked and seized.

The Brothers who survived took the vessels remaining to them and went to sea to find vengeance and loot from the Spaniards. They raided the Caribbean from one end to the other and marched hundreds of miles to strike at rich inland towns, crossed the Isthmus of Panama, went down the west coast of South America and looted, pillaged, burned, killed in memory of their lost dream.

Many of them were with Captain Henry Morgan in 1671 when he made the great raid on Panama City. They had long since taken back Tortuga, but they only used the place as a home port where they outfitted, careened and repaired their vessels, caroused and gambled away their loot. When the Sieur de Pointis came after recruits for his Cartagena raid in 1697 over five hundred Brothers were willing to join him. They were not fairly treated, though, when the heavily fortified city was captured in a long siege and the loot distributed. De Pointis tried to pay them the same small amount given to the regular troops under his command.

The buccaneers were promised more loot and kept from mutiny. But de Pointis delayed, and finally they took it for themselves. They treated the people of Cartagena with frightful cruelty until they received a vast sum of gold and silver. Then they boarded their ships and shaped a course for Hispaniola.

They were met at sea by a combined Spanish-English fleet formed to catch de Pointis. Eleven buccaneer ships were lost in the battle, among them two that carried most of the loot. The rest were so severely holed and pounded that they could barely keep under sail until they reached port at Ile aux Vaches, off Hispaniola. It was the last voyage together for men who had been members of the Brothers of the Coast.

The old, free life was finished. The men who chose to remain in the ships became common pirates. But the buccaneers left behind them an almost unbelievable record. They had during the years 1665 and 1671 alone sacked eighteen cities and four towns and more than thirty-five villages. All of these were Spanish-owned, and they later sacked Puerto Bello, Campeche and Cartagena and went to Panama with Morgan.

The buccaneers were to be remembered for their phenomenal skill as musketeers and gunners. They also had great ability to camouflage a vessel, hide her within a brief period of time in a tropical river or cove under foliage, branches, ferns and palm fronds. Men who were their companions on shore raids could never equal the stamina and speed they showed while marching, nor the jungle lore the buccaneers had gathered from the shy and gentle Arawaks who had once lived peacefully near them in the mountain valleys of Hispaniola. Some of their stories were recalled, how whole roasted steers were eaten with a pimiento sauce, the way wood doves and pigeons should be fixed on a spit and the correct herbs to be added to a cask of rum for flavor and as a preventive against the fever.

Soon, though, the buccaneer stories were nearly forgotten. The pirate crews were hard-pressed. Action was quite constant as the vessels ranged outward from the Caribbean into the Atlantic, went as far North as Nova Scotia to raid the fishing fleets. A pirate could only live in the present. Even the most profligate and stupid of them knew that time must run out; it would not be long now before death came, not long at all.

Captain John Roberts, a New Englander turned pirate, had called often at Tortuga and learned several lessons from the buccaneers that he adopted as sound. The profit motive, so strongly stressed in the northern colonies, was behind his choice to turn pirate, and he went about the trade in a very efficient manner.

He took trouble to discover that for some years buccaneer crews had sailed in possession of a Portuguese letter of marque. This was issued to them at a reasonable price by various governors of Tortuga, although the officials had nothing to do with Portugal and refused to speak the language. Then, while at sea on the lookout for possible prizes, the buccaneers flew a very peaceful-looking white flag. They only took it from the halyards and bent on a red battle banner after the first, usually crippling broadside had been fired into the prey.

Roberts kept a concealed drawer in his cabin full of letters of marque, false certificates, cargo manifests and port clearances. He stuffed a signal locker with different flags, and none of them was the skull and bones or Jolly Roger. He regretted the loss of the buccaneers and proposed to live longer, by guile and not gunshot.

It was known to him that slavers engaged in the new and growing trade sailed close to the coast of Martinique and flew the French flag at the masthead. Merchants eager for a favorable deal saw his ship from ashore, believed that he carried slaves and hurried to get their own vessels under weigh and out to meet him. They came with considerable sums of money to pay for the slaves they intended to buy. Roberts met them, robbed them and hauled offshore flying the Dutch flag.

He took fourteen vessels, one after the other, in the same really very simple fashion. But because he flew the Dutch flag on departure the people on Martinique insisted to themselves that he was a Dutchman. Then he captured the governor of Martinique aboard a prize and hanged him at once from the main yardarm. The governor died convinced that Roberts was neither Dutch nor a gentleman.

Legality had several meanings, and there were always methods like those Roberts used to keep within a semblance of the law. Men of a venal nature and with no particular moral scruples and a bit more daring than other merchant ship captains went on the account, became active pirates. New England, because of its flourishing maritime industry, attracted a number, although none of the rest ever displayed Captain Roberts's flair at seagoing masquerade.

A further factor was that the crews of the pirate ships had acquired international status along with the flags they flew. Men who served in a ship taken as a prize were often willing to sign articles with their new shipmates. If they failed to join the pirate company, they would very probably get shot, hacked to death or marooned on some Caribbean reef without food and water. There was a further consideration: when the law caught up with them they could always swear in vice-admiralty court that they had been forced to join at pistol point. Meanwhile, life was not much worse than aboard one of His Majesty's ships of the line, where the crews were held from shore leave for years at a time.

The Rhode Island pirate vessel *Good Fortune* had a Negro and a mulatto among her sailors and a man known only as Old South as one of her mates. Many Negroes, and some Arawak and Carib Indians, were in the outlaw crews, as well as Portuguese, a few Spaniards who were proven renegades, Scots, Irish, French, a good number marked men and felons, runaways from indenture, the Royal Navy and the press gang. They did not own much sense of mercy, and yet it amazed their captives to find how many people they let live. This was done mainly for profit, because often, as part of the share-out, pirates were allocated "slaves" whom they could sell as they wished.

Still there was a small, stubborn feeling of sympathy for the underdog that persisted, saved a number of lives. Hatred was confined to the masters of seized ships. When those men were discovered to have been brutal with their crews, their deaths were awful, if swift.

A popular form of protest against the system of British taxation was to give aid to piracy. It was also profitable, and there was actually much more to be gained ashore from "the account" than afloat.

The American colonies competed with each other to supply the pirate vessels, all at extraordinarily high prices, and to attract them into port and receive the loot. New York for a while was much more active in the trade than Boston. But Providence and Bristol, in Rhode Island, were also strongly interested, and men along the New Jersey coast, in Baltimore and Philadelphia, Virginia and the Carolinas.

Pieces of eight were common currency in New York, also doubloons, and what was called "Arab gold" and came from the loot taken by ships that cruised off Madagascar in the Indian Ocean. The New York Governor, Benjamin Fletcher, entertained certain pirate captains in his home at dinner, welcomed them as his friends and was seen with them in public. He was happy that his lady wore fine Madras silk shawls, gifts of the pirate captains, and massive pieces of jewelry that not too long ago had belonged to Indian princesses.

Colonel Frederick Phillipse, a leading member of the city council, made no effort to conceal the fact that he dealt with pirates. He sold them gunpowder and alcoholic spirits, flour and all sorts of ship's stores. Other New York merchants sent out articles the pirates needed, established factors on Madagascar and took a double profit, the rest on the loot given them in return. Robert Livingstone, a manor lord and a colonel of militia, was known as a backer of Captain Kidd on his unsuccessful voyage. He had better luck, though, with other captains, and was aided by friends in the Royal Navy.

His Majesty's station ship *Richmond* was anchored in the Lower Bay and according to regulations supposed to keep a sharp lookout for all illicit traffic. Pirates as notorious as Glover and Hoare and Moston and Tew and Coates came right up past her while her crew suffered a severe case of temporary mass blindness. They were rowed ashore from their vessels at the Battery, went openly through the streets to report to Livingstone, then went to pay their respects and the expected share of the graft to Governor Fletcher.

The usual bribe was seven hundred pounds to land an illicit cargo. There was often in addition another sum asked, one hundred Spanish dollars per man for the number of men in the crew. A wily harbor diplomat, a man named Giles Shelley, arranged most of the landing details. He owned a fleet of fast-sailing sloops, sent them to meet pirate ships offshore, carry messages, bribes and cargo. This supplied him with quite a nice living.

But the Deputy Governor of Rhode Island, John Greene, felt that less business should be given New York. When Captain John Avery and his crew landed on Fisher's Island at the head of Long Island Sound Greene moved fast. He knew that Avery and the crew were internationally notorious as cutthroats. His reasoning was that they should not stay around, and might possibly be enticed to New York by Giles Shelley.

So Greene supplied the whole Avery crew with a change of clothing. He procured horses for them, and a guide who put them safely on the Boston road. They left still in possession of "great treasure" and with a warm feeling of gratitude for Rhode Island and the Deputy Governor. What his recompense was from Avery is unknown.

Rhode Island was already being called "the chief refuge of pirates," and Sir William Phips, the governor of the Massachusetts Bay Colony, regretted the fact. He cooperated with the local merchants to become recognized as one of the outlaws' best friends. His effort was intensified when he learned that Governor William Markham of Pennsylvania had married off a daughter to one of Captain Avery's pirate lieutenants and that in Rhode Island a cargo of Indian Ocean loot worth £100,000 had just been received.

Puritan ethics had suffered a drastic change in Boston in the last few years. Mr. Gough, who ran the mercer's shop, admitted to having once taken part in a raid on an Arab junk bound for Surat. He had "got a good estate thereby" and afterwards retired to more peaceful and legal business in Boston. Crews of pirate ships who reached the city in 1694 carried as their whack of the share-out £1,500 a man. The merchants, along with the dramshop keepers and the agents of Governor Phips, took most of it and wanted to know why the men did not immediately seek another ship headed for Madagascar.

New England thinking put a very low opinion on the practice of piracy in local waters. There was, first off, not much profit in it for anybody, and the men who worked at it should be sailing the Indian

Ocean, far from home. The natives who went on the account and attacked coastwise shipping were accused of lack of imagination, navigational skill and the energy to go after foreign trade. Still a local pair named Thomas Hawkins and Thomas Pound became a real menace in 1689, and the Massachuserts people sent a sloop out to catch them.

She was the *Mary* and commanded by Captain Samuel Pease. He took her to sea October 4 and was informed that he could find the pirates in Tarpaulin Cove, a fine anchorage in one of the Elizabeth Islands, across from Martha's Vineyard.

Captain Pease saw the pirate craft in the center of the smooth-shored cove. He entered and came within hailing distance and called for surrender. One of the pirate captains, Pound, gave his answer by running up the red battle banner on the halyards. Pease told his gunner to lay a shot close aboard, and a second shot to be fired to emphasize the first.

Pound drew his sword. He shook it and yelled at Pease, "Come on, you dogs, and I will strike you!" His crew knelt at the bulwark beside him, and they then fired a musket volley into the *Mary*. The fire was accurate, and *Mary* suffered a good deal of harm.

But Captain Pease put grapnels aboard the pirate craft. He secured, and sent boarders to take her. A severe handystrokes action was fought which the government people finally won. Pease was wounded during it and died five days later. The pirates, tried and convicted, were hanged.

Piracy also had its lighter side for many of the New Englanders who were led to cynicism by the lack of action of their officials. James Franklin, Benjamin's older brother, got himself in trouble with the law when he printed June 7, 1722, a humorous account in *The New England Courant*. This was a weekly newspaper he owned and published in Boston, and Benjamin, although only seventeen, was already writing for it.

The offensive piece carried a Newport, Rhode Island, dateline and told of a pirate ship that had been sighted off Block Island. Prompt steps had been taken to capture the vessel, *The Courant* said. Two ships had been sent out against her. Then at the end of the account Franklin reported: "We are advised from Boston that the government of Massachusetts are fitting out a ship to go after the pirates, to be commanded by Captain Peter Papillon, and 'tis thought he will sail sometime this month, wind and weather permitting."

The Massachusetts government had done nothing about outfitting a ship, and there was no man hired by it whose name was Captain Peter Papillon. The supposed captain's last name, after all, meant butterfly in French. It was not hard for the King's officers in Boston to reach the belief that the Franklin brothers were making fun of them.

The article was read before the Massachusetts Council on June 12 and an order was issued for James Franklin to appear and be examined. He admitted that he owned and published "the said paper," and he was told that the council had resolved that the article was "a high affront to the government." The sheriff of Suffolk County then took over, and Franklin was committed to the town jail.

Benjamin ran the paper with great skill while his brother was in jail, and a number of the readers were given to think that he had written the objectionable article. James was in jail for four weeks. When he was released another affront was offered the government on the front page of the July 16, 1722, edition. It read: "And then after they had anathamatized and cursed a man to the Devil, and the Devil did not, or wold not, take him, then to make the Sheriff and the Jaylor to take the Devil's leavings."

James Franklin had only been able to leave jail on a promise of good behavior. The authorities had further ordered him to post a bond of £100 and to submit all material for the newspaper to the Secretary of the colony for his approval. They were not pleased by the further blast at their dignity, and *The New England Courant* was finally put out of business February 11, 1723. Benjamin, who had been serving his brother as combination publisher-columnist-printer's devil, left for New York to find work and went on from there to Philadelphia.

One of the most notorious and sought-after pirates along the New England coast was Captain John Phillips. He captured the

Cape Ann sloop *Dolphin* in the fall of 1723, but not for her cargo of cod. What he wanted was hands to replenish his crew, and he took the best men from the *Dolphin*.

Among them was a twenty-one-year-old Ipswich fisherman named John Fillmore. He had shipped for work on the Grand Banks and had no intention of turning pirate. But Captain Phillips stayed at sea for seven months, and Fillmore got homesick and impatient. He conspired with three men taken from a big Boston ship seized as a prize, and one night after the pirate crew had been carousing, suddenly attacked them. Phillips, his sailing master and his quartermaster were killed, the rest subdued.

Fillmore brought the pirate ship into Boston on May 3, 1724, then went home to Ipswich. Three of the pirates, after trial, were hanged in chains on Bird Island in Boston Harbor. Three more were sent to England, tried in London and hanged on Execution Dock.

The sun-swarthy "Madagascar men" with their heavy gold loop earrings, their shoulder-long hair and wide black belts and floppy pants found that they were no longer so popular along the New York waterfront. Piracy had somehow during the first part of the eighteenth century become old-fashioned, and any really bright man who followed the trade called himself a privateer. But there was as yet no consistent, strict enforcement of the law.

Known, proven pirates were still the big spenders and favorite patrons in the taverns along Dock Street and Great Queen Street and the Beaver Path. They sprawled wide-legged at the broad plank tables and ate meat pies and rusks and wild turkey, venison, duck and leg of lamb steeped in wine, partridge barbecued in bear fat, cauldrons of clams and lobsters, vats of buffalo and beefsteak stew, sausages stuffed with nuts and raisins, candied apples and pears heated with cinnamon and grape wine, Dutch cheeses and brandied plum puddings. They drank Madeira, rum, brandy and aqua vitae, and when their senses reeled and they could hardly see the door, they paid, clutched their cutlass grips for support, set the stocking caps on the backs of their heads, staggered out into the night and to their ships.

But fewer of them returned to the port each year. They preferred Port Royal, in Jamaica, as a base. It was small, and they could still dominate the place, live in the belief that the governor was their friend. The center of the noisy, dirty town was called the Vegetable Market, and beyond it were High Street and Queen Street and, near the citadel, Half Moon Beach. The houses were mostly built of wood, with rickety galleries where the doxies crowded, and ornate fretted work, tin or tile roofs.

Big banyan trees gave shade, and there was a steady concourse of goats and mules and donkeys through the streets. Negro women who wore straw hats and smoked seegars peddled pineapples and bananas, custard apples and peppers, papayas, musk melons, mangoes, passion fruit, star apples and the local, watery vegetable that was called chocho, and a coarse kind of bread known as bragadraps.

A man who had drunk up all his money in the dramshops or had it stolen from him by the doxies could still survive. There were sweetsop trees and soursop trees where the fruit could be picked without restraint, and the bay inside the Palisadoes held many kinds of fish, among them reds and kings and blues and stripers, even bonito. Sugar cane was easy to find, and tobacco, smoked as a cheroot or in a little clay-bowled pipe Arawak style. Life was never too hard until a ship entered port to recruit men for the account.

Governors grew less lenient, though, and more difficult to bribe. King's ships of the Royal Navy were often in port, and their commanders had orders to round up pirates or impress them. The pirates got out quietly and went to Providence Island in the Bahamas. It was their last base, because the Indian Ocean trade had declined past the point of profit, and here in the Caribbean guard ships cruised on steady patrol duty.

Then in 1729 a former governor, Woodes Rogers, returned to the Bahamas. He was famous for his voyage of circumnavigation and for his honesty and profound dislike of pirates. He brought with him this time his family and a royal proclamation that declared piracy was finished.

The pirates, with careful mockery, lined up in a double rank on

Providence Island and fired a volley from their muskets that barely missed Rogers's head as he landed. He did no more than blink a bit and then sent out to the ship for his family to come ashore. He walked along the pirate ranks and chose men to whom he openly offered King's money. They were to go to sea and capture their mates who were still on the account and refused to meet the governor.

Pirate hunted pirate, and there were bloody fights on some of the back cays and out islands. Prisoners began to arrive at Providence, and Rogers duly tried them under the powers given him by the crown. He waited until he had about a hundred of them. Then he hanged them all together. They made quite an impressive sight, dangling from the palm boles along the beach, and he left the cadavers there for the vultures and until the bones were bleached and rattled at night with the Trade Wind sweep.

No more came after them. He had made his point. The remaining riffraff on the island disappeared, went away to the mainland. Rogers was a very dangerous man, they realized, and piracy a trade that did not pay.

The seafaring people in New England had reached the same conclusion some years before. With their acute commercial sense they foresaw the diminution of the profit ratio as various governments moved to protect their own shipping, particularly the British in the Indian Ocean, the main area of piratical enterprise. There was no change in basic viewpoint; Salem, Boston, Bristol, Portsmouth and Portland men despised British laws more than ever, but were willing to offer superficial obedience.

They sailed as privateers whenever there was an outbreak of the long-lasting conflict between England and France. Or they went to sea in whalers or regular trading vessels, but always armed, always ready to take a prize if a little stretching of the law permitted. Several oceans were open to them where for long periods of time Royal Navy vessels could be avoided.

CHAPTER ELEVEN

GREAT VENTURE

With the losses at sea from piracy less, and despite occasional foreign privateer seizure of vessels, a number of New England shipowners were wealthy by 1700, and most of their competitors in the trade were solidly prosperous. Massachusetts merchants exported a vast amount of goods in their own ships or in ships they held under charter from England or the other North American colonies. Boston was the great center through which the flow of cargo passed and where a good deal remained for retail sale.

Long Wharf was built in 1710, and extended 2,000 feet from the end of King Street out into deep water. Boston Light, the first in the New World, was built in 1716 on Little Brewster Island, and then the "great gun," a warning cannon, was installed to help harbor traffic while the bay was fog-bound. The population had been about 7,000 in 1690 and in 1740 was 17,000 and steadily growing.

Back in the early days of the Massachusetts Bay Colony the prominent merchants were all men of English blood, with close contacts still in England. Among them were Stephen Winthrop, the governor's son, and Henry Shrimpton and John Leverett, and David Yale, the father of Elihu, for whom Yale College was named and who became governor of India. They had traded boldly and sent their ships on voyages to Alexandretta, to the Guinea coast, to Madagascar and to the Indian Ocean as well as working the regular triangular route to the West Indies, the Continent or England and the return to Boston.

But the complexion of the city had changed greatly during the first century of its existence. Now, in the period of prosperity which was to last until the Revolution, other families arrived and became leaders, and they were of various nationalities. There were French, Germans, Irish, Scots and Welsh. They carried the names of families that they made famous: Bowdoin and Faneuil, and Cunningham and Shaw, and Tracy and Magee, and Crowninshield, a name that had been altered from the original German spelling.

These people dealt wherever they could pick up cargo and a profit. They were both wholesalers and retailers, but much more than shopkeepers or commission merchants. They engaged in many ventures, bought and sold land, financed private banks, discounted notes for other merchants, extended credit on long terms, underwrote insurance policies, used a complex system of barter and handled several different kinds of monies even after 1652, when the colony decided it sorely needed its own mint. Beyond such activity they were busy with the management of the vessels they owned, coasters, fishermen, whalers and the craft sent constantly on foreign voyages.

The usual shipowner-merchant transaction involved barter in good part; and paper, promissory notes, personal bonds, bills of exchange and transfers of power of attorney; and also cash. All three forms of payment were common in foreign or domestic trade. A Boston merchant would settle an account by an exchange of Virginia tobacco for muscovado sugar that one of his ships had carried from St. Kitts. He paid an outstanding debt in Barbados with a cargo that was one fourth refuse fish, a quarter salable fish and another quarter train oil. He sometimes settled similar indebtedness with a transfer of a sum of cash, plus bales of beaver pelts, and beef and pork and fish that were sold at the current local market prices.

The debt system was widespread throughout the colonies, and powers of attorney for collection were passed from merchant to merchant. Interest was at the rate of 8 per cent, though, and whenever a man could he dealt in cash or barter. Most of the hard money in circulation came from England, and was known as "good and lawful" money, and was so regarded. There were also in common use Spanish pistoles, dollars, rials and pieces of eight; Portuguese crusados and reis; French livres; and a certain amount of Dutch guilders and Barbary gold, the last freely accepted in New York.

There was however only a small amount of gold in circulation. Most of the coin was silver, and in the early days of the colonies this was badly worn, and reduced in size by clipping, sweating and washing. A lot more of the silver was counterfeit. So in 1652 the Massachusetts Bay Colony decided to establish its own mint.

Pine tree shillings, sixpences, threepences and twopences were made. The metal came from silver plate and bullion, and coins expressly brought into the colony to be melted. The mint house was on John Hull's estate, on what has since become Washington Street.

From that time, although the fact was by no means fully realized in England, the colony became dominant in the affairs of New England. Trade centered there, and quite inevitably Boston took on much greater stature. It was foremost in the movement to resist the policies of the home government where they conflicted in any way with the maritime and commercial interests of the North American colonies. The causes of the Revolution were at work well over a hundred years before the actual break from England and the Declaration of Independence.

Boston and Salem ships took cargoes into almost every port except those in China, a trade region whose sources of wealth were as yet little understood by the colonial merchants. But their ships cleared regularly for New York and Philadelphia, the Chesapeake and the Carolinas, and then squared away for the West Indies, the so-called Wine Islands, the Mediterranean countries and northern Europe and England.

The ships' manifests listed many mixed ladings. The mates as they tallied what came aboard checked off masts and other spars; clapboards, pipe staves, headings, treenails and bolts and props and woodenware; wheat, peas, pork and beef; dry fish in casks, raw fish in bulk; and cod, mackerel, pilchards and alewives, smoked, dried or salted.

A good deal of this kind of cargo came from Maine and Gloucester and Marblehead and the Isle of Shoals Alongside it were stowed sturgeon and train oil and oysters, bread, butter, treacle, onions, nuts and soap. Then, in the 'tween-decks space in the holds, where they were quite sure of dry stowage, the mates would load moose skins (an old manifest lists 300 in one lot, 172 in another) and bear and beaver and otter pelts.

There were also a number of items shipped for re-export. Tobacco was part of it, some from Virginia, some from Barbados, in leaf form or in rolls or in casks, and more from Rhode Island and the nearby areas in Connecticut. English goods took up a large amount of space because Boston was not only a distributing center, it shipped the produce from its own back regions and what came from all of New England in small coasting vessels.

The tide of imported cargo was just about as great and infinite in its variety. Ships brought enormous quantities of tobacco from Virginia, and from England boxes of clay pipes in which to smoke it. Cotton, sugar and indigo were picked up in Barbados. Butts and pipes of wine were from the Canaries and Madeira, and from France and Spain were fresh fruit and olive oil and soap, and salt, which was in keen demand in New England and was often shipped from the Isle of May in the Cape Verde group.

Raisins came from Málaga, and ironware from Bilbao and the other Basque ports. These were usually exchanged for fish and wheat, but most Spanish merchants and those in Portuguese ports wanted cash for their goods. England still continued to supply many items to the Boston market: articles of dress and house furnishings and farm tools. Women waited for months to be able to buy cotton and silk and many coarser, heavier materials produced in English mill towns. They bought, too, silk notions and thread and buttons of various kinds, and pewter ware and pots and carpeting.

Their men bought much more: window glass, fish lines, hooks, powder and shot, muskets, pistols, fowling pieces, saddlery, canvas in bolts, suits of sails cut to specification, Russian leather chairs, hats, shoes, boots and fine clothing. The longshore gangs that worked Long Wharf handled with care the cases marked on the manifests as containing drugs, wormseed, senna, mace, nutmeg, alum, pepper, cloves and "salve," and sacks that held seeds and roots and plants.

There was also, of course, an amazing amount of liquor transported: sack, and a powerful potion called metheglin, and madeira, and canary, and just ordinary "strong water," which could mean rum, aqua vitae or French or Spanish brandy.

The trade soon created its own aristocracy. Men who had made their wealth in the Boston and Salem ships, or in the countinghouses, assumed just as much control of the community as any members of the original families. They were not to be denied position, and society widened to accept them. They were the new "codfish" wealthy, and took the name with good grace. Benjamin Pickman, when he built his splendid house in Salem, put a half model of a codfish on each front stair end.

These people lived well. They built their handsome brick homes along the narrow, winding Boston streets around Louisburg Square. Then they expanded further to country houses in Cambridge and beyond it. The more pious of their number, and they were in the great majority, attended service three times a Sunday at the Old South Church, known to them familiarly as Old South. Nearly all of them were officers in the Ancient and Honorable Company of Artillery and other militia organizations. They turned out with their units for drill on the Common and paraded in full-dress uniform to celebrate the King's birthday, when there were fireworks displayed over the harbor.

Many of the men openly copied the latest London fashions, tried to lead a London existence in every detail. They wore swords along with their fancy wigs and watered silk waistcoats, and would draw the blades if given what they believed to be the correct reason. Their sons were dressed in imitation of themselves and were taken along on hunting trips and summer small-craft cruises to Maine or Rhode Island or out past the sandy headlands of Cape Cod.

The boys were trained early in the use of arms. They were taught to hunt pigeons from blinds, and with live decoys, and they also "prated"—imitated the pigeons' calls. A bounty was paid for each wolf killed, but the boys had to bring in the heads as proof. Bounties for squirrels and rattlesnakes were easier to make, and most boys waited for the annual "wolf rout."

This was really a concerted drive, in which men joined, and a wide circle was formed in forest land outside a village. The wolves were forced inward toward the center until they were short-range targets. Then they were rapidly slaughtered.

Another annual event in almost every New England community was a wide-open hunt for anything living and wild. The slaughter was wholesale, and prizes were awarded for high score as killers. Wildlife seemed boundless, if not in many ways a menace.

The wives and daughters lived a sheltered but no less sophisticated existence. They, too, dressed in the height of London fashion and went to lengthy "routs" and balls and receptions where only a small number of men or boys were present. Hundreds of candles in crystal chandeliers lit the paneled ballroom. Minuets opened the dancing, and young girls gravely bowed and led each other forth while the fiddlers played. "Country dancing" followed the formal series, and then refreshments were served, and the party became much gayer in aspect. The guests were offered cakes, raisins, nuts, wine and punch in great quantity.

Games came next, and the girls squealed and wriggled and rustled as they "wooed the widow," "hunted the whistle," "threaded the needle" and played pawns. Around ten o'clock in the evening the party was over, and fathers took their families home, and the winter street was empty, quiet.

But while the men of these families prided themselves upon the manner in which they lived, and sought out John Singleton Copley, the most popular portraitist of the day, to paint a likeness of their wives and daughters, they were extremely active in their business affairs. They felt no hesitancy about advertising in either the *Post-Boy* or the *Boston Gazette*. To make money in trade was not yet a sin in upper-class Boston in the middle 1700's, and men bought advertisement space that announced they had all sorts of items they were eager and ready to sell.

Below this class, supporting it and in some cases moving into it, was the much bigger and more truly representative part of the Massachusetts population. Here were the men who actually sailed the ships, and built them, and by their labor and skill and knowledge kept the maritime commerce prosperous. They were the masters and the mates and the crews of the vessels, some of the masters in their early twenties, many of the sailors still in their teens; and the shipwrights and master carpenters, the riggers and mechanics, the ropemakers and sailmakers and blockmakers, the ship chandlers and longshore gang foremen and dockside teamster bosses. All of them were aggressive, ambitious, and many of them looked forward confidently to the day when they, too, would be living on Louisburg Square and driving to church in a London-built coach.

Their sons wore leather shirts and britches or tow shirts and homespun pants. The boys, when still too small to work beside their fathers, made birch splinter brooms that they sold for six cents apiece, a fair price for the time. They did better during the berry season and while the wild cherries were ripe. These they called choke cherries, and the fruit was used to make cherry rum, or cherry bounce. A dollar a bushel was pretty much the standard price a boy could expect, and a good-sized tree gave a yield of as much as six bushels.

The prize purchase for any New England boy was a jackknife, preferably one with a blade of English steel. He used it to make the birch splinter brooms and fashion out various pieces of wooden ware that were sold on the open market or added to his mother's kitchen collection. He cut line with it when he learned to splice and took it with him when he went to sea. And he went to sea just as soon as he could get there.

This was already a great tradition in New England in the eighteenth century. It had been in force now for over a hundred years, and boys respected it, followed it, although many of them made no more than a couple of voyages and then settled down ashore. The sea, for all of the population, was still much more lucrative than the land, and a boy should get his share of education on it.

The first voyage was usually in some sort of coaster, running to the southward in general cargo. The boy kept his eyes open and spent a good deal of his off-watch time on deck. If he stayed with this vessel three or four voyages, he might go mate in her, and after two years or so of that, be made master. More ships were being constantly built, and advancement was fast. It was also good sense to get to know the coast, find out how other folks lived, what kind of craft they built and sailed and how they fished and farmed the land.

There were often Long Island Sound ports where the coasters touched, Stonington, white, neat and tight on its point, Saybrook at the broad mouth of the Connecticut River, and New Haven and Stamford, possibly a night at the anchor in Huntington before the final run with the tide right down the East River and Hell's Gate to New York.

New York was quite foreign, even to a boy raised on the waterfront in Boston and accustomed to the sight of strange ships and seamen. The houses were different, and built of stone, and the church steeples were like a small forest, and ashore at least a dozen languages were being talked. The boy walked Great Queen Street, and Whitehall, and the Battery, and went on up Broadway past the trim expanse of the bowling green. Ladies in carriages trailed scents of exotic perfumes never smelled in Boston and talked with each other in what the boy believed to be French. There were a number of Negro slaves, and on Wall Street, heading back toward the ship, he saw the slave market.

A King's Attorney wearing his red cloak of office and tapping the sidewalk emphatically with the ferrule of his long ebony cane stared at the boy until he stood aside and let the man pass. It was his almost uncontrollable impulse to make a vulgar noise for the King's Attorney. But there were English officers in scarlet coats and white britches at a tavern doorway and with them a provincial officer in plain blue. It might only make trouble for the provincial, the boy thought, and most likely much more of the same for himself.

He bought a gob of toffee from the next street seller he met, debated buying a ring-tailed monkey he saw on South Street. But he decided against the monkey, remembering the various tasks of cleaning and swabbing already assigned to him by the mate. He was glad to return aboard. The vessel seemed very familiar to him and somehow almost like home.

The captain picked the tide again and headed for sea, down through the Narrows on the ebb. Then the sloop was off Sandy Hook and past sight of the land as the captain held her well out to be clear of the New Jersey shoals. Cape May was the next landfall and after it the entrance to the Delaware. The boy was awed as he stood on deck and for another moment forgot his work.

Here was a body of water as great as some sea. The far shore was not visible to him, lay below the horizon, and the wind blew just as hard as upon the open Atlantic. But now the mate was calling, and the boy went back to his work with sand and canvas to scrub a tar-spattered grating spotless white.

He felt a sensation of disappointment. There wasn't even another vessel to be seen on all this expanse of water. Then, though, he heard the captain and the mate in talk in the cockpit. The captain said that over there on the starboard hand among the marshy creeks at the mouth of the Cohansey River was a hangout for old pirates, and some not so old yet that they didn't pluck off a becalmed vessel or one caught in the ice during the winter gales. Over on the other shore, in Lewes, the mate said, pirates had made a very thorough raid and plundered the whole town.

The boy scrubbed a bit harder as he listened. Maybe Philadelphia might not be so dull after all. But when he reached it and the sloop was tied up alongside the wharf and he was allowed to go ashore, he found it was just another brick-built small city that looked too much like Boston for him. If there were any pirates in the place, he could not find them, and they must be hidden away in the back rooms of taverns or stuck deep by the Quakers in cells of the town jail.

The Chesapeake, the great, forest-bound body of water on to the southward, was better. The boy felt excited from the moment the sloop hauled her wind off Cape Charles and stood in from the sea. Men in rakish craft with extremely low freeboards were working the oyster beds in past Hampton Roads. A boy in a dugout canoe made a sudden, deft sweep with a net on a pole and caught a flopping, wriggling crab that must have weighed three pounds. The Boston boy felt both envy and satisfaction. This was what he was after; he could tell them at home how that crab was brought aboard, snap, just so.

The sloop kept on up the river and touched at St. Mary's, at Solomon's Island and Annapolis. The boy saw Indians, sullen, miserable, rum-raddled, but still Indians of the tribe that had massacred the early settlers here. He saw Negro slaves who wore uniforms furnished them by their masters and who rowed mahogany-hulled barges that the captain said were just as fancy as those waiting for the Lord High Mayor at the water steps in the Thames at London. The slaves wore long red silk ribbons on their straw hats, and the cotton uniforms were white. They sang as they rowed and maintained a superb rhythm.

They came from the plantations up the river, the mate said. The sloop would go there to load tobacco before she started north. The boy was glad. Virginia and the tidewater country were exotic, strange and nothing like New England. The few plantation houses he had already seen made anything around Boston look paltry.

He studied the vessels as well as the houses and, certain now that he was going to be a sailor, became excited over them. Most of them here, he saw, were designed for shoal water use, and were sailed in the backwaters, the meandering rivers and creeks that led off from the immense bay. Ballast was carried, bags of sand, or just plain rocks taken out of a field, to give the craft her balance and help the effect of the shallow keels. The sails were of leg-of-mutton cut, and some of them hung on two masts. The cargoes aboard them were mainly oysters dredged from the beds out in the channel, and some were loaded with farm produce, even noisy chickens, and a few pigs.

Those boats had dugout canoe hulls. They were really heavy and awkward, must be slow sailers, the boy thought. There was another type, though, which he could only call a shallop because it was planked in pine and had overall shallop lines. Her bow was quite sharp for her kind, and the mast was raked aft out of the ordinary.

She was about thirty-five feet in length, with a big jib and a leg-of-mutton mainsail. Her decking was solid fore and aft, and she was well-caulked.

"Cargo boat, that's what," the mate told the boy. "Hauls stuff from way up in them back cricks. No oysterin', or fish. She ain't got but less than four feet draft for all that beam. We ain't got her kind up North. Water's too rough. But what do you figure her beam to be?"

"Ten foot," the boy said.

"Close," the mate said. "Twelve's more like it. But why's the mast rigged so far aft?"

"Get the cargo down the hatch without too much work," the boy said.

"Right you are," the mate said. "They're about to take the bow lines for this kind o' craft off our whaleboats."

"I'll be happy," the boy said, "to see a real whaleboat soon, and eat a bowl or two of clam chowder the way my Ma makes it."

"You're homesick, you mean," the mate said.

The boy nodded. "Yes, I am," he said.

He lost his homesickness on the run north. There was still too much new to be seen and experienced, and all of his first impressions to be sorted out, put in place in his mind. The greatest thing he had learned, he told himself, was the dependence of the mainland colonies on the sea. A creek was a road through wilderness that led to tidewater and the sea. And for the many folks who had settled on the offshore islands the sea was of course their chief source of food and their lifeline as well as their protection.

John Gardiner, for example, red-bearded old Lion Gardiner's descendant on Gardiner's Island at the head of Long Island Sound, and Nathaniel Sylvester on Shelter Island, and the families on Block Island and the Isles of Shoals and Martha's Vineyard and Nantucket and the Maine islands, lived a sea-surrounded existence. Their only contact with the mainland was by some sort of vessel, and although for weeks at a time they were isolated by storm or fog, they flourished and took a good living from their islands and the sea.

John Gardiner maintained on his heavily wooded, star-shaped

island a manorial establishment just about as splendid as any in Virginia. He still held the trust of the local tribes, the Manhansets and Montauks, and went alongshore whaling with them, spoke their language, greatly admired the prettier and younger of their squaws. He also dealt quite diplomatically with the pirates who used the surrounding waters as a hideaway after an Indian Ocean voyage. William Kidd, the Scottish sea rover who had the bad luck to become entangled in the political and financial schemes of Lord Bellomont, was one of Gardiner's visitors.

Kidd brought ashore onto the island a considerable amount of loot from an Indian Ocean voyage he had just completed. He gave a magnificent piece of cloth of gold to Gardiner's wife, then buried the loot. His warning to Gardiner was blunt: "If I call for it and it is gone, I will take your head or your son's."

But Kidd was in disfavor with Bellomont, and Bellomont was the Royal Governor. He tricked Kidd into his custody at Boston and arrested him in 1701, sent him to England for trial. Kidd did not have a chance; he was the political scapegoat for Bellomont and others of a court group who had hoped to make secretly a fortune from piracy. It was Kidd who lost his head and not John Gardiner nor Gardiner's son. Kidd was hanged in chains at Execution Dock on May 23, 1701, his body left to rot above the Thames tide. King's men from Boston came to the island and dug up the loot, took it away on an order from Bellomont. Mrs. Gardiner still had her piece of cloth of gold, though, and cherished it as another gift from the sea.

Nathaniel Sylvester on Shelter Island a few miles to the westward of Gardiner was also visited by pirates and various types who wished to keep clear of the King's men. But in the main his life was quite calm. He was an Englishman who had gone out to Barbados early and made himself wealthy as a sugar planter. He had come north in 1652 with his eighteen-year-old bride Grisell and settled on the island, for which he had secured in considerable part a King's grant.

He was in search of timber for rum kegs, and the island was covered with superb stands of white oak. Sylvester left his ship on the westerly side of the island, proceeded ashore in a pinnace with

his wife and met the local Manhanset sachem and the other members
of the tribe who were soon to be his friends. He was a gentle and
pious man, very close to Quakerism in his religious beliefs, and he
compensated the Indians fairly for what he took from them.

He built a sturdy hip-roofed house on a knoll above a narrow
bight winding in from deepwater and began to till the land as he
cleared it of timber. This was to be his permanent home, he decided,
and he would not return to Barbados. He harvested the marsh hay,
raised stock, imported slaves and sold his produce and his timber to
coastal vessels that made the island a regular port of call.

George Fox, the Quaker leader, heard of Sylvester's sympathy
for the sect and took trouble to visit him. Quakers were being
savagely persecuted in the Massachusetts Bay Colony, and Sylvester
had given some of the survivors haven on his island. Fox arrived
there in July, 1672, and described the voyage in his journal. He
wrote:

"We went at night on shore and were not able to stay for the
mosquitoes, so we went on the sloop again and put off from the
shore and cast anchor and stayed all that night. The next day we
went out into the sound but our sloop was not able to live in the
water so we turned in again, for we could not pass, and came to
anchor again at Fisher's Island, two nights, and there was exceeding
much rain whereby we were much wet, being in an open boat. So we
passed all day and night there, the 28th of 5th month (July). And
we passed the two Horse Races, waters so called, and passed by
Garner's Island [he means Gardiner's] and so came to Shelter Island, which was 27 leagues from Rhode Island."

Fox was used to a rough life and soon recouped himself in the
comfort of Sylvester's home. Then he addressed a gathering of about
a hundred Indians who had been summoned by Sylvester. He spoke
to them through an Indian interpreter whom he described in his
journal as a man who "could speak any English very well." He sat
afterward for two hours with the Manhanset sachem and the senior
warriors of the tribe, no doubt pointed out to them some of the finer
points of Quaker theology.

Word of Fox's presence was passed along the Long Island shore,

and hundreds of people gathered on August 6 to hear him preach. They came, he wrote in his journal, "a great way to it from many places." He must have met settlers from Rhode Island as well as Connecticut and both forks of Long Island. It was surely quite an extraordinary sight as the craft came in from the open sound and up the windings of the bight to Sylvester's water steps at the foot of his broad lawn.

There were shallops and ketches and wherries and pinnaces and dugouts, and very probably many of them were used as workboats and still smelled of oysters, marsh hay and fish. But the people were immaculately clean and dressed in their best, and as they climbed from the water steps and clustered on the lawn, they formed a compact, solemn group. They had come here because of a deeply religious need which they hoped Fox would satisfy.

Fox spoke standing bareheaded in the summer sunshine. The Manhansets had joined the people from off-island and rested motionless as they listened, unaware that their quill-decorated buckskins, their wampum necklaces, face paint and eagle feathers made them as vivid as birds beside the somberly dressed settlers. Sylvester's force of Negro slaves had come, too, and listened with the same silence and immobility of the Indians. Their eyes shone, though, as Fox spoke of the ways of the Lord, and when he was through Sylvester read for quite a time from the Scriptures.

The people left at dusk, just as the evening planet rose above the dark mass of trees. Farewells echoed over the water, and booms and gaffs creaked as sails were hoisted, and one by one the craft tacked out into the bay, and then even the dim blur of the hemp sails was gone.

Another man sympathetic to the Quakers created a refuge for them thirty miles at sea on Nantucket Island. He was John Macy, a Baptist, who while living in the Massachusetts Bay Colony had come to detest the Puritans' cruelly inflexible laws. He sailed for Nantucket in the fall of 1659 and with no desire to go back. He had been fined thirty shillings by the General Court because he had asked a group of

Quakers into his house out of the rain. He was a strong-willed man, and must have considered himself a competent sailor. He had aboard the small sloop in addition to himself, his wife and five children, a man named Edward Starbuck and a boy, Isaac Coleman.

They were caught by a heavy squall when well out into Massachusetts Bay. Water came aboard the boat, and the gear was strained. Mrs. Macy suggested to her husband that he put back to the mainland. He told her in a firm Baptist voice, "Woman, go below and seek thy God. I fear not the witches on earth or the devils in hell!"

Mrs. Macy accepted the advice, the sloop survived the squall, and all hands arrived in good shape at Nantucket. The island had belonged to a wealthy Puritan, Thomas Mayhew, who had sold it to Macy and a man named Tristram Coffin and seven others. They paid him thirty pounds and a pair of beaver hats for it, hoped to make a living by raising sheep on the wide-sweeping spaces of the island moors.

They were soon engaged in coastal whaling, though, and so were the men of the small colony started on nearby Martha's Vineyard by Mayhew. The Gay Head tribe of Indians, so called because where they lived on the Vineyard a headland was brilliant with contrasting colors of several kinds of clay, were both friendly and excellent whalers. They took the white men to sea with them and taught them the niceties, the exactions and dangers of the pursuit. Much the same thing happened on Nantucket, and the settlers on the eastern end of Long Island at East Hampton and Southampton were already highly skilled at the trade, had learned it from braves of the Montauk and Shinnecock tribes.

The Long Island people made a large part of their living from whaling, and most of the men preferred it to farming. They had set up the business in a regular fashion in 1640, and by 1650 they had organized companies and built bigger boats to cruise well offshore.

Beach lookouts who sat high up on log masts had been kept on watch since the beginning of the trade. For the boys of the region, the whaling season, from December to April, had a special meaning. School was closed then so that they might help on lookout watch and in the boats and when the catch was hauled ashore and prepared for the cauldrons and the trying out. Some of the large boats were gone for as much as three weeks at a time, and the boys took intense pride in being aboard one of them. The crews hunted at sea during the day, camped ashore at night, and there was always some new experience to be found.

The Nantucket men had picked up their knowledge of the trade fast, and by 1700 had begun to stay offshore overnight in the cedar-hulled boats. They sought the sperm whale, which they recognized as a fighter but also worth a good deal more than the right whale species. Captain Christopher Hussey and his crew fought, killed, then towed ashore through the tail end of a storm a sperm whale that was the best catch ever brought into Nantucket harbor.

Men no longer thought of dividing the catch by island districts, a system by which each of the four divisions of the south shore of the island had crews of six men who kept watch for whales. They now worked together, and bound offshore at least several days of sailing from the island. The beast that Captain Hussey had landed was one of a school of sperm whales. There must be more, many of them, and with their capture went wealth.

This was around 1712, and the Nantucketers were the first to make the venture. Then, though, crews from Martha's Vineyard followed them onto the offshore grounds, and mainland crews from Boston and Salem and New Bedford and the Maine ports. Whaling was suddenly a major source of wealth for New England. Crews were to finally pursue the whale to the Arctic, the South Seas, and anywhere over the oceans of the world where the beast could be killed.

The men at the ledgers in the countinghouses said that there was as much money in it, possibly more, than in privateering. The Puritan conscience was pleased by the fact also that whaling was fully within the law. Owners of whaling ships had no difficulty in recruiting crews.

CHAPTER TWELVE

REVOLUTION

While prosperity continued in the northern colonies during the first decades of the eighteenth century, the breach between them and the home country widened as a result of their involvement in English politics and European rivalries over which they had no control. Following the capture of Port Royal in 1710, and the Treaty of Utrecht in 1713, which gave Newfoundland and Acadia to the British, this was a period of relative peace, interrupted only by the depredations of the Indian "Navy" off the Maine coast. Yet the British, and particularly the French, used this respite mainly to strengthen their positions on the new continent.

France built the powerful fortress of Louisburg on Cape Breton Island to guard the entrance to the St. Lawrence River and erected other forts in the interior. New Englanders built forts on the northern frontier to guard against Indian raids, and for reasons of self-preservation were forced to give their support to the home government. Peace was broken in 1739 by new European quarrels that for once did not involve the colonists extensively. There was a French attempt to recapture Port Royal, Nova Scotia, in 1744. It failed, and the next year, a retaliatory expedition of New Englanders under William Pepperell working with a Royal Navy fleet commanded by Sir Peter Warren was launched against Fort Louisburg. It was a ragtag force, but with good luck in the weather and some skillful improvisation on the part of the attackers an unopposed landing was made and the fort surrounded, and the supposedly impregnable bastion capitulated.

With the Treaty of Aix-la-Chapelle in 1748, Louisburg was returned to France, and a period of uneasy truce reigned in America. This was shattered when the so-called French and Indian War, an outgrowth of the Seven Years' War in Europe, broke out widespread across the northern frontier in 1754. In the first few years honors went to France, but after a slow start the British eventually captured Louisburg and followed this with an historic victory by James Wolfe over the Marquis de Montcalm at Quebec, effectively ending French influence in North America. Mainly a land war, there were large numbers of colonial forces actively engaged, and they suffered severe losses. But the rigidity of British command had a far more corrosive effect upon colonial loyalty than the casualty lists.

Time and again, either in some wilderness combat or at sea, the question of rank arose. Some "King's man" quoted London as his authority, and was disputed by a "Colonial" from one of the poorly paid and often badly disciplined militia contingents. The ultimate effect was a hatred of the British that was to endure and be a major motive to keep on fighting in both the Revolution and the War of 1812.

British political leaders added to the colonial sense of injustice by their attitude after they had made peace with the French. His Majesty's government, plagued by chronic and enormous debt, looked unhappily upon the maintenance of the army stationed in America. The army was big, and expensive, and the reasoning at Whitehall was that a lot of money had been spent to defend the colonists against the French and Indians. So in 1765 an American Revenue Act was passed by Parliament, the first law ever specifically created to raise money in the colonies for the crown.

It was known as the Quartering Act, and came into effect in March, 1765, at the request of General Thomas Gage, the commander of British forces in America. It was to be enforced for two years, and would compel the civil authorities to provide barracks and supplies for the troops. Another act, passed the next year, demanded billeting and quartering space in unoccupied dwellings, inns and alehouses.

The Stamp Act had also been passed in 1765, with the purpose of raising £60,000 a year from the colonies for the support of the troops. This sum was to be contributed to the colonial revenues for 1764 and make a total of about £300,000. The receipts were to be paid into the royal exchequer, and the new taxes were upon newspapers and pamphlets and broadsides and almanacs, all kinds of legal documents and insurance policies, and ship's papers and licenses, and playing cards and dice.

Protest flared from Georgia to Massachusetts. The fact was forgotten or ignored in the northern colonies that for years their self-financed campaigns against the Indians had often failed because of broken promises and lack of funds. Fury was concentrated upon the British in a deliberate fashion. During the summer of 1765 secret, rebellious organizations were started.

They were called Sons of Liberty, and men of wealth and position led them. Their immediate, announced objective was the repeal of the Stamp Act, and their slogan "No taxation without representation." The records of the vice-admiralty court were burned in August, 1765, by a Boston mob in defiance of the act. Then the home of the comptroller of the currency was looted, and the fine home and library of Chief Justice Thomas Hutchinson. Hutchinson's son-in-law, Andrew Oliver, who served as stamp agent for the Boston area, was forced to resign, and soon afterward all the agents in the colonies quit, afraid of the Sons of Liberty.

Three years later, in further defiance of the officials sent out as replacements from London, John Hancock proved his right to belong to the organization. He came into Boston harbor aboard his sloop *Liberty* and sailed her up alongside Long Wharf. She carried a full cargo of Madeira wine in the hold, for which Hancock refused to pay revenue tax.

Liberty was boarded by officers sent from His Majesty's frigate *Romney*, at anchor in the harbor. Hancock was thrown ashore from his own vessel. But he came back, and with him were friends and admirers. They tended to the royal revenue agent stationed aboard, hustled him into the cabin and locked him up there. They put the wine on the wharf, and Hancock paid no tax. When the Royal Navy towed the sloop out to an anchorage alongside *Romney* in the bay Hancock led a riot ashore.

Customs men were chased off Long Wharf and the other wharves. They were forced to stay in their homes while crowds paraded outside and threatened them. They escaped later to Castle William, on an island in the bay. Boston was cleared of revenuers for a time, and Hancock became a popular hero.

Formal rejection of the Stamp Act was made in May, 1769, when George Washington introduced in the Virginia House of Burgesses a set of resolutions that were unanimously adopted. They affirmed that the sole right to tax citizens of the colony rested with the governor and the provincial legislature.

South Carolina and North Carolina and the people of Savannah, Georgia, followed the action of Virginia. People in the port towns in Maryland and Delaware and Pennsylvania and New Jersey and New York, and in Connecticut and Rhode Island and Massachusetts joined them. By the end of 1769 only New Hampshire among the colonies had failed to boycott British goods.

The result was severe for the British economy. Imports from the home country fell from £2,157,218 in 1768 to £1,336,122 in 1769, and in that latter year in New York diminished from £490,-763 to £75,930, and in Philadelphia for the same year from £441,-829 to £204,978. Not only the royal exchequer, but British merchants and manufacturers and shipowners were very hard hit. Other, more restrictive acts were passed, and the revenue laws tightened. The colonists resisted with greater stubbornness, and then in Boston there was violence, and men were killed.

Two regiments of royal troops, the 29th Worcestershires and the 14th West Yorkshires, had been stationed on the Common through-out the winter of 1770 simply because the citizens would not obey the Quartering Act and give them shelter. The regimental morale was poor, and most of the rank and file were either drunks or malcontents who had enlisted in the army to keep out of prison in England. They spent the winter miserably in crude tents, and the population snubbed them, and the boys pelted them with icy snowballs, rocks and garbage.

The night of March 5 was very cold and icy, after a thaw. A single sentry was posted in front of the Customs House on King Street, his hands crossed numbly over his bayoneted musket, propped against his chest. The usual gang of boys arrived and began to revile him with good, ripe New England epithets and limber up their throwing arms in a snowball barrage. Boston was a rough town, where sailors from a thousand ships took shore leave each year and sailors had worked out even more vigorously on the royal soldiers. The Customs House sentry lost his temper. He cursed the boys back, stabbed at them with his bayonet and a crowd gathered. This was about to be ugly riot. Then, at nine o'clock, somebody rang the bell in the Brick Meeting House.

The signal meant fire or a general alarm. People came out of their houses with fire buckets and with muskets, pistols, a few swords. They heard the commotion in King Street and went there. The British had heard it also and reinforced the sentry with a detachment.

Men took over from the boys. They menaced the sentries and shouted, "Fire, you damned lobsters! Shoot! Shoot!"

When a heavy stick was thrown and hit one of the soldiers on the shoulder the detachment fired a volley, and in fear, another after that. Three men were killed and two mortally wounded. The crowd broke and ran. But Samuel Adams, a leader of the Sons of Liberty, went to see the Lieutenant Governor and gave him serious warning of what might soon happen in redress.

The troops were withdrawn from Boston. They were stationed on islands in the bay. It was the only way that peace could be kept and mass rebellion averted.

Peace was to be balanced precariously for several years to come.

But hatred of the British was intensified, and the situation steadily deteriorated and approached war. The British themselves were responsible for a great part of the mounting, bitter friction.

Officials who represented the crown, and senior officers of the army and the navy, were adamant in their attitude toward the colonials. They remained callous, cocky and inept in nearly all of their relationships. It was their unshaken conviction that they were a superior sort and that without them, and without unflaggingly strict direction from London, the colonies could not exist.

Rhode Islanders responded to this in much the same fashion as the Boston people. The inhabitants of the small village of Providence took action in the summer of 1772. A drummer went banging and shouting through the streets and carried the news that brought men on the run to hear what he said. He told them that His Majesty's revenue service schooner *Gaspee,* a vessel of 102 tons, was firmly aground with low tide on Namquit Point. The point was seven miles to the southward from Providence, and high water would not return until three o'clock the next morning to float her free.

She had been chasing the New York-Providence packet *Hannah* up the bay when she grounded. *Hannah* was out of Newport and bound for Providence, and her master, Captain Benjamin Lindsay, with great care and pleasure, tricked the revenue schooner into shoal water. Her commander was Lieutenant William Dudingston of the Royal Navy, and in the space of a few months he had made himself violently hated in the Narragansett Bay area which he patrolled.

Since his arrival in March Dudingston had shown nothing that resembled mercy or local common sense to anybody suspected of smuggling. Captain Lindsay refused to let him board and inspect the *Hannah* outside Newport, then, under a fresh southerly breeze, led him for twenty-five miles to the sand bar at Namquit Point and sailed right on over it with his considerably shallower draft.

The able-bodied men and a good many of the boys in Providence gathered fast at John Sabin's tavern. Lead was molded into bullets over the kitchen fire. Rum punch was served against the chimney-place heat to celebrate the opportunity to repay Lieutenant Duding-ston several debts.

John Brown, a village merchant who had suffered severe losses because of the excessive British tax system, acted as chairman of the meeting. It chose Captain Abraham Whipple without hesitation or question as the leader of the attack upon *Gaspee*. He was a stocky, round-faced man with humorous eyes and a quick smile. His sea service extended over many years in privateers, and he had been master of the letter of marque ship *Game Cock*.

When he started to move toward Turner's Wharf, the crowd quietly followed him. A lean young Providence veteran, Captain John Burroughs Hopkins, walked at Captain Whipple's side and had been accepted by the others as his second in command. The crews for eight whaleboats were picked at the wharf and an experienced shipmaster put in command of each. The crews took their places and stowed their weapons, mostly barrel staves and paving stones. They muffled the oars and rowlocks with canvas so that no sound would be made to warn the British. The men who owned muskets were told to prime them and keep them dry.

It was just ten o'clock in the evening, and there were seven miles to be rowed against the rising tide. Captain Whipple gave a low-voiced order. Bow and stern men in the boats pushed off from the wharf. Boat commanders leaned down over the long steering oars and softly called the stroke.

No lights were carried, and on the dark surface of the bay the oar blades cast only slender flashes of silver, and from the cutwaters came a faint, continuous gurgling that was less than a whisper. The people on the wharf could no longer see the boats. They turned back toward the village and their homes.

Captain Whipple kept the flotilla in single file down the bay. He stood at the steering oar in the sternsheets of the first boat and watched for the loom of Namquit Point, then the silhouette of *Gaspee*. Her topmasts showed in the starshine, and her high-steeved bowsprit, her long yards and gaffs and booms, slick with dew. A lantern sent light through the broad stern windows, and another, weaker light burned on deck. She rode pretty well to the tide although still firmly aground, Captain Whipple saw. It would be an hour yet before Dudingston would be able to get her off the bar into deep water.

Captain Whipple raised a hand above his head in an arresting gesture. The men in his boat and the men in the boats astern held their oars in the water without motion. The boats drifted, soundless, and came down on the schooner from off her bow. She carried four cannon of three-pound caliber and a crew of twenty-seven men. Those could rather easily take care of whaleboats armed with only a few firelock muskets.

The watch on deck did not see the boats or hear the men who stood up, musket in hand. But from off the outboard quarter of the schooner came another whaleboat, and Captain Whipple did not have to hail her. He recognized at once her commander. Captain Simeon Potter gave a hand signal, and his craft pulled abreast and he talked for an instant with Whipple, confirmed the plan of attack.

Captain Potter was from Bristol, fifteen sea miles away. He had as crew in his boat twelve husky Bristol boys. Four handled the oars for him, and the other eight relieved them and tended the weapons. Potter was famous for his slave-running, his years of privateer service and his abilities in any kind of a fight. Whipple was glad to have him here, and said so, and told him to join in the attack, move immediately to board the schooner.

The crew of His Majesty's revenue vessel were a sleepy, careless lot. When the Rhode Island men came vaulting over the main rail, nobody was awake on deck, and Captain Whipple called for Dudingston by name. The lieutenant rushed out of the after cabin bravely enough and fired a brace of pistols to repel boarders.

But the lieutenant was not in the best of shape for action. His shots were wide, and he was dressed in no more than his drawers and singlet, although he had poked his gold-laced tricorne hat on his head as a sign of authority and that he was in command of *Gaspee*.

Some of the Providence men did not like that. One of them, a man named Joseph Bucklin, fired his musket at Dudingston. The ball took the lieutenant in the arm, tore onward into the groin. Dudingston moaned, reeled, dropped to the deck. But there was no great desire to kill, and a surgeon was among the boat crews. He took care of Dudingston's wound while the schooner sailors were kicked, cuffed, stripped naked and offered as targets to the Narragansett Bay mosquitoes.

Then everything that could be broken was broken and the cabin and the fo'c'sle looted. Dudingston and his crew were put in a boat, rowed to a rocky, inhospitable island, sent onto it and told to stay there. Dudingston was speechless; he saw what had just been done by experts aboard *Gaspee*. The Rhode Islanders had set fire to her. She would burn right down to the water's edge or until her magazine exploded.

The lieutenant must have been a very sad man that night. He could expect little advancement in His Majesty King George's navy. But when he was brought before a court martial in England he was given surprising treatment. He was acquitted of the charge that through negligence he had lost his ship, and he lived to advance to high rank and become a rear admiral.

The same spirit of good nature, though, did not carry over from the home country to New England. The British government offered a reward of a thousand pounds for the arrest of the leader of the attack on *Gaspee* and five hundred pounds for any of the men who were engaged in it.

The chief justices of Massachusetts, New York and New Jersey were appointed to serve as commissioners of inquiry in the case. The people who were identified by the commissioners were to be sent to England for trial, a wholly new and very grave change in colonial legal procedure. Two sessions were held at Newport, but nobody appeared to testify. There was open animosity shown by the Rhode Islanders for the commissioners, and the body adjourned in June, 1773, and never met again. After incidents like this war was inevitable. There was no way to close the widening breach.

With the battles of Lexington and Concord and the outbreak of concerted fighting in 1775 the patriots found great, immediate need for men to meet the British on the sea. The British troops had fallen back on Boston, and a good part of their supplies had to come to them by water. Hog and Noodle's Islands and several other small islands in the northeast part of Boston harbor had been used as cattle pasture, and during May the British sent boats after the livestock.

Rebel seamen in small craft were ahead of them. The hay stacks were set afire, and the frightened cattle driven off the islands or slaughtered. When the British troops landed there was nothing for them to take back but a few carcasses already well picked by the crows and gulls and inhabited by swarms of ants.

This was the first of an almost endless series of sea raids and hit-and-run harassments of a commando character that went on all through the Revolution. The Royal Navy, with strong, powerful armed vessels, was able to dominate the coast and maintain an effective blockade throughout, but American ingenuity and daring and fine seamanship often pierced it and allowed vessels to escape offshore.

General George Washington, as soon as he took command of the Continental forces at Cambridge, realized how important the sea conflict was. He talked with Colonel John Glover of Marblehead, and from the rank and file of the regiment Glover led he drew the sailors and fishermen who formed the nucleus of what was called Washington's Navy.

Washington appointed on September 2, 1775, a Marblehead man and a captain in the Army, Nicholson Broughton, "to take command of a detachment of said Army and proceed on board the Schooner *Hannah*, at Beverly, lately fitted-out and equipped with arms, ammunition, and provisions at the Continental expense." Broughton was ordered to get to sea at once and "to take and seize all such vessels laden with soldiers, arms, ammunition, or provisions."

It is quite likely that the men in Broughton's crew for the *Hannah* shared the belief with him that they had been assigned to something very much like privateer service. Broughton, his officers and men were given over and above their pay in the Continental Army one third of the cargo of each vessel taken, with the exception of military and naval stores. The captain was entitled to six shares of that one third; the first lieutenant got five; the second lieutenant, four; and so on down to the privates, who got one share.

British blockade ships chased Broughton back into port twice. But on September 7 he overtook and captured a vessel named *Unity*. He brought her into port on Cape Ann without a fight and found she carried naval stores, timber, provisions and fish. General Washington was very much pleased, although he regretted that powder had not been in the *Unity* cargo. He ordered other ships outfitted during the fall and winter, and by the time the British left Boston in March, 1776, the Washington "fleet" held seven schooners and a brigantine.

Major General Sir William Howe of the Royal Army was worried by the effects of the sea raids upon the British lines of supply. He reported to the Earl of Dartmouth early in the war: "I am also concerned to observe that the uncertainty of defenceless vessels getting in this harbor [Boston] is rendered more precarious by the rebel privateers infesting the bay, who can take advantage of many inlets on the coast, where His Majesty's ships cannot pursue them, and from whence they can safely avail themselves of any favorable opportunities that offer."

It was Howe's recommendation that in the future valuable stores be sent over from England aboard men-of-war. The lower gun decks would be removed to give sufficient stowage space. But before anything like that was done in Royal Navy dockyards Captain John Manley in command of the Continental schooner *Lee* took a real prize. He brought his 72-ton ship alongside the fully loaded British ordnance vessel *Nancy* on November 29, 1775, and quickly seized her. Some of the items on her manifest were 2,000 muskets, 31 tons of musket shot, 3,000 round shot, barrels of powder and a brass mortar with a 13-inch caliber. Admiring officers on Washington's staff calculated that the contents of the prize captured by Manley would have taken the colonists eighteen months to manufacture.

The brass mortar, which weighed 2,700 pounds, was hauled ashore by eager hands and emplaced in the Continental Army camp outside headquarters. General Israel Putnam, known familiarly as "Old Put" by the troops, climbed up on the mortar and brandished a rum bottle. Then he refreshed himself, and with some of the rest of the rum christened the weapon, and it was duly accepted by the Continental Congress.

General Washington was so pleased by Manley's seizure of *Nancy* that he wrote in his commendation: "Your general good behaviour since you first engaged in the Service, merits mine and your Country's Thanks. You may be assured that every Attention will be paid to any reasonable Request of yours, and that you will have the Command of a stronger Vessel of War."

Manley was the former master of a schooner that worked in the West Indian trade. He was a resident of Boston, and had been going to sea for years before he captured *Nancy*. But, like many other officers who served in the Continental Navy, he found it difficult to fight with any great success against the veteran British naval officers and their powerful, well-armed ships of the line.

It was the privateer vessels and the small coastal craft that really carried the war at sea to the enemy. The Continental Navy, as such, was shattered soon after the service was formed. Some of the ships were fought with extreme bravery, but at the end nearly all of them had been sunk or beached or blockaded in various ports. There were thirteen frigates commissioned as fast as they could be built and equipped for sea duty. But by 1781 they had been reduced to two vessels, the *Alliance* and the *Deane*.

Privateers captured or destroyed three times as many ships as the Navy claimed. And among their prizes were sixteen warships, a type of vessel that a privateer did not usually like to engage. It was a clear demonstration of the fire power and the speed and maneuverability of the privateer ships and of the superlative sea skill of their officers and crews.

Official figures were never compiled on the sea warfare of the Revolution. But it has been estimated that American privateer owners kept between 200 and 450 vessels in operation throughout, and perhaps more at the end. There were then approximately 9,000 colonial men at sea in privateers, or about to go to sea. This was a larger force than General Washington could sometimes muster in the Revolutionary Army.

However, the fight for independence was in very great part the Army's war. Seamen helped as much as possible, and under the tight grip of the British blockade managed to perform a surprising number of successful operations. One of the most important was carried out by men of the Marblehead regiment who served under Colonel Glover. They were all former fishermen or sailors, and were responsible for saving the bulk of the Revolutionary Army after the disastrous battle of Long Island that took place on August 27, 1776.

General Washington had matched 5,000 green American troops against a combined force of 17,000 veteran British and Hessians. Loyalists who had escaped through the American lines gave Generals Clinton and Cornwallis an accurate description of the disposition of the Revolutionary Army, and with that information the British were able to turn General Putnam's flank.

American retreat became a rout, the troops fleeing down the dusty roads toward Brooklyn as fast as they could run. Just in time, 4,000 Maryland troops under the command of General William Alexander arrived. They took up positions in and around the sturdily built Cortelyou house, close to Gowanus Bay. There they held, and stubbornly drove back the British attacks. Most of them were killed, or taken prisoner, and in the evening General Alexander was finally forced to surrender to the Hessian general, de Hesiter. But because of the bravery of the Marylanders, the rest of the American troops were able to escape across the Gowanus marsh to the bay.

Washington was aware that General Howe, the British commander-in-chief, could rather easily trap the remaining American troops entrenched in Brooklyn. But when daybreak came thick with fog he knew that he might evacuate his force across the East River. The fog would hide the movement from Howe and the big British fleet that lay at anchor in the Lower Bay.

Washington called Colonel Glover to his headquarters on Washington Heights. He explained the problem to the Marblehead man and then told him to proceed on his own. Glover went back to the regiment and passed an order: all available small craft were to be collected at once and rowed or sailed to Brooklyn for evacuation purposes.

The Marblehead contingent worked quickly, shielded by the fog and without enemy interference. They went across to the Brooklyn shore in the assorted craft they had found and that night started moving out the troops to Manhattan Island.

It was often very tricky work. The British trenches were so close to those the Americans were leaving that they could plainly hear the British picks and shovels and the guttural cursing of a Hessian sergeant. But the evacuation was continued steadily until dawn.

With nightfall on the next day it was resumed, while remnants of the Delaware and Maryland regiments and Colonel Hand's rifle corps held the positions as a covering force. Ebb tide came at nine o'clock, and there was heavy rain. Sail craft were of no use, and many of them were filled with troops and their gear. Then, at eleven o'clock, the northeast wind that had blown for three days swung suddenly into the favorable southwest quarter.

Boat after boat was sent away, spread canvas, trimmed her sheets and headed for Manhattan. Salem men had joined the Marbleheaders in the boat crews, and the operation was working very well. But the tide turned during the night, and the wind hauled around into the northwest.

General Washington was worried about the last of the troops in the Brooklyn entrenchments. He sent his aide, Colonel Alexander Scammel, to move them out faster. But the order was misunderstood; General Mifflin gave an order to evacuate the entire line. When the weary, hungry troops reached the ferry wharf to embark they found several regiments ahead of them, waiting nervously in the foggy darkness.

General Mifflin was able to hold his men together, and the British had as yet not penetrated the empty American lines. Boats kept on sailing deep-loaded, and across the river General Washington sat his horse at the head of the ferry stairs and watched the troops come ashore.

Dawn was gray, without sun, when the last of the boats ran the river. Captain Alexander Hamilton was in charge of disembarkation in Manhattan. He ordered the troops to fall in and take formation once they were out of the boat. Then he marched them proudly past General Washington. The job was done.

It was some days later that Washington's staff learned through information from spies how lucky the evacuation fleet had been. A Brooklyn woman of strong Tory leanings, Mrs. John Rapalje, had sensed during the final night of troop movement that too many boats were busy on the river. She sent a slave to give warning to General Howe. But a Hessian sentry grabbed the slave and believed him to be a spy for the Revolutionary Army. He held him through the rest of the night, until a British officer making a dawn inspection round met the pair.

The Hessian could speak very little English, and the slave was not willing to speak much. Still the slave passed his mistress's message on to the British officer. The Americans were all gone, though, and the slave was released and sent back home.

When General Washington was forced to retreat again later in the war and make his famous crossing of the Delaware on December 11, 1776, it was Marblehead men who handled the boat. More than six hundred of them who served during the Revolution were buried later on old Burial Hill in Marblehead, and many more died at sea, or where no formal burial was possible.

But men from all of the colonies distinguished themselves in the Revolutionary services. A peculiar form of small craft warfare existed after the British took New York City and sent troops out to occupy Long Island as far as Montauk Point. They were opposed in the main by Connecticut troops, who held their own shore of Long Island Sound and who made commando-like raids against the

British. Their purpose was to keep the British troops tied up, destroy installations and supplies of rations and forage and, whenever possible, kill the enemy or take prisoners.

It was on one of these raids that Sergeant Elijah Churchill of the Second Continental Dragoons gained the first part of his Purple Heart decoration. He went back later in another operation that was just about as remarkable and gained the second part.

Both raids were planned in detail by Major Benjamin Tallmage, of the same regiment, who was chief of the Revolutionary Army intelligence service. Tallmage performed a great deal of scouting of enemy territory himself, and was often accompanied by Lieutenant Caleb Brewster, also of the Second Dragoons, whose special duties were the command of the Army's flotilla of armed whaleboats on Long Island Sound, the transportation of spies and the transmission of intelligence information.

Tallmage was intelligence chief from 1778 to the end of the war, and General Washington remonstrated with him a number of times because of the risks taken by the young officer. Still, Tallmage volunteered on November 7, 1780, to make a surprise attack across the Sound. He had learned through spies that the British had stored three hundred tons of hay, winter forage for their cavalry mounts, at Coram, a small Long Island village. The hay was near a stockaded fort the British had built on the south shore of the island and called Fort St. George. It was Tallmage's plan to take the fort and as many prisoners as his force could handle, then march to Coram and burn the hay.

Fifty men, all volunteers, went with him, Sergeant Churchill among them. A rough gale was whipping the Sound, and they had to wait hours, until it was almost dark, before they were able to shove off from Fairfield, on the Connecticut shore. The men used both oars and sails in the slim-hulled whaleboats, their muskets, pistols and powder horns covered against the spindrift.

They were four hours making the passage, and landed on a deserted beach without any sort of enemy challenge. But the weather had carried them well past the landing point Tallmage had chosen, and they had a much longer distance to march to reach their objective. The gale was still blowing hard. The men were half frozen, their long coats and leather gaiters crackling with ice as they moved.

Tallmage gave an order to Churchill to hide the whaleboats as much as possible under piles of sand, driftwood and seaweed on the beach. Then he ordered the force into the scrub pinewoods back from it. There were a large number of British troops in garrison on Long Island for the winter, and several thousand Loyalist militia stationed at various points. Tallmage wanted to keep his unit intact.

They waited in the woods during the light of the next day, November 8, and at dusk began a fast march down the frozen and empty road across the island. It was miserable, blustering weather, the ruts of the road white with frost, and the night so cold even the foxes did not move. The troops kept in close column, and by three in the morning were within two miles of Fort St. George.

Tallmage halted the men. He inspected them and their weapons and assigned Churchill to lead the first attack wave. This was made up of sixteen men, and the sergeant took them forward on the double, bayonets fixed. They headed straight for the main blockhouse, one of three within the log stockade.

They were very spry for dismounted dragoons and were only a few yards from it when a sentry challenged them and fired through a loophole. Churchill kept the men running, and when they reached the stockade designated men bent and braced themselves, and others scrambled onto their backs and leaped up and over onto the footwalk where British musket flashes cut scarlet streaks in the darkness.

Ladders led down from the footwalk, and the raiders sprang from them into the compound of the fort. All three of the blockhouses were being briskly defended, but Churchill found a long, heavy log at the woodpile that would serve as a battering ram. He and his men picked it up and ran with it at the door of the central blockhouse. They wrecked and smashed loose the planks of that, picked up their weapons and went inside after the defenders.

There was some mean hand-to-hand fighting until the British surrendered. Seven of them were killed or wounded, and more than fifty were taken prisoner. Churchill had seized the main blockhouse almost instantly, and the other two held out for only ten minutes. Major Tallmage collected his men and the prisoners in the compound and considered himself lucky. The Revolutionary Army casualty list was one man wounded.

With dawn the patrol was ready to burn the fort, start for Coram to burn the hay and then march to the north shore with the prisoners. But in the dawn light they saw a British schooner, her topmasts visible over the stockade. She lay at anchor in an inlet near the fort, and she was too fine a prize for Tallmage to ignore.

He divided his force into two detachments, leaving one to destroy the fort and the schooner and taking the other with the prisoners to Coram for the destruction of the hay. It was broad daylight before the hay stacks were well afire, and Loyalist militia were out on the roads to cut off retreat.

But Tallmage kept his people moving steadily at forced march pace, and they rejoined the detachment which had burned the fort and the schooner. They kept on, and at four o'clock in the afternoon were back at the boats. Pursuit was not too close. The raiders put their prisoners aboard and climbed in themselves. They cleared the beach with oars and sails, picked up a fair wind for Connecticut and were safe.

Sergeant Churchill received the right to the second half of his Purple Heart in a raid on October 2, 1781, which again crossed the Sound to Long Island. This was directed against a British installation called Fort Salonga, east of Northport on the north shore. It was led by Major Lemuel Trescott. He commanded about one hundred men, Churchill among them, and all volunteers from the 5th Connecticut Regiment and the 2nd Continental Dragoons.

The British had sent a number of troublesome raiding parties of their own from Fort Salonga, and General Washington wanted the place destroyed. He had ordered Major Tallmage to scout it and have maps drawn if possible. This was so well done that when the raiders landed they knew the exact station of each British sentry.

The raid was staged from Compo Point, at Westport, Connecticut, and the men went into the whaleboats at dusk and hoisted sail. They crossed without difficulty, and at three o'clock in the morning on October 3 had the fort secured.

Churchill was once more the leader of the first attacking party and made a direct assault. British sentries were either silently captured or killed, and the sergeant did not lose a man. He struck with such speed that only four British were killed before the rest surrendered. Fort Salonga gave up twenty-one prisoners and considerable quantities of powder, artillery, stores of small arms, ammunition and clothing.

The return to Connecticut was made in untroubled fashion, and the prisoners given to headquarters for interrogation. When General Washington devised the Purple Heart decoration in 1782 only three men were put on record as having received the award. One was Sergeant Churchill.

CHAPTER THIRTEEN

NEW NAVY

Twenty-two New England captains were on the appointment list of the early Continental Navy. This was understandable because of the great part men from that region had played in the maritime life of the colonies. Family connections and influence also had a lot to do with it. Esek Hopkins of Rhode Island, who had been at sea for forty years in merchant ships and as master of privateers, was made commander-in-chief with the rank of commodore. Critics of the appointment system pointed out that his brother, Stephen, was the chairman of the Naval Committee of Congress and his son, John B. Hopkins, had been given command of a frigate.

But during the war various other men emerged as fine sea fighters and masters of vessels. Among them were Henry Johnson, John Rathbun and Joshua Barney, and Nicholas Biddle, who had served in the Royal Navy and been a messmate of Horatio Nelson, and Jonathan Haraden, and John Barry, and the most illustrious of all, the vain and fearless and brilliant little Scot, John Paul Jones.

Most of these men served as the masters of privateers rather than in the Navy for the quite simple reason that privateers offered better pay and much more chance to fight the British on something like an equal basis of fire power and ship maneuverability. It was further true that privateers recruited better crews, due to the pay inducements, and Navy ships waited in port sometimes for as much as a year before they had enough hands to put to sea.

The Naval Committee of Congress had appointed Esek Hopkins commodore November 5, 1775, and on December 22, 1776, it issued commissions for the officers assigned to the first four Continental Navy ships. Then, on March 19, 1776, authorization was given for privateering, and Congress issued to shipowners letters of marque and reprisal.

A letter of marque was a form of commission that permitted a privateer vessel to seize the goods and vessels belonging to an enemy country. Certain regulations were established to limit seizure, but they were usually ignored. Privateer captains took almost any prize that seemed worth while.

A letter of reprisal was a special commission, much more limited than a letter of marque. It was issued to the owner or master of a merchant vessel so that he might obtain at sea reparation for losses he had suffered because of enemy action. It was to be issued only after all attempts by the owner and his government to get legal redress had failed. Issue of the commissions became quite common, though, as the war progressed and very few shipowners remained who had not suffered some kind of loss at enemy hands.

The original Continental Navy squadron was much too small and weak to put up concerted action against the Royal Navy fleet in American waters. The best it could do was to make individual ship raids, and in March, 1776, the commodore himself conducted one of these, slipping through the British cordon and sacking Nassau in the Bahamas. But after that Esek Hopkins was rarely at sea, and the majority of his captains were frustrated by the blockade, and the lack of ships and crews.

It was the privateers who carried the war to the British, and at first they flourished. During the summer of 1776 privateers put to sea all along the coast, from Maine to Georgia. With the greatest of haste New England shipyards converted fishermen for privateer duty. They took ketches, sloops and topsail schooners, increased the length of their spars and expanded their sail plans, put a few fourteen-pounder cannon and some swivel guns aboard and called them ready for sea.

None of these vessels was much over sixty tons, and many of them were less. Their crews were usually ten to fifteen men and a couple of boys; their personal weapons were fowling pieces, hatchets and pitchforks. They were cocky, careless and covetous, sailed sometimes alone and sometimes in wolf pack formation and took prizes wherever they could find them.

Their favorite area in the early days was the Gulf of St. Lawrence, and among the maze of islands, in the prevalent fog, they got in each other's way, often attacked each other. The bigger vessels, and those with better-disciplined crews, hauled off and ran for European waters to molest the British close at home.

The New Englanders had keen competitors in the privateer fleet, and often met coastwise ships that were commissioned as cruisers by New York, Pennsylvania, Maryland, Virginia, South Carolina and Georgia. Officers aboard the cruisers carried a variety of documents, and some had as many as three: a letter of marque, a commission in the Continental Navy and a commission from their home state.

They took a heavy toll from British shipping until the Royal Navy was organized in strength to combat them. During the year 1775 alone American privateers seized 143 prizes. But by 1777 the prize total was reduced to 73 ships. The Royal Navy's fast-sailing frigates and brigs and the big, clumsy but powerful ships of the line had caught up to the Americans and made them pay a severe price for their depredations. There were many occasions when privateer crews also were reduced dangerously to send men aboard captured vessels and sail them into port. British seamen rose in sudden, violent mutiny against their captors, seized the privateer vessel and brought her to a friendly port where the Americans were quickly condemned by an Admiralty court.

A considerable number of teen-age American boys who had started out gaily enough in privateers fetched up in the notorious British prison ship, the old 64-gun *Jersey*. She was in such bad shape that she had been condemned by Royal Navy surveyors, and her last purpose was to rest at anchor in the East River between Manhattan and Brooklyn in New York harbor and serve as a hulk. The calking was gone from her deckhead; the seams lay wide and rain and snow fell unimpeded below upon the prisoners packed in her holds.

Fierce rats ran the holds. The ship was verminous, and stank of rotting timbers, rotting men and death. The daily ration for the prisoners was worm-filled ship biscuit and decayed salt beef; once a week, they got a watery oatmeal gruel. Those who had money and the energy to climb to the deck were able to buy a bit of sausage and some fresh vegetables from bumboatmen who came alongside. But not many men had money, and prices were high.

British hospital ships lay off at the anchor from *Jersey* and received her sick. The hospital nurses were male civilians, hired because they were Loyalists and hated rebels. There were sadists and drunkards among them, and they were untrained and uncaring, skilled only at robbing the dead. The sick were forced to sleep two men to a bunk, and when a man died his bunkmate remained with him for the rest of the night.

It was estimated at the end of the war that between the years 1776 to 1783 at least 11,000 American seamen had died aboard *Jersey* or her hospital ships.

For an American privateersman who was captured at sea or in waters around the British Isles there was the formidable Mill Prison. This was situated between Portsmouth and Portsmouth Dock, a huge granite structure that was notorious among Englishmen before the war. But Mill Prison, while grim, and with a record of very few escapes, was not as bad as the lower holds in *Jersey*.

Prisoners were allowed to govern themselves, set up their own rules of conduct. They slept dry, and there were enough blankets. A man if he wished was able to take books from the prison library, read and study. Others made odd bits of carving and fashioned ship models that the guards sold for them on the outside. Still it was nothing like the pay supposed to come to a bold privateer. The complaint must have been often, "Ha'pence is what we get, m'lad, instead o' pounds, and demmed few o' the first."

The year of 1777 was the worst for privateersmen. Capture, shipwreck and loss at sea in storm had taken severe effect. The low morale at home was also a factor. Public confidence in the war had faltered, and the Continental currency was almost worthless. Then General Sir William Howe led the bulk of his New York City garrison south in a squadron of ships to the Chesapeake. The British occupied Philadelphia, and General Washington, beaten in the Battle of Brandywine, was forced into winter quarters at Valley Forge.

It was very hard to recruit a privateer crew during that time. Shipowners had to spend money to get recruits aboard their vessels, and for some New England shipowners such a practice was against all their principles.

A ship's officer in his best coat, cocked hat and new stockings, sword at his side, paraded through the narrow, cobbled streets of the seaport town where the privateer lay at her wharf. He called out the virtues of service aboard the vessel, and he appealed to all young men of high spirit and patriotic feeling to join him at the tavern. A color bearer, a fifer and a drummer strutted the streets ahead of the officer, and the martial music, the appeal of high wages and adventure at sea and in foreign ports, along with the invitation of free food and drink at the tavern, were almost irresistible.

The ship's officer waited there with rum, cherry flip, piled platters of food and the articles of service. When a man had satisfied his hunger and nearly quenched his thirst he usually signed articles. Thousands of young Americans, more drunk than sober, joined the privateers straight from a tavern taproom door.

While morale was still at a low ebb, and before Louis XVI decided to bring the support of the French to the new American nation, a number of New England shipowners held to their belief about how the war at sea might be won. They were convinced that privateers could eventually destroy the major function of the Royal Navy, the maintenance of the supply line from the British Isles to North American ports. But first, American privateer ships must be better built.

Elias Hasket Derby of Salem was the chief protagonist of this theory. He was a merchant-shipowner who had made a fortune before the war, lost it since and gone to privateering to recoup himself. He held the theory that many of the American ships lost to the British had been captured or sunk in action because they were not correctly designed for the service. So Derby worked out new designs on the drafting board in his countinghouse, then with half models carried them further, to the molding loft and finally to the shipyard.

He carefully computed sail plan, hull form, speed and armament. Then he built a new class of topsail schooner. She was big enough to carry the guns to fight off a British sloop-of-war, fast enough to run from frigates or ships of the line, and could be converted into a regular letter of marque cargo ship.

Other sharp-eyed shipowners followed Derby's example. They built in the years 1779 to 1783 ships designed to take more than 20 guns and a crew of 150 men and boys. With the entrance of France into the war on June 17, 1778, privateering again became a very popular endeavor for Americans. There were so many ships built for the trade that crews were short, and once more the ship's officer, the color bearer, the fifer and the drummer paraded the seaport streets, calling the reluctant to the tavern.

A number of American privateers had already been working out of French ports on the Continent and in the West Indies. There was in particular a shortage of crews in the Continental ports, and American privateer captains used much the same stateside recruiting strategy and a lot of free liquor to get men. When they had anything like a reliable crew they stood out to sea, gave the green men a little gunnery practice off the coast, then headed for the English Channel and possible prizes. But once France had entered the war, American privateersmen became extremely bold, aware that they could count on French warships for combat assistance.

The English Channel no longer deserved its name. American and French vessels, gun ports triced high, guns run out, lookouts at the mastheads, dominated it. King George's splendid navy was being shattered piecemeal, and her merchant ships seized, burned or driven from the sea.

The same day, June 17, 1778, that France declared war on England and took the side of the Colonies, a very somber report was made in the House of Commons in London. This stated that since the war with the colonies had begun the British had lost 733 ships, of which 174 had been recaptured. An earlier report, presented to the House of Lords by William Creighton on February 6, 1778, gave the calculation that the British had lost to American privateers cargoes and ships worth £200,200,000. He estimated further that these losses had been effected by 174 privateers carrying 1,838 guns and 9,236 men and boys. The Americans had seized along with the ships almost 11,000 men in British crews, an alarming figure. His Majesty's press gangs were very nearly at the bottom of the manpower pool, and had emptied jails and prisons to find replacements.

Royal Navy ship captains had vigorously complained to the Admiralty about the quality of the men sent them. What was the value of a ship, they asked, if her crew could not handle her guns or hoist her sails or take her to sea? The Admiralty did not have any immediate answer. But it did know through spies that the French had 80 ships of the line in service, with 6,700 men aboard them. Louis XVI also had just dispatched from Toulon 17 ships of his fleet under command of the Comte d'Estaing. They were ordered to duty in American waters.

Blockade of British-held ports along the American coast, and the eventual entrapment of the British army in a place such as Yorktown, must have been foreseen, if only dimly, by some of the smarter officers of the Admiralty. From June 17, 1778, onward Britannia definitely did not rule the waves.

Jonathan Haraden was one of the American privateer captains who gave the British great trouble during the war. Born at Gloucester, he chose to make his home across Massachusetts Bay at Salem, but was seldom there while he could be aboard ship. He started the war in General Washington's "Navy" as a lieutenant assigned to a small vessel named *Tyrannicide*. She distinguished herself in several engagements, and in a two-hour battle fought gunwale to gunwale against the much bigger British frigate *Revenge* she made the latter strike her colors and surrender.

Haraden came back to Salem and was offered command of a locally owned letter of marque ship. She was the 180-ton *General Pickering*, armed with 14 six-pounder cannon and carrying a crew of 45 men and boys. Haraden was thirty-five years of age, and known as a quiet, gentle man except when roused by battle. He was extremely popular among privateer crews, and it was not difficult to convince him that he should take the *General Pickering* to sea.

He sailed for Bilbao in May, 1780, with a cargo of sugar and a duly authorized letter of marque. Well out to sea in the Atlantic, he met a 22-gun British cruiser, and beat off from her after a two-hour fight. Then at night in the Bay of Biscay and near the Spanish coast he ran alongside the British privateer *Golden Eagle*. She was a good deal larger than his ship, and carried twenty-two guns, but that did not bother him.

Haraden took a deep breath and bellowed through the speaking trumpet that he was ready to blow the British ship apart unless she immediately surrendered. Her master meekly obeyed and only lost his temper when he was taken aboard *General Pickering* as a prisoner and was able to see how small she was. Haraden was amused in a mild way and kept on with the prize astern for Bilbao.

He was almost in port on June 3 when his lookouts called down from aloft that they had just sighted a vessel carrying a lot of sail. The British prisoners listened to the lookouts and studied the sail, then told Haraden that it belonged to the British privateer *Achilles*. That ship mounted forty-two guns and had a crew of 140 men. She was a much more powerful fighting machine than *General Pickering*, and should be feared.

But Haraden was determined to get into Bilbao if he could and take the prize with him. The wind had begun to subside into light airs, and Haraden knew that he might very readily be overhauled. *Achilles* with her large sail plan was the faster ship, and before the wind failed had drawn alongside the prize and captured her. She also pitched a number of bracketing shots at *General Pickering,* and Haraden was lucky to find the wind to sail out of range.

He was familiar with the approaches to Bilbao harbor from past voyages there, and chose his battle station in behind a line of shoals. *Achilles* had too deep a draft to navigate them, and must fight him from outside. This would reduce the advantage the British ship held and give him the chance to fight her on almost equal terms. If she ever closed with him, though, Haraden and his crew clearly understood, *General Pickering* was finished, and so were all hands.

The American crew spent the night getting ready for battle. There was little sleep; the men and the boys were too tense. Those who were not busy with their duties swarmed into the rigging to stare out to sea for sign of *Achilles* or watched the harbor mouth and the headlands along it where already thousands of Spaniards had begun to gather. The Spaniards built fires, danced, drank, sang and shouted into the night insults against the hated English. *Achilles* represented for them Drake and Hawkins and Raleigh and Cavendish and all the men who from the time of the Armada had defeated Spain on the sea. This, the Americans' battle, was also their own.

Dawn brought breeze, and *Achilles* moved promptly in from seaward to begin fighting. Haraden waited until she was within sure range of his guns. Then, still inside the barrier shoals, he maneuvered, brought his ship around and presented for just an instant his broadside to *Achilles.* During that instant his gunners let go in unison at the British ship, and the shot struck solidly, lunged thumping into hull and bulwarks and deck planks, slugged through sails and rigging. *General Pickering* had scored, and *Achilles* had not; the British gunners had been too slow and had not been able to deliver a broadside.

Achilles braced her yards around, hauled off, wore ship and returned to the attack. She tried various maneuvers that would bring her broadside batteries to bear upon the American vessel. Sailing in a cramped space, and in shoal waters where he might readily ground his own vessel, Haraden answered the attacks, and each time raked the British ship with broadside fire.

It went on for three hours. Ashore, the Spaniards emptied their wineskins and shouted themselves speechless. The British bull was being gored repeatedly by the smaller, smarter American, whose real weapon was his ability to handle ship. Now the British captain was running. He cleared for sea on a fresh breeze, and *General Pickering* came out from the shoals in pursuit.

Haraden drove his ship to engage with *Achilles* on any terms. The British captain, though, had too much respect for him. He took *Achilles* away on the increasing breeze, and the best Haraden could do was to recapture his former prize. When his crews were ready he sailed *General Pickering* and *Golden Eagle* into Bilbao and went to the anchor. He and his men received a tremendous welcome. They were for the people of Spain great heroes.

Homeward-bound, having sold his prize and his cargo of sugar, Haraden met off Sandy Hook three British merchant ships. They were armed, and if they had stayed together, could have beat him off or sunk him. He cut them out singly, though, and by surpassing seamanship and gunnery seized all three. Then he went on to Salem and was most happily received.

The call of the sea and the demands of the war soon sent him back to *General Pickering*. He cruised to the southward and entered the Caribbean and met a big British brig, a King's packet, carrying dispatches for the Admiralty. Haraden fought her for four hours at close quarters and at the end won her by bluff, in very much the same way he had taken the *Golden Eagle* outside Bilbao.

This time, while the deck reeled beneath him with concussion and the air screamed with the passage of British shot, he took out his pocket watch and shouted across to the packet commander that he gave him five minutes in which to surrender. The ships were only a few feet apart, and the British captain could clearly see and hear him. But he did not know that Haraden's men were down to their last round of ammunition and that *General Pickering* was really in very bad shape.

Haraden gave the order to his gunners, and that last round was rammed into the pieces and the guns trained. The gunners stood ready, stooped over the touchholes with their slow matches glowing.

Haraden, watch in hand, counted off the minutes: One, two, three, four. It was with the fourth minute that the packet captain surrendered.

Haraden crossed to her to accept the captain's sword and to inspect her. The battle fury must have left him then, to give way to sadness. Her main deck was awash with blood. Dead men were strewn upon it, and the captain led only a very few survivors, most of them wounded.

Good luck stayed constant for Haraden. He served through the rest of the war in command of various privateers, his reputation so great that he never failed to have his pick of crews. It was estimated after the armistice that he had taken more than sixty ships which mounted a total of at least one thousand guns.

Right along with Haraden in the top rank of privateer captains, and just as daring, Henry Johnson of Massachusetts established a splendid record in the war. He began early as master of the Massachusetts sloop *Yankee.* But, like many other privateer masters, Johnson weakened his crew strength by putting men aboard prizes taken at sea. This brought about his own capture in July, 1776, when British prisoners were able to get on deck and take *Yankee* from him and sail her into Dover.

Johnson and his crew were moved, still aboard *Yankee,* to the Thames and London, then transferred to confinement aboard a British warship. But Johnson had friends in London, and the friends collected a sizable bribe that took him out of the warship and into freedom and, a few weeks later, to Baltimore. He reported at once for service in the Continental Navy, and was given command of the 16-gun brig *Lexington.*

Lexington had been captured by the British and recaptured from them by her former American crew, and this fact must have amused Johnson to some degree when he took over aboard on February 5, 1777, with the approval of the Continental Congress. Three weeks later he had the brig at sea. *Lexington* carried dispatches and blank naval commissions for the use of the American Commissioners in

France. So Johnson had been warned before he sailed, "The British Emissaries in France are very inquisitive about all Vessels and Persons coming from America, and therefore you will be very cautious of talking with any Person concerning the place from whence you came, where you are going, or what is your business."

Johnson obeyed the warning pretty well. He showed himself to the enemy at close range only twice while at sea and each time seized a prize. He came into Bordeaux on April 3, 1777, went ashore at once and took a fast coach for Paris.

There is no record that he talked to any "Person" along the way, and he got to Paris safely with the dispatches and the blank naval commissions. But the American Commissioners had, wholly unknown to themselves, two very active spies as members of their organization. One was Benjamin Franklin's confidential secretary, Dr. Edward Bancroft, who was paid £1,000 a year by the British for espionage. The other was of smaller caliber, a man named Van Zandt, who used the alias of George Lupton.

It was Lupton who reported promptly to his employers in the British Foreign Office about the arrival of Johnson. He wrote:

"And now for a piece of news. The noted Yankey, Capt. Johnson, who was taken sometime last summer and brought into London, but afterwards made his escape from on board the man of war in which he was confined is arrived here. He brought dispatches from the Congress and this day delivered them to Mr. Deane in my presence while we were at dinner. He left Baltimore 28th Feby last. The Congress was at that place at that time. He arrived at Bordeaux where his Ship is at present.

"She is called the Lexington, mounts 16 four pounders, is a remarkable fast sailing Ship. She has about 60 men on board, on his passage he took two prizes, the one an empty Transport which he set fire to at Sea, after taking everything that was valuable from onboard. The Scoundrel says she lighted him along very pritely for the best part of a night, and at last went to the bottom. The other was a Scotch Brig bound from some port in London to Jamaica loaded with Herring & Coals. This vessel, he brought into port with him. 'Tis thought she will sell for near one thousand pounds Sterling. This Captain is the most conceited Chap I ever met with, and I am much mistaken if his own imprudence don't bring him into your hands once more, from which I am convinced he'll not make his escape to easily. . . ."

The spy's report was duly received in London, but not before Johnson had received his orders from the American Commissioners. The commissioners were Benjamin Franklin, Silas Deane and Arthur Lee, who had agents of their own operating in the British Isles. They knew a very great deal about Royal Navy ship movements, and with the help of Caron de Beaumarchais, a French writer and musician who believed devoutly in the cause of American independence, they kept a steady supply of munitions in transit overseas.

Beaumarchais, working out of the former Dutch embassy in Paris and under the name of a fake export firm, sent a million dollars' worth of powder, weapons, uniforms and other military supplies to the small Dutch island of St. Eustatius in the West Indies. The cargoes were picked up there by American Navy ships, which ran the British blockade at the times designated by the Commissioners in Paris or whenever possible. Among the blockade-runners were the sloops *Independence, Reprisal, Sachem* and *Hornet* and the brigs *Lexington* and *Andrew Doria*.

It was on the blockade run from St. Eustatius to the Delaware River that *Lexington* had been captured and then recaptured just before Johnson joined her as master. Now he was ordered to take *Lexington* to sea in company with two other American ships on a raiding voyage.

The American Commissioners were fully informed about the make-up and sailing dates of the huge British convoys that assembled at Portsmouth, in England, and at Dublin, in Ireland. Months were needed to gather the ships and the Royal Navy escort vessels to protect them, and meanwhile the press gangs were busy ashore, and the doxies and the spies. Franklin and Deane and Lee had detailed information about the departure from Dublin of a fleet of merchant ships carrying very valuable cargoes of Irish linen.

Lexington cleared from Bordeaux chased by an enormous 80-gun British ship of the line, *Foudroyant.* She was just as clumsy as she was big, though, and Johnson outsailed her and kept his rendezvous at Nantes. The American ships he met were *Reprisal,* commanded by Lambert Wickes, and *Dolphin,* whose master was Samuel Nicholson. The senior officer was Wickes, and he decided to put to sea although *Foudroyant* lumbered around outside the harbor waiting for them.

They outsailed her on May 23, 1777, and got safely to sea and set a northwest course to intercept the linen ships. But they missed the linen ships, doubled back and boldly entered the Irish Sea and afterward the English Channel. They cruised together for a month, and in one five-day period took fourteen prizes. Their total catch was eighteen ships, and the Royal Navy gave increasingly hot pursuit.

The little squadron was forced to separate off Ushant, and *Lexington* put into Morlaix and *Reprisal* and *Dolphin* into St. Malo. The British ambassador to France, Lord Stormont, had a lot to say about the French lack of neutrality and how captured British ships were sold in French ports and American "pirates" allowed shelter. This was more pressure than the American Commissioners thought wise to ignore. It would be better to get the raider to sea and out of immediate sight.

Johnson was ordered on September 16 to sail for Boston with packets of dispatches and letters. He cleared *Lexington* from Morlaix without trouble, but two days later, on the first leg of his Boston course, he met the Royal Navy cutter *Alert.* She mounted ten guns, and she was fast, and her commander, Lieutenant John Bazely, was eager to fight.

Johnson exchanged broadsides with her and suffered severely; he beat off and ran, and was overhauled. *Alert* kept pounding, and the gunners aboard *Lexington* could not match the rate of fire. *Lexington* was in very bad shape after three and a half hours of it. His sailing master and his lieutenant of marines dead, his first lieutenant and gunner wounded, and with a number of more dead and wounded among the crew, Johnson decided to surrender.

The dispatches were in a weighted bag. He brought it from his cabin and pitched it into the sea. Then he told the Royal Navy captain that he was willing to strike his colors, and asked for quarter. Quarter was granted and a prize crew put aboard *Lexington,* and Johnson went back to a British prison.

This time it was the formidable Mill Prison. But Johnson managed to escape, and was home in New England in July, 1778. The Marine Committee of the Continental Congress had ordered an inquiry into his conduct aboard *Lexington* during the battle with *Alert.* This was done despite his previous record and the recommendations given him by the American Commissioners and Captain Wickes.

Johnson was not deeply pleased. He relinquished his commission in the Continental Navy and returned to the privateers, where he was happy. During voyages he made until the end of the war he was often off the coasts of the British Isles, after prizes and profit, rather than naval approbation.

Wherever American seamen out of privateers and letter of marque ships met during the last years of the war there was almost always intense dispute about who was the finest master of those vessels. Many of the crews chose Haraden, and almost as large a number were in favor of Johnson. But by what was often an overwhelming majority the men's favorite was Gustavus Conyngham.

Conyngham was their kind of sailor, top and bottom, and, they insisted, their opinion should prevail. Believers in the merits of the Pennsylvania shipmaster thumped vigorously with their pewter mugs on the tavern taproom tables, slopping themselves and the opposition with ale, grog or cherry flip. This led to further, more extensive argument, in which fists and mugs were used, and sometimes dirks and cutlasses. Then the town watch arrived, and the disputants, impartially drubbed by the bailiffs, were hauled off to jail for the night.

Gustavus Conyngham deserved every bit of credit given him by his admirers. He had become famous in France as *"le terreur des*

Anglais" because of his raiding exploits, and his reputation was nearly as bright as that of John Paul Jones.

Conyngham came from Philadelphia in the early spring of 1777, sailed from there in command of the supply ship *Charming Betty,* bound for France. He reported to the American commissioners in Paris upon arrival, and Franklin who knew and liked him, saw that he was issued a privateer's commission and given the fast 10-gun lugger *Surprise.*

He recruited a crew for her and shoved off to cruise the English Channel. His first prize was a King's packet carrying mails. He sent her to France with a prize crew, shaped a course for the Isle of Guernsey and stood in close alongshore and landed from a small boat with a few of his men.

The Lieutenant of the island and the adjutant from his Majesty's garrison were out on the moors shooting rabbits. Conyngham and his party captured them without trouble, took them and their rabbits aboard *Surprise.* Then he headed for Dunkirk, and joining his prize along the way, considered that he had done quite well.

But the British made such an outcry about his seizures that the French were forced to lock him up in the Dunkirk jail. It was a gesture to assert their already highly dubious neutrality, and Conyngham understood why he was there. Still he preferred freedom and a ship command, and friends provided them for him.

This time Franklin gave him a commission in the Continental Navy, and he took to sea a fast 14-gun cutter named *Revenge.* It was while he was captain of *Revenge* that he made most of his reputation as a sea raider. For eighteen months Conyngham sailed the rakish-lined cutter around the British Isles, across the Atlantic and into the Caribbean. He took sixty prizes during that time, as many as credited to Captain Haraden, and he used friendly Spanish ports for refit purposes and sources of stores and munitions.

Then, under orders, he sailed early in 1779 back home to Philadelphia and was given a rousing welcome. The Marine Committee of the Continental Congress had decided to sell *Revenge,* though, and turned her over to a group of local merchants. There was no command open for Conyngham in the Navy and very little prospect of one. The merchants who were the owners of *Revenge* somehow must have considered that in their calculations, because they at once offered her to Conyngham as a letter of marque ship.

Conyngham was elated, and recruited a crew and made her ready for sea. He shoved off down the Delaware, found a fair wind, cleared the coast and eagerly began another cruise after prizes. But His Majesty's frigate *Galatea* overhauled him, and she was too fast for him to elude, and carried too many guns for *Revenge* to fight. He surrendered.

The officer in command of the boarding party from *Galatea* recognized Conyngham. He was given rough treatment when he was taken to the frigate, and aboard her he was put in chains in the lower hold. *Galatea* took him to England, where he was tried, found guilty, and remanded to Mill Prison.

His lack of popularity persisted among the prison guards. They kept him in the noisome, cruelly uncomfortable "black hole" in solitary confinement. But Conyngham had friends both within the prison and outside. It took some effort and careful planning, and then, in November, 1779, he and fifty other inmates dug a tunnel that led them to freedom and across the Channel to Holland. John Paul Jones was there at the time, aboard the Continental Navy frigate *Alliance*, anchored at the island of Texel, below Amsterdam. He was happy and proud to have Conyngham as his guest aboard until Conyngham could find a new command. Jones knew a real sailor when he met one.

It was men like Haraden, Johnson and Conyngham who carried the war to the most sensitive part of the British economic system, their home-based shipping. John Paul Jones struck in the same fashion, but went further and hurt them more. His raids along their coasts flouted their national pride.

CHAPTER FOURTEEN

RICHARD AND SERAPIS

This was the final, terrible instant before battle. John Paul Jones was acutely aware of it, and every man and boy aboard the slow-sailing, old *Bonhomme Richard* shared the knowledge with him. He stood alone on the ship's broad quarter-deck, the other officers withdrawn a bit so that he might concentrate fully upon the plan of action he must take.

The sun of late afternoon was at his back. It exaggerated the height of his stocky figure, seemed to widen the shoulders beneath the heavy gilt epaulettes of his commodore's rank. The crescent hat with the cockade on the left side, the smoothly tied stock, the blue, white-lapelled uniform coat, the sword sash, the white breeches and stockings and the shiny slippers were all impeccable. Commodore Jones was a dandy, a fop.

But it was the expression of the deeply tanned, gaunt-jawed face that held the attention of the men of the crew who were able to watch him. They stared at him from their stations beside the shotted and ready cannon on the main deck, and down from the fighting tops of the three masts where they crouched and tightly clasped the grips of swivel guns, muskets and pistols.

The cheekbones showed sharp in Jones's face, and the nose thrust forward like a blade. The lips were pale with compression.

189

The gray eyes were low-lidded as he glared out over the almost calm sea at the powerful enemy vessel.

Here was a fighter. Here was a sailor and a man to hold command. The entire crew of 380 had volunteered for service under him. Now, even though their knees quivered, and they gasped for breath in anticipation of pain, wounds and death, they were proud to be his shipmates.

It was six-thirty in the evening of September 23, 1779. *Bonhomme Richard* was about to open broadside fire on His Majesty's 44-gun frigate *Serapis*. The two ships sailed parallel courses off the high, white chalk cliffs of Flamborough Head on the northeast coast of England, while the rest of Jones's squadron of three ships hovered on the horizon, too timid to come closer. Jones had deliberately chosen to engage, sought battle with the stronger and faster British ship with his characteristic eagerness.

A long road of sea experience lay behind Jones. He had come through a great deal before he was able to take command of *Bonhomme Richard* and the rest of his so-called fleet and maneuver into action against *Serapis*. Some of that strange and often violent past must have returned to the channels of his mind even while he waited in the stillness of the final instant to give the fire order to the gunners bent over their pieces.

He was thirty-two, a Lowland Scot born in Kirkbean, Kircudbright-shire, and the son of a gardener. He went to sea early in coasters and then deepwater ships, taught himself good grammar, the mathematics necessary to understand navigational principles and the basics of naval architecture. He was mate aboard a slaver and captain in various British cargo ships running the Caribbean and the American coast before the Revolution broke out and he chose to make his career in the Continental Navy. It was his intense desire to rise to high rank in the new service, and he had a very firm belief in what he called *"Pro Publica,"* a liking for freedom from tyranny.

Jones was disputatious, though, and insufferably cocky, quick to quarrel with anybody who doubted his superlative seamanship or his right to hold command of first-class vessels. This and the fact that he was not American-born weighed heavily against him in a service dominated by New Englanders who had small use for foreigners in general, and less for allegedly penurious, overproud Scots. They deprived him later of command of *Ranger* while the ship was in a French port. The American Commissioners at Paris were far from agreed about his preeminence as a ship captain, and in the end he was fortunate to get command of leaky and cranky old *Bonhomme Richard.*

He served the first part of the war in secondary capacities before he reached France, and it was only when he was given command of the sloop-of-war *Providence* that he could prove himself to the members of the Marine Committee of Congress. He seized sixteen prizes while her captain, and as a result was told to take the fine, new sloop-of-war *Ranger* to sea.

That was in June, 1777, and he went to join her at Portsmouth. He spent some months in the pleasant New Hampshire town before he finished outfitting her and could collect a crew. Portsmouth held a number of wealthy families whose money had been made in ship-building, the sale of lumber and general trade with the West Indies. The cocky little captain stayed at the best inn, but he was often entertained in the spacious white Georgian houses with their grace-ful porticoes, elliptical fanlights, long, wainscoted rooms and enor-mous fireplaces.

He paid to have printed and distributed throughout the northern New England region a recruiting handbill that carried at the head a bold line of type: "Great Encouragement for Seamen." It went on to induce them to serve under him aboard *Ranger* and to report to the Ship's Rendezvous in Portsmouth or at the Sign of Commodore Manley in Salem, "where they will be kindly entertained, and receive the greatest Encouragement."

It was impossible to gather the kind of crew he wished because of the "Encouragement" offered competent seamen aboard the privateers at more than double the amount of Navy wages. The officers given him by the direction of the Marine Committee were not particularly to his liking, either, and he had taken *Ranger* to sea with some misgivings.

When he cleared from Portsmouth he had bent onto the mizzen gaff halyards the new American ensign with its red and white stripes and white-starred blue field. He carried news of the surrender of the British army under Burgoyne at Saratoga, with orders to take it as fast as possible to the American Commissioners in Paris. His very great hope was that because of the Saratoga victory the French would enter the war against the British. He was right in this, and later, on February 14, 1778, while bringing *Ranger* in along the French coast, he had been given a formal salute of the flag by units of the French Navy.

Ranger handled well enough for him on the outward-bound run, and after a few months in ports in France while she was refitted he went raiding into the Irish Sea. He had always maintained the conviction that land raids against the British, right in their home ports, would have a crippling and demoralizing effect upon them, severely slow up their war effort overseas.

So he struck at Whitehaven and at St. Mary's Isle, in the southern part of Scotland near where he had been born. Vessels were seized or burned at their moorings in port, and the bailiffs went rushing across the countryside to spread the alarm. Jones, looking for bigger booty, sent *Ranger* out to sea, and off Carrickfergus harbor, in the North of Ireland, on April 24, 1778, he found it in His Majesty's sloop-of-war *Drake*.

Drake was at anchor in Carrickfergus harbor and came out to meet him, and about an hour before darkness the two ships engaged. They were about equal in size and gun power; *Ranger* mounted 18 nine-pounders, and *Drake* carried a similar armament of 20.

They fought furiously in broadside exchanges for about half an hour while on the smooth green shoulders of the lochside the cattle stared aghast at the enormous bursts of sound, and the alarm fires set by the bailiffs sent somber banners along the last daylight in the sky. Jones did not dare to close with *Drake;* she had a bigger crew, would undoubtedly repel his boarding party with severe losses. His tactic was to direct concentrated fire at her masts and rigging, smash them, render her rudderless and without maneuverable headway. Meantime, his fighting top men could keep their volleys going against the British gunners, drive them from their pieces.

The tactic worked. The fore and main topsail yards in *Drake* toppled as their rigging was shot away and went overside with a great, grinding lurch. *Drake* lay helpless, and almost all her cannon were silent, the cannoneers dead, wounded or deserters from their stations. Captain Burden, her commander, was dying, and the first lieutenant was also mortally wounded. It was the second lieutenant who surrendered her after an hour and four minutes of fighting. She had lost 42 men out of her crew of 160, and that was enough for the second lieutenant.

Despite his victory Jones was relieved of command of *Ranger* when he brought her into port at Brest. The American Commissioners in Paris were still far from agreed about his preeminence as a ship captain. It was only after months of waiting, and through the intercession of Benjamin Franklin, that he was able to take over leaky and cranky old *Bonhomme Richard.*

Now, on the evening of September 23, Jones faced his supreme test. He looked aloft at the big British ensign *Bonhomme Richard* flew to trick the enemy. Pretense was just about finished. Captain Richard Pearson, the master of *Serapis,* had bawled across the water at him, "What ship is that?"

Jones told his sailing master the reply he wished given, and Samuel Stacey called deep-voiced, *"Princess Royal!"*

But Captain Pearson had no belief in that. He had been warned by a boat from shore that the ship he confronted in the dusk was the *Bonhomme Richard* and commanded by John Paul Jones. He challenged again, got no answer and, lifting his speaking trumpet, shouted, "Answer immediately, or I shall be under the necessity of firing into you."

Jones turned and nodded to a quartermaster who stood by the main halyards. The British ensign came quickly down; the American ensign was bent on and sent aloft. The final instant was gone; this was battle. Jones stood taut and called to the starboard broadside gunners, "Fire!"

Dusk had left the sea. But the great, full harvest moon, honey-yellow, was rising over the horizon, and dimmed the glow of the slow matches the gunners held. The gunners blew upon the match ends once more and reached down to the touchholes and leaped aside as the pieces went slamming back in recoil against the preventer hawsers.

Muzzle flame was scarlet on the moon-touched sea and reflected in darting streaks along the black hullside of the *Bonhomme Richard*. The air was split by detonation, and the cannon balls made a high, quick whine in flight. Powder smoke began to drift black and thick up toward the sails and the fighting tops.

Serapis veered from her course under the impact as the American shot came aboard her. She had just triced up her gun ports, and replied immediately in kind with a broadside salvo from her double gun decks. The ships were only a couple of hundred feet apart, and the rest of Jones's squadron stayed clear, refused to obey his signals for assistance. He must fight *Serapis* alone and close with her before she sank his clumsy old vessel with superior fire power.

Bonhomme Richard had been built in 1766 for general cargo service in the French East Indies trade. She was approximately 145 feet long, with a 35-foot beam, and weighed about 900 tons. Her hull was badly weakened by dry rot and years of exposure to parching tropic sun, and had been pierced to mount 45 cannon, more than she could take and remain fully seaworthy.

There were 6 nine-pounder guns on her fo'c'sle-head and the same number and caliber on her quarter-deck. She mounted 16 new and 12 old 12-pounders on her covered gun deck as her main battery and 6 old 18-pounders in the gun room aft. The 18-pounders were dangerously worn, the barrels and breeches thin.

Two of the gun room 18-pounders exploded with the second salvo fired. Their crews were instantly killed, torn apart by the rending metal. Almost all of the other gun crews stationed in that confined space were either killed or wounded, their guns made useless. The shipside was jaggedly smashed, the deckhead was about to collapse, and the deck had become a gore-strewn shambles.

Jones must have experienced an awful moment when he realized what had happened below. The wrecked battery contained the ship's only large caliber guns, and *Serapis* mounted 44 pieces, among them a powerful 18-pounder battery. Now the vessels were no more than a hundred feet apart, and crashing broadside answered crashing broadside. *Bonhomme Richard* was being severely riddled, would soon founder and sink under such punishment.

It was completely clear to Jones that he must close with *Serapis,* lock his vessel to her with grapnel hooks, hawsers and fouled spars and then send away a boarding party to take her in direct assault. But he was still uncertain of the battle quality of his men. There were among his crew only about eighty men who were Americans. Almost one hundred of the others were British sailors recently released from French prisons. The rest were a motley collection, Portuguese, Swedes, Scots, French civilians, whatever men he had been able to get to volunteer from off the dockside at Lorient.

His officers were excellent, and he could trust them, and the French Marines up in the fighting tops and on deck had already proven themselves by their shrewd and steady fire. So the only tactic was to close with *Serapis* and board, fight it out with pike, cutlass, ax, pistol and grenade.

Captain Pearson understood his intention, though, and kept off from collision with *Bonhomme Richard,* continued to tear and riddle her with rapidly served broadsides. Then Pearson backed the topsails of *Serapis* in an attempt to check her speed so that he could put a totally devastating broadside into *Bonhomme Richard.* The light, fitful breeze betrayed him. He was not able to carry out the maneuver, and the advantage went to Jones.

Jones told Stacey, his sailing master, to "lay the enemy's ship aboard," and a course was steered directly at *Serapis.* The ships met bow to quarter, the *Bonhomme Richard* bowsprit lunging up into the mizzen rigging of *Serapis* along the British ship's after quarter.

They locked inextricably, as Jones had hoped. The heavy, thickly rigged *Bonhomme Richard* bowsprit pierced through the tangle of cordage and shrouds and shot-ripped sails, and aloft, the long yard-arms tangled, some that belonged to *Bonhomme Richard* half across the enemy's deck.

The first lieutenant aboard *Bonhomme Richard* was a strapping young Virginian named Richard Dale. He was a veteran with nearly ten years of service, although only twenty-two. He had shipped with Captain John Barry and been aboard the brig *Lexington* under Captain Johnson when she was captured in 1777 homeward-bound. Since then, he had been in Mill Prison, escaped, was recaptured and put in the "black hole," escaped again and reached Lorient. He volunteered at once for duty in *Bonhomme Richard,* and Jones was very happy to have him, gave him great trust and charge of the vital main battery work.

But the terrific and rapid British fire, delivered at point-blank range, almost muzzle to muzzle, had wrecked every *Bonhomme Richard* main battery gun. The British gun crews were so close to their targets that they leaped aboard *Bonhomme Richard* to swab their pieces after firing a round. The long-barreled, black-mounted guns reared back in the breeching tackle, fetched up against the preventers and, smoking and steaming, were frantically reloaded and once more fired.

Bonhomme Richard was a shambles below her weather deck. Round after round of heavy shot had smashed her timbers, her bulk-heads and planking. She was holed below the waterline, and took a lot of water aboard; the carpenter reported five feet of it in the lower hold. One hundred British prisoners, crews from prizes taken by Jones's squadron, were confined there. They screamed in maddened fear, and the sound they made was so intense that Jones heard it above the clangor of the battle.

He gazed around for a moment, away from these mortally clasped ships, and looked to seaward to find some sign of help from the squadron vessels that were supposed to support him. The huge convoy of British merchant ships that *Serapis* and another Royal

Navy man-of-war, the *Countess of Scarborough,* had been escorting home from the Baltic had fled away on a northerly course. One of the French ships that belonged to Jones's squadron had dared engage *Countess of Scarborough.* She was *Pallas,* and she fought the Royal Navy ship with some fury several miles off. But *Alliance,* the French vessel whose master was the weird, psychopathic character, Pierre Landais, took no part in that, nor did the other ship of the squadron, *Vengeance.*

Bonhomme Richard was exposed both to cowardice and treachery by her alliès. For now, deliberately in the clear moonlight, the target unmistakable because *Bonhomme Richard* was painted black and *Serapis* yellow, Landais sailed down and raked Jones's ship fore and aft, holed her repeatedly and killed several of her men.

Still Jones would not consider surrender. He was determined to keep on fighting until *Bonhomme Richard* took *Serapis* down with her when she sank. Pearson had ordered an anchor lowered aboard *Serapis,* with the expectation that wind and tide would swing the American ship free from her. The grapnels and the lashings held, though, and sails afire, bulwarks shattered, dead men sprawled across the bullet-chopped remains of the hammock nettings, the two vessels remained embraced.

Jones swept the powder grime from his eyelids. He straightened, and touched his sword hilt and the pistol butts in his sash. One of his chief petty officers, maddened by battle shock, had just released the British prisoners from the main hold. They came up on deck screaming and wild, ready to kill their captors. Jones yelled at them in his loudest voice of command, beat them with the flat of his sword blade and a pistol butt. Lieutenant Dale joined him, and between them they drove the British to the pumps amidships, made the men take the handles and set to work.

But when Jones swung around to go back to the quarter-deck the chief gunner, a man named Henry Gardner, ran past him. Gardner was staring-eyed and deep in the clasp of hysteria; he yelled that the ship should strike her colors, surrender. Jones took out a pistol and poised the weapon on the palm of his hand with a practiced gesture, then threw it end for end through the black drift of cannon smoke. It caught Gardner behind the ear and knocked him sprawling and unconscious.

Over aboard *Serapis* Captain Pearson had seen and heard. He called to Jones, "Do you surrender? Do you strike?"

Jones shouted fiercely back at him, "I have not yet begun to fight!'

But *Bonhomme Richard* had only three cannon left that could be served. These were nine-pounders on the poop. Jones beckoned men to his side, gripped the bulky elmwood carriages with them, swerved the pieces on the rough wooden wheels by using wedges and crowbars. Then they hauled the cannon over to the port side and into firing position.

The exercise of cannon was for Jones an exactly timed, highly skilled performance that demanded great technique. A crew of at least ten men was needed to fire a piece, and each had his precise function, and there were thirteen separate parts of the procedure. The gray, canvas-covered powder cartridge went home in the barrel bottom first and seams down, a wad behind it, and after that the shot, and then the gun was trained, elevated, steadied on target by the chief gunner with his tautly stretched piece of white cord led back from the breech. The fire order was given in unison by all the gunners in a battery, just as the ship was at the top of a roll and at the best possible moment for execution of the pieces when the platform of the ship was stable beneath them.

Within this sulphurous pall nothing like ordinary performance could be maintained. Jones stumbled over dead men as he hauled, loaded, trained and fired. He slipped on deck planks slick with blood and what had been bodies. He pushed aside men who were blank-faced with horror. They could not keep their voices still or keep out of his way. Fear had consumed them, and they screamed constantly, at the British, at the flames that rippled along the sails, at themselves and at death.

Jones could no longer serve the cannon. He had reached the point of total fatigue. For the past few nights he had taken no more than three or four hours' sleep. His body was numb; it would not

accurately obey his will. He groped to a hen coop, sat slack upon the slats.

He was close to absolute despair. He knew that *Serapis* could not be seized by a boarding party assault. His men were too tired, too few, and she had double, covered gun decks where her men could protect themselves and fight with immense advantage. The only effective order for him to give was to tell the men in the fighting tops to keep up their swivel gun and small-arms fire.

Jones stood, and called aloft. He beckoned at the *Serapis* in indication of the meaning of his order. Then he went aft to his station on the quarter-deck and the work with the nine-pounders.

The French Marines in the fighting tops of *Bonhomme Richard* wore their long red uniform coats with the white facings and crossed white belts. Their tall, cockaded shakos and the crossed belts made them fine targets for the British topmen, but they were taking almost full measure of the enemy. Lieutenant Stack commanded the detachment in the main top, and with them were sailors, and the detachment amounted to twenty men. Stack was an Irishman, a volunteer from a French regiment in which he served as a professional. He handled the detachment with superb skill. The short-barreled coehorn mortars, the longer swivel guns and the big French muskets kept a frightful cascade of death upon the main deck of *Serapis,* and the British topmen had been thrown bodily out of their own maintop platform.

Nathaniel Fanning, a young midshipman from Stonington, Connecticut, was in the *Bonhomme Richard* foretop with fourteen men, and another young American officer, Midshipman Robert Coram, was in the mizzentop with a detachment of nine men. They also maintained rapid, murderous fusillades, mostly from the Charleville muskets that the Marines fired with great accuracy. The coehorns and swivel guns hurled grape, pieces of chain, glass and scrap iron. Grenades were being passed aloft in buckets, and slow matches for their fuses.

Jones recognized what must be the principal target for him. It was the mainmast of *Serapis*. Chop that down, and with the losses she had already suffered, she would be in very poor shape. Jones loaded his nine-pounder with double shot. He fired, swabbed and hauled the gear, fired again, and beside him his aide, Midshipman John Mayrant, worked in silence. But Mayrant stopped once and with Jones stared aloft at the *Bonhomme Richard* main yard above them.

A Scottish sailor, a man named William Hamilton, had just swarmed out along the yard. He pushed himself belly-down, his bare, calloused toes strained to the footrope, a bucket of grenades in one hand, a red-glowing match in the other. Hamilton went all the way to the outboard end of the yard. Then he set himself and lit a grenade fuse, dropped the missile downward through the black, slow waver of smoke over the main deck of *Serapis*.

A hatch was part open down below aboard the British ship. The powder monkeys had used it constantly to bring cartridges to the main deck gunners. But the gunners had been driven away from the pieces or were wounded or dead. There was a pile of cartridges at the foot of the ladder into the hold, and dazed, frightened British seamen stood next to it, afraid to go on deck. That was where a grenade dropped by Hamilton struck and exploded.

The blast killed about twenty men and burned and maimed many more. It did great damage to the lower structure of the vessel, weakened her in her main beams. But Jones hardly looked up any more except to take aim on her mainmast. He was busy directing the fire of his nine-pounders as they sent round after double-shotted round into the stubborn British oak.

The huge mainmast had begun to sway, stripped of the supporting web of stays and shrouds and riddled by Jones's fire. Captain Pearson surrendered *Serapis* a few minutes later, just before ten-thirty in the evening. Lieutenant Dale took a boarding party over with Midshipman Mayrant, and they met Pearson, conducted him back to their commodore.

The mainmast went finally, nodding, swerving in a wide parabola first and taking overside a shower of blocks, fouled stays, sheets and braces and a clutter of smashed yards. The sea sprang white under that blow, and Jones and Pearson waited until it had subsided before they stiffly offered each other a short half bow. Then Jones accepted Pearson's sword and led his prisoner below to his cabin for the traditional glass of wine at the end of battle. They walked around and over dead men. Jones felt saddened, not yet elated by his great victory. Half of the crew of *Bonhomme Richard* were casualties.

Two days after the battle, as Jones led his raiding group and his prize in the North Sea, he was forced to abandon *Bonhomme Richard* for *Serapis*. The old ship was fire-gutted, and it sank in the heavy sea that was running. Jones kept on aboard *Serapis,* avoided the British Home Fleet ships sent out after him, and took refuge in the Texel, where the supposedly neutral Dutch welcomed him.

Appreciation of his victory came to him there. Letters reached him from Paris and Lorient and London. The flat, sandy shore of Texel Island behind which he took refuge was incessantly patrolled by British ships. One of his London correspondents had passed on to him the reason for this.

The *Bonhomme Richard–Serapis* action had deeply disturbed not only Whitehall but the mass of the English people. John Paul Jones had become for them a fabulous figure, a man with supernatural strength and fighting skill. He had scored what the British looked upon as their worst defeat of the war.

Lord Sandwich, according to Jones's correspondent in London, had written a Home Fleet captain: "For God's sake get to sea! If you can take Paul Jones you will be as high in public estimation as if you had beat the combined fleets!"

CHAPTER FIFTEEN

BOSTON COMES OF AGE

The peace, signed finally in Paris on September 3, 1783, was uneasy and strange. A great many benefits had come from the wars. The thirteen colonies were joined together as states under the Confederation of the United States, with title to an immense territory that stretched from the Atlantic coast to the Mississippi. Abolition of the royal and proprietary ruling class and the participation of all kinds of men in the Revolution had considerably widened the political base; quitrents, entail and primogeniture, three of the main stumbling blocks in the way of freedom, were out forever.

But a large part of the population had been dislocated, and the Loyalists paid bitterly for their devotion to the King. Almost 100,-000 of them were forced to leave the country, 7,000 in a single contingent from New York on April 26, 1783. They had been barred from all offices and professions, and were made to pay double or triple tax assessments if they chose to stay in the country. The State of New York got more than $3,600,000 from the sale of confiscated Loyalist property, and Maryland over $2,000,000. Distribution of this land helped the poor somewhat and let a number of tenant farmers establish themselves as independent homestead owners. Penal codes and prison conditions improved to a degree, and yet debtors' prisons remained in several states.

The Anglican Church was banned in all states where it had been tax-supported, and was missed by thousands of worshipers. Slavery was prohibited in Massachusetts in 1780, and in New Hampshire in 1784, and emancipation begun on a gradual scale in Rhode Island, Connecticut and Pennsylvania. By 1786 eleven states all told had declared slavery illegal. Still the Rhode Island shipowners took huge profit from the African slave trade, and Baltimore naval architects designed new and extremely fast clipper type of vessels for them.

Freedom had released the new nation from the galling pressure of the Navigation Acts, but then, in 1783, a British Order in Council barred importation of meat, fish, cheese and butter from the United States into her West Indian islands and restricted trade in all other cargoes to British ships. At the same time France, without whose aid the Revolution could not have been won, was now at war with Britain, and the French complained of the fact that American ships ran in full cargo to the British Isles. War threatened between France and the United States, and privateers were fitted out by both nations, sent to sea to seek and seize the other nation's ships.

New England shipowners looked bleakly upon the possibility of further war. Massachusetts in particular had suffered an extremely severe depression at the end of the Revolution. The New Bedford whaling fleet was gone, destroyed by the very efficient Royal Navy blockade during the last war years. Nantucket was in a condition of semistarvation, the best of her men and her ships lost. More than a hundred Nantucket widows moved along the narrow red brick streets, shawls pulled tight around their ravaged faces, or, out of long habit, stood on the captains' walks on the roofs of their silent houses and gazed forth at the sea or sat behind drawn blinds and let their sorrow go in weeping.

The fleets of Massachusetts small craft that had worked the Grand Banks and the other coastal fishing grounds had been too slow to escape the Royal Navy cutters, sloops-of-war and frigates. They, too, were gone, and along with them nearly all of the state navy vessels and a great many of the fast privateers whose masters had dared too much too often. Shipbuilding was down to one eighth of what it had been before the war.

The large amount of cheap money issued by the government had started inflation. Tariff discrepancies among the various states were extreme because of the weakness of the confederation system and the fact that financial controls were not yet centralized. So coastal shipping steadily diminished, and merchants shut up shop and crews went on the beach, hungry and jobless.

Then the British offered what Boston people believed to be the supreme insult. British freight ships, loaded to the hatch coamings with fancy European cargo, came into port and went alongside the wharves and started to discharge as speedily as possible. They were followed by French and Spanish ships that carried the same kind of de luxe freight, silks, satins, bonnets, slippers, shoes, gloves, shawls, corsets and men's attire, each item shrewdly picked for a market that had been deprived during seven years of war. Merchants watched red-faced with anger at the doors of their countinghouses. They pointed out to their clerks in vivid phrases that both the French and Spanish had forbidden American vessels to enter the colonial ports of those two countries.

Trade was still trade, though, and the Boston merchants went down to the wharves and began negotiations for the cargoes. They bought on credit and in a feverish, quite uncharacteristic abandon, with little of their usual haggling over prices. Clerks reported that customers had already formed queues outside the retail shops, and that country storekeepers were coming into town to place orders in great quantity for the backwoods trade.

There was a vast amount of land speculation all through New England and in Maine in particular. Prices rose with the effects of inflation upon the entire economy, and the inevitable collapse came. Banks were overextended and called in loans, demanded mortgage payments and denied further credit. Then the Massachusetts state government began to tighten up on people whose taxes were in arrears.

Farmers lost their places by foreclosure or tax lien. Country storekeepers, unable to maintain credit any longer in Boston, failed by the scores and added to the financial wreckage of the small towns. There was unemployment, and then hunger, then a series of sporadic uprisings fomented mainly by Revolutionary veterans who believed they had been unfairly treated. Militia and federal volunteer troops put down the uprisings without much bloodshed, and gradually the economy recovered.

Sharp-witted Yankee shipowners had a great deal to do with the return to normalcy. They had pondered from every angle the trade restrictions placed upon them by the British, the French and the Spanish and found various methods to get around them. Ships left fully loaded with cargoes of corn, codfish and salt beef for the West Indies. Their masters had instructions to enter into smuggling alliances with Dutch, Swedish and Danish traders in the islands owned by those nations.

Ships from Massachusetts and Maine and Rhode Island began to arrive steadily in Curaçao, and in the Virgin Islands, then a Danish possession, and the little Swedish island of St. Bartholomew. Cargo transferrals were made, and bills of lading accepted and paid for, and the former American commodities went forth in other vessels for resale by the local merchants.

But the New England shipowners began to look upon this trade as too small. They were emboldened by the success of the smuggling operation, and saw no reason why they should not play charades with the British, the French and Spanish. Captains sailed south mainly with food cargoes but also carrying the usual New England truck goods and harness, hardware and wooden utensils turned out by hand in many backwoods communities. The captains brought their vessels alongside the ports of call during darkness, then, at dawn, began the charade.

Bosuns and sailors slacked off on shrouds until the rigging hung awry and yards tilted high and fouled canvas. The ensign was reversed on the main gaff halyards—the international signal of a vessel in distress. Then, putting on their most solemn expressions and working their vessels very gently, the captains entered the restricted ports. They were met invariably by irate port authorities, but there was a cash donation in a sealed envelope for those men and other, larger donations for the senior naval officer and the governor.

It became the habit of the colonial officials to declare a "condition of starvation" for the people they governed. They welcomed the Yankee captains and their cargoes, commiserated with them at dinner about the disrepair of their vessels and privately and warmly asked them to come back soon. There was just enough real starvation in some of the colonies to make the presence of the American vessels plausible. France was still fighting Britain, and a blockade along the European coast had cut short a large part of the ordinary food shipments to the West Indies.

Their ships' rigging set up again, the holds empty except for ballast, the captains cleared for home. The ledgers kept by the ships' clerks showed that a fairly good profit had been made on the voyage. Bribes were of course expensive, but in wartime prices were high, and would be higher yet next voyage. These waters were roamed by French privateers, British men-of-war and outright pirates of three or four nationalities. There was a definite risk attached to this trade, and a shipowner was wise to make his customers pay for it.

The opening of an overseas market for New England products had eased economic tension, swung the political tide toward the reactionary Federalist Party. The Federalists, who were for a strong central government, were led by Alexander Hamilton, and he counted among his most active supporters the Massachusetts bankers, merchants and shipowners. The struggle for ratification of the Federal Constitution by Massachusetts was held in 1788 and was fought hard. A number of men who had expressed sympathy for the recent uprisings against the tax laws now took the side of what they called law and order and which meant to them in practical terms work and wages. The decision went to the Federalists with opposition of only 19 out of a total of 355 votes.

New England had regained prosperity, was once more the dominating force in the American commercial structure. Boston merchants looked much further than the West Indies or the Baltic and general European trade. Certain hints in the published accounts of Captain James Cook's voyages of exploration were recalled, and the statements of far-roving Russian fur traders made in conversation in Riga.

The so-called Northwest Territory, the enormous region that comprised all of the American northwest coast between California and Alaska, was as yet untouched by American enterprise. But for generations Russian traders based on Alaska and the Aleutian Islands had collected the magnificent sea otter skins, sold them at a high profit in Canton. The Russians dealt with Indians in the North, bought most of their pelts from them. New Englanders had successfully traded entire Indian nations out of their traditional homesites on the Eastern seaboard. It was only logical that trading vessels be sent to the Northwest Territory, their cargoes the famous assortment of truck goods and some rum and lead and sheet copper to be used for barter. The ships would then proceed to Canton, trade pelts for tea, and come on home.

This was the triangular market arrangement which Boston merchants dearly loved. They were very eager to establish it. Competition between Salem and Boston was as keen as ever, and the Boston merchants were afraid that Salem ships would take the lead in the Canton trade, secure the major sources of profit.

There had already been an attempt to enter the Canton trade during 1783, the year the peace was signed. The 55-ton sloop *Harriet,* owned in Hingham and under command of Captain Hallet, sailed from Boston with a cargo of ginseng. But while in Capetown, his ship at anchor in Table Bay, the captain met several officers in the employ of the Honorable East India Company. The Englishmen, in their light blue coats with black velvet lapels, broad gold braid and gilt buttons that bore the crest of the company, were very friendly, played the host lavishly for Hallet.

Before the evening was over they asked him what his cargo was and where his ship was bound. Captain Hallet fully understood the reasons for the hospitality he enjoyed and what lay behind the seemingly offhand questions. He answered, though, without hesitation. He and his owners had little to lose under the present circumstances.

Ginseng was his cargo, he told the East Indiamen, and *Harriet* was bound for Canton. The East Indiamen almost immediately made him a proposition. The Honorable Company would buy the ginseng, and the purchase would be made in high-grade Hyson tea, the weight of the tea to be double the weight of the ginseng *Harriet* carried.

Captain Hallet agreed. It was a fair enough proposition, and would ensure his owners a nice profit. More, he would not have to sail the sloop across the dangerous waters of the Indian Ocean and then the China Seas, ducking pirates and typhoons nearly all the way. He shook hands with the East Indiamen and the transaction was made formal. *Harriet* discharged and reloaded in Table Bay, sailed for home without disturbing the delicate balance of British trade in Canton. That had been the major factor in the British offer to buy the ginseng, Captain Hallet told his owners when he was back home with *Harriet*. The Honorable East India Company wanted to hold onto all of the China trade, and the profits it took there must be huge.

But the wealth to be found in the Orient was too great to be ignored any longer by American merchants. The New York-owned brig *Empress of China* entered the trade in 1784, sailed for Macao on February 22 under the direction of Major Samuel Shaw of Boston. The major, whose actual rank aboard was that of supercargo, was a member of one of the few big mercantile families in New England that had chosen the side of the Revolution. He was greatly respected for his character, his sagacity and powers as a diplomat.

Her master, Captain John Greene, brought *Empress of China* into the Portuguese port of Macao, below Canton, on August 30, and she was well received. Major Shaw traded her cargo for tea and silk, then she got under way for home, reached it in May, 1785. The profit her owners made put Boston, Providence and Philadelphia merchants quickly into the trade.

The North River sloop *Experiment* had cleared New York for Canton while *Empress of China* was still at sea. She was an 85.5-ton vessel, bluff-bowed, with a very long main boom and bowsprit. She flew square-rigged upper and lower topsails and carried a crew of fifteen men and boys under the command of Captain Stewart Deane, who had perfected his navigation as a privateer master during the Revolution.

Experiment was the first American-flag vessel to make the run direct to Canton. She made it in four months, twelve days. The boys aboard her were given a marvelous opportunity to learn their work as sailors. Captain Deane kept the sloop moving in almost any kind of weather. She had the low freeboard of her North River design, but she was strongly built and well rigged. He drove her hard once she was across the Gulf Stream, squared her away to the northeast trades and put her on her heading for Cape of Good Hope.

The boys met turtles and tiger shark, sargasso weed, bonito and barracuda, and days when there was no wind at all, and *Experiment* lay without motion under the equatorial sun, tar sticky to the touch in the deck seams, the planks so hot they blistered right through callouses. The sails gave a little shade, and the boys gathered in it, and the mate did not say anything about further work.

Then, with dusk, breeze came. The jibs snapped and filled, and the upper topsails. The man at the wheel stood straight and began to steer. *Experiment* once more left a wake, silver, touched with golden foam, the sea beyond still cobalt.

The boys looked at the ship and newly understood her. They had just experienced what Greek and Phoenician and Viking sailors had felt in their time. They told themselves, because of their intimate contact with her, that they were a part of this vessel. She in a sense also belonged to them and not to the owners.

They knew each spot along the hullside that needed paint. Some of the baggy wrinkle, old hawser laid up on the shrouds, had chafed loose, would wear a topsail through, must be renewed. There was splicing to be done, too, and canvas to be sewed, and the ship's jolly boat calked so that she would hold sea water for a while and not get too dried out for quick use. And the decks needed to be swabbed down, right now, before it was too dark to see.

The world of the ship held the boys until Captain Deane sent her in from the North China Sea past the dark, narrow peak of Lintin Island and up the Pearl River. Then, in a moment, the ship was very small and China immense. The boys stood amazed and almost stunned. Nobody had ever told them the Orient would be like this.

Sights, sounds, smells that were completely foreign overcame them, and they were slow, clumsy with their work while *Experiment* tacked along the reaches past the Bogue forts, took aboard her upper river pilot and went to her anchorage off Whampoa Pagoda. The boys laughed and talked a lot after the anchor was down and the bosun had told them to knock off for the day.

They were intensely excited, wanted to go on, get at once to Canton twelve miles away upstream. It was their abrupt desire to become a part of China, as they were a part of the ship. Canton was called the City of Rams, the mate had said; he had heard stories from East Indiamen. There would be girls with jade earrings and little, very little snub-toed slippers and tight black pants. Birds would be singing in gilded cages, and the tea and the rice wine were served in carved cups. When a new hand went home from here, he could start to tell himself that he was a sailor.

Experiment returned with a cargo whose profit profoundly pleased her owners. Major Shaw, after writing a lengthy report about the China trade for the government, sailed again for the Orient, this time aboard the ship *Hope.* She was another New York ship with a Boston master, Captain James Magee, and upon her arrival at Canton a fine homeward-bound cargo was arranged for her by Shaw. The major stayed on as honorary American consul in the Pearl River city and in 1786 founded the first American commercial firm there, Shaw & Randall.

Then a Massachusetts ship, *Grand Turk,* famous as a privateer during the Revolution, came out under the command of Captain Ebenezer West. She was followed by a Salem ship that was one of Derby's fleet. She was the *Astraea,* and Derby had given her command to Captain James Magee, now a proven China hand. Captain Ichabod Nichols then brought out the bark *Light Horse,* and each vessel made the return passage in highly profitable cargo.

But the China trade did not promise well for the future. The great difficulty seen by the American merchants was the lack of a proper bargaining element with the Chinese. There was not enough ginseng available stateside to supply the trade as a form of specie, and there was a great lack of silver money. This once again gave evidence of the importance of the Northwest Territory and what might be done with sea otter pelts as a form of barter.

Boston merchants decided to enter vigorously into the Northwest trade, although in Salem canny and wealthy shipowners like Derby and Crowninshield still sent their vessels straight to the Orient. An expedition was organized in Boston in the summer of 1787 and command of it given to Captain John Kendrick of Wareham. The sum of $50,000 had been raised and the ship *Columbia* bought, along with her the smaller, 90-ton sloop *Lady Washington,* which was to serve as her tender on the prolonged voyage. *Columbia* had been built in the Briggs yard at Hobart's Landing on the North River in Scituate in 1773, was of 212 tons burden and 83 feet long.

The owners armed both her and *Lady Washington* against possible Indian attack, and the crews for the two vessels were chosen with much care. Captain Robert Gray, a Continental Navy veteran of Tiverton, Rhode Island, was made master of *Lady Washington,* which was just 40 feet long and could be expected to take some bad weather off Cape Horn, the route to be used by American ships for the first time. *Columbia* was given in addition to her regular crew a surgeon, a trained furrier and an astronomer. The astronomer would help with the navigation if Captain Kendrick so wished and double as schoolmaster for younger members of the crew, whether they wished it or not. Captain Kendrick was also supplied with a clerk, special medals to commemorate the voyage and impress the Indians and a sum of Massachusetts state coin for cash transactions when necessary.

The two vessels stood out to sea together and kept company pretty much on their southing. Then, off Cape Horn, they got into trouble. Gales that lasted six and seven days blew the sails right out of the bolt ropes. *Lady Washington,* heavily laboring, wind-driven water in solid, dark masses over her fore deck, was separated from *Columbia.* The boys in the crews had no time to look for molly hawks or Cape Horn pigeons and only saw the Cape itself through a lash of spindrift that almost blinded, left the skin abraded and caked with salt.

Both ships rounded Cape Horn and made good their courses into the Pacific. But they were not to rejoin until at their rendezvous point in Nootka Sound at Vancouver Island. *Lady Washington* came in first, although she had lost her cabin boy, who had been unwary with Indians met ashore along the way. Then, a week later, *Columbia* picked up her landfall on Cape Flattery, ran the majestic Juan de Fuca Strait and proceeded through the foggy, somber waters of Puget Sound to the rendezvous. Her crew were glum, the boys disconsolate. Two of their number were dead of scurvy, the rest so lacking in energy they could only handle the lightest and smallest sails. Their bodies were covered with sea boils, their teeth loose in the gums, their eyes rheumy and bloodshot. They had been eleven months at sea, and they longed for the feel of land under their feet.

They found it on Vancouver Island. The season was too late for any trading to be done, and Captain Kendrick ordered both ships' companies ashore to live. Strength and vigor returned, and the very familiar New England practice of use of the double-bladed ax was started. Huts were built in a clearing above Nootka Sound. The winter of 1788–89 was spent there, and Captain Kendrick kept his people busy.

Forges were built, and the bar iron that the ships had carried was worked into chisels. The Haida, the local Indian tribe, were already interested and came visiting across the Sound. They arrived in dugout log canoes whose bows and sterns were ornately carved. There should be, Captain Kendrick and Captain Gray agreed, a good market for the chisels.

Trading began in early spring, and by then all of the iron had been turned into tools, and in addition a small boat had been built. There were bad reports about the Indians on this coast, and Kendrick proposed to keep both his men and his vessels safe. The new boat was given an armed complement and moved back and forth around the vessels as the Haida canoes gathered and the braves by sign language asked to come aboard.

Kendrick and Gray let them aboard in small groups, and on the after decks of the two ships examined the pelts offered. The Haida had many that were of fine quality, dark brown, short-furred, and lustrous, most of them about two by five feet in size. Blunt arrows and harpoons had been used to kill the sea otters, so that the pelts would not be injured. They would make splendid adornment for the robes of Chinese mandarins and those men's concubines and would fetch as much as $150 apiece for the best in the Canton market.

The Haida braves, squat and flat-faced men, were willing at first to trade a prime quality pelt for a chisel. But then, as the trading continued, they began to understand the white men's psychology. The white men were too eager to trade, and quite gradually the Haida increased their price. They received, along toward the last of the bartering, eight chisels for a skin.

They had picked up a bit of English in addition to their knowledge of Yankee sharpness, and they would not lower their prices once they had established them. They called the whites Boston Men and occasionally smiled as they pronounced the phrase. Then a few of them appeared bearing small hardwood statuettes, and the whites recognized the reason for the Indian smiles.

With their skill at carving, and with the chisels purchased from the New Englanders, they had subtly portrayed representative figures. The most striking was a statuette that might well have been created with Captain Kendrick as the model.

The Indian sculptor had caught the long and lean, bony face, the deep-set eyes beneath the visor of the leather-topped cap with a button at the crown. Muttonchop whiskers gave brooding severity to the face and met a high stock wound around the throat. The lanky body was covered by a flared, three-quarter-length nautical coat. Hands were held immobile in the pockets, and the legs set wide and stiff. The entire pose was one of uncompromising rigidity and aloofness, yet there was also an indication of great inner tension, as though a powerful, hidden spring were coiled too tight.

Rations for the ships' crews became short in the summer of 1789, and the Haida remained stubborn, would not change their prices. The two captains consulted and Kendrick decided that time had now run out for the expedition. He changed commands with Captain

Gray, took over *Lady Washington* and the cargo she had collected and sailed for the Hawaiian Islands. His orders to Captain Gray were to proceed to Canton and trade the peltry there at the best terms possible for cargo to be delivered in Boston.

Captain Gray interrupted his Pacific traverse to put into Hawaii for water, firewood and fresh fruit and vegetables, also to the enormous delight of the crew. Hulas were stamped out on moonlit beaches, soft songs sung, and some hard liquor drunk. This was as close to Paradise as they would ever get, the New Englanders told themselves, although they were not surprised when a young Hawaiian volunteered to join the crew.

His name was Attoo, and he was a prince's son who had felt the sea urge, and came aboard *Columbia* dressed in his full regalia of rank. But Captain Gray made him understand how impractical that would be at sea, and Attoo surrendered it, gave it to Gray for safe stowage. *Columbia* called in at Canton according to her orders, where Gray made the best deal possible with the hong merchants, then sailed for home.

When he brought the ship into Boston harbor she had logged 41,899 miles in her circumnavigation and had been out of her home port almost three years. The Boston authorities gave her a thirteen-gun Federal salute and then had it repeated. This was a great triumph, and it was followed by a parade up State Street.

Captain Gray called Attoo below to his quarters and gave back the ceremonial Hawaiian garments, explained what a triumphal parade was like in Massachusetts. Attoo, who had been working aboard as cabin boy to replace the boy killed on the Northwest Coast, dressed himself in his regalia. Then he followed Captain Gray ashore where they were joined by the rest of the crew, all strictly spick-and-span.

Attoo marched right behind Captain Gray to the Old State House and was the hit of the parade. He strode head up, proudly, and he wore a feathered, finely worked scarlet cloak that was resplendent with golden suns. His helmet was shaped in the same style as that of a Trojan warrior, with a high, tufted ridge along the center.

The Boston people cheered wildly as they saw him, and at the Old State House he was led forward to shake hands with Governor Hancock.

Later, after a state banquet for the owners of *Columbia* and her officers, an assessment of the voyage was made. Some of the sense of triumph left the owners. Costs for the ship had been heavy. Commissions, and various duties, the graft paid at Canton, and the gifts given to officials had sorely lowered the margin of profit. Her 1,050 sea otter pelts had sold for $21,404.71 in Canton. She had brought home a top-chop quality tea cargo that sold well in the Boston market. Still, everything taken off the debit side of the ledger, including necessary ship's repairs, *Columbia* had only returned $11,241.51 to her owners.

Canton was a costly port for American shipowners, would remain so for years to come. There was, though, no other like it open in China, and as long as Americans wanted tea, silks, nankeens and chinaware, Boston ships would call there for whatever could be made from cargo.

Columbia was put in a shipyard for overhaul and a month later, in September 1790, was back at sea, bound out on the same enormous set of courses, Attoo still aboard. During the second voyage, Captain Gray found the great river on the Oregon coast which he named after his ship, proceeded to the Northwest country and procured a load of furs. Then he ran his westing down to Canton, entered into the lengthy negotiations necessary for a China-side cargo, sailed for home and arrived on July 29, 1793, in Boston.

Captain Kendrick had been in touch with his owners and made an arrangement with them for the disposition of *Lady Washington*. He ran the sturdy sloop between the Northwest Territory, the Hawaiian Islands and China. The vast reaches of the Pacific fascinated him, and he spent the rest of his life sailing that ocean.

The Boston ships steadily increased their Northwest trade and, after the second circumnavigation by *Columbia* whalers and sealers, began to sail the South Atlantic, stand around the Horn and run the length of the West Coast from Chile to Puget Sound. They used the Falklands as a sealing base, and the Juan Fernandez group off Chile and Santa Catalina off California. Both whalers and sealers carried a considerable amount of New England truck goods when outward-bound.

The Spanish population on the lower West Coast, mainly disappointed gold seekers, bored government officials and missionaries sent to convert the Indians, were in short supply of many needed items. The New England crews happily smuggled those ashore, went on North for further trade with the Indians of Puget Sound.

They brought for them the same cargo as the regular traders: scrap iron, sheet copper, old tools and muskets, nails, blankets and notions of all sorts.

The Indians were soured, sullen, having been badly cheated by former visitors. Some of the tribes were of an extremely warlike nature and known to practice cannibalism. There were swift, sudden and bloody fights aboard a number of the Boston ships, and a few of them were taken by Indians, burned to the water's edge or sunk, lost without survivors to report exactly what had happened.

Still, the trade remained attractive to the Boston merchants, and they kept on sending out ships. A considerable group of sailors, several hundred men who worked in these vessels, came to be called Nor'west men. They wore the title with pride.

This was the beginning of the great, golden age of New England maritime prosperity. John Adams, who had served two terms as Vice-President under Washington, was elected President in 1796. He was Massachusetts-born and fully recognized how important ships and unrestricted sea trade were to the new nation. He wrote: "Neither nature nor art has partitioned the sea into empires, kingdoms, republics or states." He added in specific warning: "Neither the Mediterranean, the Baltic, the four seas or the North Sea are the peculiar property of any nation."

The declaration ended solemnly: "With all the materials our country abounds; in skill our naval architects are equal to any; and commanders and seamen will not be found wanting."

Congress established the Navy Department on May 3, 1789, and

President Adams appointed Benjamin Stoddert as the Secretary of the Navy. Stoddert, well-known for his patriotic activities, was a merchant who made his home at Georgetown on the Potomac. He claimed at first that he was not equipped for the assignment, but President Adams knew better and only told him to get along with his work and build a fleet. All the Navy had to send against the French in the ugly, unofficial war that began in 1798 was three frigates.

Charles Maurice de Talleyrand-Périgord, Minister of Foreign Affairs under the French Directory, was in large part responsible for the war. He believed that his country could benefit by direct restrictions placed upon American maritime trade. He issued early in 1798 decrees to stifle it and even tried to exact tribute from the United States government. President Adams's response was an order to the United States Navy, effective May 28, and reading:

"You are hereby authorized, instructed and directed to subdue, seize and take any armed vessels of the French Republic."

The group of naval architects whose ability the President relied upon in this critical period was made up of men who were almost entirely self-educated. They had learned their profession before and during the Revolution, designed the best of the vessels to come from American shipyards. Among them were James K. Hackett of Portsmouth, the Cross brothers and Jonathan Greenleaf of Newburyport, Sylvester Bowers and Benjamin Tallman of Providence, Benjamin Hollowell of Boston and Joshua Humphreys and James Penrose of Philadelphia.

Their designs had formalized the lines of the Continental Navy frigates and sloops and in addition those of the postwar merchant ships. They believed in the efficiency and seaworthiness of relatively small vessels, and as a consequence the lengths of the Massachusetts ships in the Orient trade were kept within a hundred feet. The average dimensions of the Salem ships owned by such men as Derby were 99 feet overall, 28 foot beam and 339 tons burden.

Grand Turk, which was the biggest of the merchantmen that ran to the Orient, had an overall length of 124 feet and weighed 564 tons. She was not popular, was criticized as too large and was sold in 1795 to a New York merchant who then sailed her out of that port. One of the major complaints regarding her was that she was difficult to handle in either Boston or Salem harbor. Any vessel that tried to enter Salem while drawing more than twelve feet was forced to discharge her cargo into lighters. Boston was not much better. Low tide gave a shipmaster only twelve feet in which to reach Long Wharf.

Rather small overall length and a shallow draft were of distinct value, too, on the rugged Northwest Coast, in the uncharted China Seas, and around the Malay archipelago and Sumatra. There was what amounted to a tradition in Boston that the Northwest trade ships be held to 200 tons, instead of 300 tons burden.

Beyond these calculations was another, which the American designers had inherited from their European ancestors. It was that if a man built a ship more than four times longer than her beam measurement, she would inevitably break her back in a heavy seaway, and sink. A direct effect of this thinking was the prohibition to build a ship that weighed more than 500 tons. She would also founder in a storm, become a total loss.

The typical American vessel in the 1780–90 period was bluff-bowed and wall-sided. She was not intended to enter the water, but to squat upon it, duck style. She was dressed up with a great deal of ornamental woodwork fore and aft; her hull was decorated with various ribands of paint, black topsides, or blue or dark green, with a bright lemon or orange waist, and with a contrasting color inboard.

Color was the one rakish element allowed. The hemp sails were well cut and in fine proportion to the hull plan; still, royals were seldom used, and skysails considered wholly impractical. Rigging, made of Manila hemp that passed through blocks of wood, was bulky and hard to handle. Work was never easy for a sailor; tacking ship, coming about from one course to another, was a complicated, lengthy procedure. A modest seven or eight knots was regarded as a respectable speed for a vessel on her best point of sailing.

Stoddert, when he became Secretary of the Navy, realized that he must change a great deal of maritime thinking. Congress had authorized funds in 1797 for six frigates, and Stoddert chartered shipyards and gave out the work to contractors. The Navy ships were built in Portsmouth, Boston, New York, Philadelphia, Baltimore and Norfolk in a deliberate attempt to stimulate industry all along the seaboard. Ordnance contracts went to New England and New Jersey and Pennsylvania foundries, and timber was supplied by contractors in the Carolinas and Georgia.

Joshua Humphreys of Philadelphia had been appointed as the chief designer of the new fleet. He was aware that the frigate class was the type of vessel needed to meet the French men-of-war and privateers. The French government had issued in 1796 a series of decrees that asserted the right to seize all neutral shipping that carried British goods or was bound for British ports. In the space of a year the French took 316 American merchant ships, and a state of undeclared war existed between the United States and her recent ally.

Humphreys, a Quaker whose abilities George Washington had recognized, was informed that the French were converting many of their old, bulky ships of the line into powerful, very maneuverable frigates. This had been done by shortening the topmasts and taking out upper decks. The French called the converted vessels *razée,* which meant "shaven," and they were just as fast as their shipyard crews had hoped.

Humphreys broke with a very great deal of American naval architectural tradition and laid out plans for a radical type of vessel. He intended to build frigates faster and more powerful than any in the European navies. He would combine, he said, the lines of a French *razée* with those of an extremely sharp-rigged Baltimore schooner and mount aboard her 24-pounder batteries. This would really make her a small version of a ship of the line, because he also proposed to put into her very heavy beams and planking around the waterline to withstand intensive enemy fire.

His plans were considered radical and impractical, but they resulted in *Constitution,* one of the finest warships of her class ever built.

Constitution weighed 1,576 tons. She was 175 feet overall, with 43.5 foot beam and 14¼ foot depth of hold. She had clipper lines, carried an immense amount of canvas for her size, and a 180-foot mainmast. Humphreys designed a unique form of extraordinarily strong trusses for her hull to support the strain of her canvas and the shock of her guns when served.

She was rated a 44-gun vessel, but mounted more than 50 pieces. Her main battery held 30 cannon of 24-pounder caliber. The secondary battery was twenty-two 12-pounders. The "long guns" when served right could pierce 22-inch oak at a range of 1,000 yards. Her own hull was made of live-oak scantlings at the waterline, and Humphreys calculated that they were thick enough to bounce any enemy cannon ball back into the sea.

President Adams was greatly elated by the construction of *Constitution.* When she was launched on July 23, 1798, and sailed out of Massachusetts Bay under full canvas, he wrote about her: "The *Constitution* took advantage of a brisk breeze and went out of the harbor and out of sight this forenoon making a beautiful and noble figure amidst the joy and good wishes of thousands."

President Adams made sure that *Constitution* and the other new frigates were manned by the best crews to be found, and the Navy Department took special efforts to recruit them. Wages were much higher than in merchant ships, or privateers, or what was paid for skilled labor ashore. They went as high as $17.00 a month, and men were recruited only for the length of a single cruise and were given prize money over and above their wages. They were allowed to board the vessels and inspect the quarters before they signed on, and they stopped by the galleys and sampled the food, which was excellent.

The Navy had little trouble in recruiting crews, although the old-timers knew that discipline would be very strict at sea. The lead-tipped cat-o'-nine-tails was still used just as much on the recalcitrant, drunken and careless as in any Royal Navy or French ship. Simple seamen were as yet treated essentially without mercy. They were expected to suffer, take orders from their superiors under any circumstances and obey them smartly and with goodwill.

Command of *Constitution* was given to Captain Samuel Nicholson, who had become famous in the Continental Navy. Her sister ships were *United States* and *Constellation*. *United States* was commanded by Captain John Barry, another Revolutionary War hero.

Constitution did not do very well despite all the hopes held for her. The first retaliatory blow of any real effect against the French was struck by the United States corvette *Delaware* on July 7, 1798, off Egg Harbor, New Jersey. She was a 20-gun craft under the command of Captain Stephen Decatur, Sr., and she met and quickly took the French privateer *La Croyable*. When the gunfire stopped echoing over the flat salt marshes Captain Decatur had the subdued enemy in tow and headed for port as a prize.

It was *Constellation* that made the best record of the new frigates, although she had been reduced in size from her original plans. Members of Congress who were not yet ready to accept the radical designs proposed by Humphreys had voted to make her lines much more conventional. She was rated a 36-gun ship with a 1,278-ton burden that made her smaller than *Constitution* and *United States*.

Her overall length was 164 feet, her beam 40.5 feet and her depth of hold 13.5 feet. Her ordnance was twenty-eight 18-pounders and twenty 12-pounders. However, Humphreys had succeeded in hanging onto her lean hull lines and sharp bow, and when all her canvas was bent on and she had gathered full way, she logged 14 knots. She was the fastest frigate in the fleet.

Her commander was Captain Thomas Truxton, a handsome, florid-faced Long Islander. He had been a privateer captain in the Revolution and master of a merchant ship in the China trade when called to serve in the Navy. He was known as a fop, and also as a lady's man who liked to drink and dance when ashore. But he was soon recognized also as the most able officer in the Navy. Although he had gone to sea very young and was self-educated, he had spent the long months of the China voyages compiling a manual on celestial navigation and a book on ship rigging.

Captain Truxton took *Constellation* to sea and headed her for the West Indies, with orders to raid the French naval bases there. But off the British island of Nevis he met on February 5, 1799, a powerful French privateer named *Insurgente*. A heavy squall swept the sea as the two vessels closed, and *Insurgente* lost her main topmast, ripped out of her by the force of the wind. Then *Constellation* began belaboring her with broadsides, and the French gunners instantly replied. It was the intention of *Insurgente* with her 36 guns to shoot away the rigging of the American ship and make her unmanageable.

But Truxton quickly shifted tacks, kept his broadside weapons in active salvo fire. The Frenchmen tried to bring their ship alongside *Constellation* and secure to her with grapnels so that they might board and fight at handystrokes.

Truxton understood the French maneuver. He told his sailing master to haul *Constellation* ahead. She drew away from *Insurgente* and put herself in a position where she could rake the other vessel fore and aft with a broadside delivered at almost point-blank range. That crippled *Insurgente,* and she struck her colors. Truxton's surgeon reported two crew members dead and two wounded. Over aboard the French ship the casualties were much more severe; she had lost 29 dead and 71 wounded.

Truxton went home and was made Commodore, given a small squadron. He took it south in search of French ships, cruised the coast of Guadeloupe until he found what he wanted. She was the big 56-gun *La Vengeance,* and both vessels cleared immediately for action, chose courses that put them within close range of each other.

They fought at close range for five hours outside the roadstead at the French naval base in Basse-Terre. The Frenchman received no help from shore, and Truxton had taken his ship away from the American squadron. Great holes were torn in the bulwarks, the hulls, the rigging and sails of both vessels. Fires were ignited by friction or hot shot, and men stumbled from the guns to douse them, stumbled back. Dead men lay where they fell, or were stacked like wood by Marines who could not take time from their musket fire to heave the bodies over the side. Wounded who could crawl went down the blood-slick ladderway that led to the surgeon, the saw and the scalpel. Some had been hit by splinters; their bodies were impaled with ragged fragments of planking or spars. Others had become blind, and groped their way, tripping and falling.

Truxton decided at the end of the fifth hour that his men had taken enough. He passed the order for *Constellation* to stand clear. She stood away from the French ship on a northwest course for Port Royal, Jamaica. *La Vengeance* did not attempt pursuit for she lay a wreck upon the late afternoon sea, her scuppers splashed with blood.

Truxton's losses were considerable. He had suffered 25 dead and 14 wounded, and his surgeon greatly needed help. It was luck that at present the United States and Britain were not at war and he could ask assistance from the Royal Navy doctors in Jamaica. But *La Vengeance* had taken an awful pounding, and through the long glass Truxton was able to estimate her casualties before the vessels were too far apart. *La Vengeance* had lost twice as many people. She was also damaged to the extent that she would not put to sea again for a long while.

The weird, never-declared war went on through 1799 into 1800, and then Napoleon, who had come to power in France, was willing to terminate it. More than the United States Navy, it had been American privateers fighting in hundreds of actions that had broken French sea power. By 1799, when Napoleon took over, the French had already lost 85 warships, and the count of merchant vessels seized in action with the Americans was not complete.

During the war patriotic citizens had invested directly in the United States Navy. They financed by "donation" the building of six frigates and three sloops-of-war. It was for them a very wise use of their money. Here was the nucleus of a permanent naval force, to be called upon instantly in time of conflict instead of hurriedly collected privateers drawn from the merchant marine fleet.

The cost of naval construction was six million dollars. The Navy ships and the privateers, all of the latter sent to sea without government expense, had saved trade worth 220 million dollars, if not more. The United States was about to become a great maritime nation. Merchants in New England and on down the coast looked forward to the peace with intense anticipation. They were ready to begin again their world-wide operations, open up not only China but all of the Orient and the Pacific islands, South America and Africa beyond Cape of Good Hope.

CHAPTER SIXTEEN

SALEM SETS TRADITION

It was without doubt the finest sea school ever conducted in the New World. Elias Hasket Derby—now so successful and wealthy that his competitors and many of his friends called him "King"—ran it on his own wharf in Salem. The students were his employees, served as clerks in his countinghouse, and when he felt they were ready he sent them to sea in the ships he owned.

It usually took four years of clerking in the countinghouse before a boy was chosen by Derby to be sent to sea. He recruited them from a certain small, well-to-do segment of Salem society, and in the years right after the Revolution, they represented an easily recognizable type.

Their faces were angular and bony, their noses long and quite often sharp; their voices already possessed the twang that along with aggressive trading practices was to make "Yankee" famous throughout the seagoing world.

Nearly all of them were the fifth or sixth generation descendants of original settlers, and sailors. Their father's fathers had been shipmasters. The sea was in their blood. It was their single ambition to sail ships. So, when fit, and when chosen, generally around the age of ten, they went to work for Derby. When they were fourteen or a bit older they went to sea.

They left behind them some anxious mothers and sisters. Still, feminine thinking in Salem was conditioned to accept the hazards and the separations of the sea. It was by chance of sex difference alone that the women were not in the ships. And if the men were successful—one voyage with Derby or any other Massachusetts shipowner made a boy a man—marriage was possible for a girl at sixteen, at the latest eighteen. Men retired from the sea around thirty, sent out their sons and nephews in the ships they now owned.

One of the typical voyages of a Derby-owned ship soon after the Revolution was made by a crew with a master who was nineteen. He was Nathaniel Silsbee, who later became president of the Senate of Massachusetts and United States Senator. His background was a bit different from the other Derby ships' officers in the fact that his family was poor, and he was responsible for the care of his mother and two sisters. He had been at sea for four years and previously served as master on a West Indies voyage. His second command was the brig *Rose,* bound for Hispaniola and the extremely troubled French colony of Saint Domingue, to be known soon as the Republic of Haiti.

Rose sailed in June, 1792, with probably the youngest crew ever to put to sea, even from Salem. Silsbee's chief mate, Charles Derby, was also nineteen. Richard J. Cleveland, a close friend and former schoolmate of the master, was eighteen and making his first trip to sea as captain's clerk. The second mate was twenty-four, and must have considered himself a seasoned veteran in that company.

Rose carried general cargo and made a slow run because she was forced to buck the prevailing summer southerlies, and then, in tropic waters, was absolutely becalmed. Cleveland could not resist the lure of the azure sea. He stripped to his drawers and dived over the side; like nearly all Salem youths, he was a good swimmer.

But he had failed to see a large shark that moved toward the ship. It was noticed by Captain Silsbee, who stood on the quarter-deck. He quickly knocked his hat from his head into the sea and called out to Cleveland to fetch it for him before it became water-logged and sank.

Cleveland swam fast to get the hat, still unaware of the shark, and was brought aboard with great speed. He then saw the shark, which lunged in fury along the shipside while a sailor stood poised with a harpoon ready. But Captain Silsbee told him to stow it; the weapon would only be lost, Silsbee said.

Rose was almost forty days to Cap Français, her port of call in Hispaniola. The youngsters of the crew were never to forget the experience of arrival there. The broad bay at the foot of the purple and russet and mauve mountains, with their great, wind-driven scarf of cumulus cloud at the summits, was filled by many ships, most of them huge French men-of-war. Bumboats steered among the ships, selling fruit that to the Salem men after a New England shipboard diet were amazingly exotic, and bamboo creels that held freshly caught fish that were the colors of rainbows.

The crew went ashore just as soon as they were given permission by the harbor officials. They found the beautiful little city of Cap Français a strange mixture of promised delights and repressed terror. This was a year after the awful slave revolt when in a single night, out on the Plaine du Nord past the city, more than one hundred great plantations had been burned, and their owners and any other white person of any description killed. Cap Français because of its extensive fortifications and alert garrison had been able to save itself. But hundreds of rage-maddened runaway slaves had died in attack on the ramparts, and some, from ignorance, had literally crawled into the muzzles of cannon, been blasted forth by astonished French gunners.

Now a taut, sullen peace endured. Napoleon was in power in France; his commissioners were here, and advanced certain promises of liberty, equality and fraternity to the vastly predominant Negro population. Saint Domingue was the wealthiest French colony. Napoleon cherished it and proposed to keep possession of it.

The Salem men passed on their way into the city many small booths where all sorts of cheap French goods were sold, mainly by grinning, shouting, gesticulating Negro women who wore gay turbans and tight, bright cotton dresses. Then, in the city proper, they came upon splendid shops. They were wise in the ways of merchandise, and carefully inspected each display of stock.

Some of the items of feminine apparel they had never seen before; several, they admitted, they had not known that women wore. There were perfumes, too, and gloves and slippers that were surely not the style in Salem. The crew looked around them with renewed interest.

They had reached the Place d'Armes, the main square of the city. Across the way was the governor's palace, and on the other side, the exquisite little theater. Here, Captain Silsbee told his shipmates in a low voice, the captured runaway slaves had been executed. They were put in a big iron cage and burned to death over a fire. Troops with bayoneted muskets kept back the crowds of slaves sent by their masters to take a lesson from the spectacle.

This evening only a few women were in the Place d'Armes, and although they were well dressed and a number of them were white, it was easy to guess their profession. Silsbee spoke of them as "fire ships" and indicated the officers who also stood and watched.

The revolutionary tricolored cockade was worn by both the white and Negro officers. They called each other "Citizen" as they saluted and bowed. But the bows were stiff and perfunctory, and their eyes were hard. When up on the dark mountainside a drum rapped as staccato as a musket shot, their heads jerked; they touched the pommels of their swords.

Captain Silsbee turned and started back toward the ship and without speech the crew followed him. All of them had had enough of Cap Français, and *Rose* had abruptly become a home away from home.

She discharged her cargo into lighters during the next few days, loaded sugar and sailed for Salem on the land breeze very early in the morning near the end of August. It was a fair passage north. She came into Salem in September, 1792, with a considerable profit for Mr. Derby.

Her crew was home about two months before assignment to a new ship built and owned by Mr. Derby. She was the 190-ton brig *Benjamin,* bound for the island of Mauritius and the East Indies. Her cargo was tobacco, Madeira wine, hops, saddlery, window glass and mahogany boards. She sailed from Salem on December 11, 1792.

During her first week at sea she met gales that blew from the north-northwest and northwest. Captain Silsbee took the topsails from her and kept her driving under full lower canvas. But as she crossed George's Bank the height of the seas became tremendous. The box-bowed little ship received a severe beating.

Several fresh-water hogsheads were smashed out of their deck lashings and swept over the side, along with two casks that contained cargo. Captain Silsbee eased her off the wind all he could; still he was threatened with the loss of the caboose and the quarter boats. The men who worked on deck suffered cruelly in the first three days of the gale, and the cook, a Negro new at sea, had his feet frozen.

He was of stoic nature or at least did not complain, and when his condition was discovered his feet were in very bad shape. It was necessary for the second mate to amputate the man's toes, and the best instrument available was a penknife. There were no medical dressings or antiseptics available, and the cook was about to lose his feet from gangrenous infection when Captain Silsbee brought *Benjamin* into port in the Cape Verde islands.

Prominent in the roadstead, her giltwork gleaming in the tropical sun, H.M.S. *Scorpion* lay at anchor. This was just a few years after the long, bitter Revolution, but Silsbee did not hesitate. He sent the second mate away at once in a boat to ask the assistance of the British frigate's surgeon.

The surgeon boarded *Benjamin* with a nod and a smile, immediately gave his attention to the cook. He treated the infected feet, left salves and medicines and instructions for their use. When Captain Silsbee offered him payment, the Royal Navy man refused. He had only done his duty; this was the unwritten law of the sea.

Benjamin took aboard fresh water and vegetables the next day, January 27, 1793, and sailed for Capetown. It was a slow, difficult and monotonous passage through the belt of calms around the equator. Silsbee navigated as he had been taught, using the few erroneously marked charts given him in Salem, and a Guthrie's Grammar, which contained further doubtful charts, and "Longitude, Bearings and Distances of Principal Places from London." His sextant was good, though, and his pocket watch reliable. He shaped an amazingly accurate course.

More than the calms and the heat, it was the condition of the ship that bothered her crew. She was no longer the smart, all ataunt vessel they had taken out past Naugus Head into the northwester that struck them what seemed years ago. Now she drifted loglike, a hulk, lifeless in the brazen, weed-thick water.

Pitch bubbled in her deck seams. A man could not put his foot down for more than a second or so, or clasp a block or a handrail, without experiencing discomfort. The sails drooped in the gear. Long, green beards of seaweed swung undulant and mocking from her sides. Her bottom, the crew knew, was incredibly foul. She was island as much as ship. Her wooden bottom sheathing attracted any kind of marine life smaller than turtle.

But the wind came. The sails filled, and sluggish, still unwilling, *Benjamin* stood away under weather helm for Capetown. She reached it April 10. Her crew had been at sea four months from Salem.

Captain Silsbee anchored in Table Bay below the neat white town and the bold rise of hills known as The Devil's Mount. The signal-man stationed at the top of Sugar Loaf had broken out a hoist telling of the ship's arrival offshore, and Silsbee got quick clearance for the crew to land. He left only an anchor watch aboard, and those men were to be promptly relieved for their share of liberty.

Fruit was the first item the crew sought, and they fancied in particular the big, smooth and firm Cape grapes. The town was very Dutch-seeming, with its rows of prim, two-story houses with plastered walls and tall trees along the wide streets. The men, as they gobbled grapes, stared at the lanky Negro slaves who passed them, loads of merchandise or vegetables balanced effortlessly on their heads, and at the small, brown and bow-legged Hottentots, eyes raised in furtive scrutiny of the white men.

Captain Silsbee separated from the crew near the big square used as a parade ground and went on alone to pay his respects to the

Governor. These were troubled times, and it was very much to his advantage to be as politically informed as possible. He learned by a bit of discreet questioning at Government House that war was about to start between France and England.

It would be best for him to discharge and sell here his Salem cargo and load *Benjamin* with local products for Mauritius. The island was a French possession, and if war broke out he could make an exceptionally high rate of profit on what he had carried from Capetown.

The brig was discharged and reloaded at top speed, and on April 23 she sailed for Port Louis, Mauritius. She ran into a gale the next day that was severe enough to have Silsbee heave her to under foresail and mizzen staysail and jettison his deck cargo. But after that she ran in fine Indian Ocean weather. May 26, while still on her Port Louis course, she was overhauled by and talked with the French brig *La Prudente*. The French ship was also bound for Mauritius, and her captain had dispatches that told of the outbreak of war between his country and England. Silsbee should now quite certainly make a large profit on *Benjamin's* cargo.

Benjamin entered the beautiful harbor of Port Louis on June 6, and Silsbee put her at the anchor. Palms touched by breeze swayed rhythmically over white sand beaches inshore. The town lay tranquil, basking in the high, hot sun. Birds whose calls were unfamiliar to Salem ears sounded from the jungle vegetation on the mountain slopes. There was the tantalizing, instantly recognizable smell of coffee—coffee beans that dried spread out to the sun, and the other, more delicate odor of the coffee plants themselves.

The crew were in a great hurry to get ashore. Cleveland felt the urge very strongly; as captain's clerk he anticipated all sorts of lucrative cargo deals to be arranged here. But Silsbee was not quite so eager to land.

When the boat had pulled away from the *Benjamin* he ordered the coxswain to steer for the man-of-war that flew the flag of the commander of the French naval forces in the port. He told Cleveland to recall the phrases of *la politesse* learned in Mr. Derby's countinghouse. Cleveland was to board the man-of-war with him, and they would present their compliments to the commanding officer.

Vice-Admiral St. Felix was the man they met on the quarter-deck. His body was cadaverous within the ornate uniform. The eyes beneath the sweep of the gold-looped crescent hat were muddy, and the admiral's skin was yellow, his teeth loose in the gums. He was suffering acutely from scurvy, he explained to the young Americans. Supplies of fresh fruit and vegetables were cut off from shore for a very logical reason.

St. Felix was a Royalist. The government ashore was of revolutionary temper and composed entirely of members of the Jacobin club that controlled Mauritius and the nearby island of Réunion. The Jacobins were trying to kill the admiral by harming his health until he succumbed to the inevitable next bout of fever. But if he came ashore for relief from the scurvy, they would hang him or shoot him, whichever was quicker.

St. Felix admitted that he had not been ashore for months. He preferred death the slow way. Captain Silsbee and Cleveland bowed to him and wished him better health, then they headed for the town.

The Salem men were received amiably enough in Port Louis. Deals for the cargo were arranged that would pay off handsomely, and lighters were sent out to take it ashore. But when *Benjamin* had discharged and was about to take in what export cargo there was available Silsbee and Cleveland had an amazing interview with St. Felix.

St. Felix told them flatly aboard his flagship that they could not clear the port. Despite all his political convictions and differences with the Jacobin government in power, he was still a loyal Frenchman. The prevalent belief was that at any moment the United States was to enter the war on the side of England against France. He considered Americans as potential enemies.

The young Salem pair went back in complete frustration to *Benjamin*. Cleveland, knowing nothing better to do, and weirdly fascinated, spent many long hours in the main hold. It was empty, a gloomy and dusty cavern. Cleveland stood very still. He listened in horror to the loud, steady munching sounds of the thousands of teredo worms that attacked the ship's hull. He had the impression they might rush in upon him, riding the crests of gigantic waves that would swiftly sink the brig.

But the Massachusetts shipwrights, although they had not yet come to the use of copper sheathing, understood the habits of the teredo. They had placed a layer of hair between the sheathing planks and the actual bottom of the ship, and there the worms stopped.

Cleveland returned topside and spent the rest of the long, waiting period under the shade of the quarter-deck awning or in hot, hopeless trips to the town.

Several American ships were ready to sail by July 6, and their masters, Silsbee among them, boarded the French flagship for a conversation with St. Felix. He was concave with scurvy pangs and talked hissing through his loosened teeth, but he refused permission to sail. There were in the port other ships due to leave for France, and the admiral had the idea the Americans might attack them at sea.

Another attempt to get permission to sail was made on July 31 and refused. The Americans were forced to wait until November 20. Then the American ship *Pigou* arrived, directly in from Bordeaux with French passengers. Both St. Felix and the local Jacobins were satisfied that the Americans meant no harm, and the blockade was lifted.

The crew aboard *Benjamin* must have sung a capstan chantey the day they brought the anchor aboard and spread sail. They had been in Port Louis for nearly six months. The vexations of the stay had made the second mate unruly, and Silsbee had put him on the beach, replaced him with Cleveland. Now the ship put to sea for the overnight run to the roadstead port of St. Benoit on the island of Réunion. She was to pick up coffee there to fill out her Mauritius cargo.

She cleared from Réunion on December 7 and reached Capetown on January 4, 1794. A few days after she had been at anchor in Table Bay the American ship *Henry* arrived, also from Réunion, but with only part of her cargo. Then, on the same day, the brig *Hope* put in from Salem. Their masters boarded *Benjamin,* and Captain

Silsbee was ready for them with a thoroughly if rapidly planned business proposition.

Silsbee was aware that he could go back to Mauritius with a Cape cargo of wine and other South African products, all in great demand on the island, and send home part of his present cargo in *Henry* and *Hope*. The two captains accepted his proposition, and he made arrangements with them for the cargo transferral. The part he sent to Salem, consigned to Mr. Derby, would pay for a good deal more than the cost of the ship plus the cost of the original outward-bound freight. The rest of his present cargo he would sell here for Cape products and those he would run right away to Mauritius.

Then he discovered that all possible haste was necessary. The British frigate *Diomede* came into the bay before *Benjamin* had all her Cape cargo aboard. Captain Silsbee heard from friends ashore that the officers of the *Diomede* disliked the presence of the Salem brig here. It was the Royal Navy custom for officers to increase their low pay by prize money provided by the sale of enemy ships seized at sea. *Benjamin* was a neutral, and had broken no British law, but she was bound for an enemy port, and her value, shared out among the officers of *Diomede,* would help to pay the wardroom liquor bill or be a nice bit to send home to families in England.

Silsbee hurried the remaining cargo out to the ship. Young Derby, the chief mate, stowed it securely while Cleveland tallied it, and the ship was ready for sea. Silsbee remained on deck and kept his long glass trained on *Diomede*. The captain of the frigate appeared extremely conscious of the fact that *Benjamin* was about to leave. Although almost a full gale had started to blow, a boat had just been sent away from the frigate in the direction of the Salem ship, and this was surely not the time to make a social call. Silsbee and his mates breathed easier when the force of the weather sent the *Diomede* boat ashore a mile short of where *Benjamin* was anchored.

The gale increased as *Benjamin* started to heave short her anchors and make sail. But she would have to take a course close to *Diomede* to get out of the bay, and Silsbee decided to wait for darkness. Then he ordered both his anchor cables slipped and ran for the open sea.

The men on the fo'c'slehead who handled the heavy anchor cables had a dangerous job in the darkness and the sprindrift slash with the slippery deck heaving under them. They got rid of the anchors, though, and the brig heeled, straightened to her canvas pull and went rushing lightless past *Diomede*. The wardroom lights burned brightly aboard the frigate; very likely, His Majesty's officers were at a game of cards.

Benjamin ran out the gale under her foretopmast staysail, then hoisted all regular canvas. She reached Mauritius on March 13 and sold her cargo immediately at an immense profit. She took aboard island products and sailed again on April 8, having in the space of twenty-six days sold and discharged one cargo and bought and loaded another. Not wishing to be detained again, Silsbee was relieved to hear that Vice-Admiral St. Felix had mysteriously disappeared from the port.

But when he was ready to leave he was told on a Sunday morning that effective Monday morning an embargo was to be put on all shipping in the port. Silsbee and his shipmates had very vivid memories of the last sweltering stay in this harbor. They wanted no more like it.

Clearance papers for the ship were obtained by a high-ranking port official, who was promised a free ride to Salem. A pilot who had an impeccable reputation in the Jacobin club—which had voted the embargo the night before—was privately hired, and he in turn hired native sailors. Pilot and sailors were brought out to the ship, and she was prepared for sea. But Silsbee held her until the church bells rang in the town, and ashore by inflexible custom everybody left work and went to dinner.

The echoes of the bells were still sounding over the water as Silsbee gave the order for a halyard hoist and for the anchor cable to be slipped. The additional sailors had been hired to handle the ship fast, and they performed well. The three topsails, the jib and spanker were set after the cable was slipped.

Benjamin ran out of the harbor with a high, white curl of bow wash as she gathered headway. The pilot and the Port Louis sailors jumped into the longboat and lowered her at the harbor mouth. She was theirs, a gift from Silsbee, to take them back to town to answer some quite embarrassing questions sure to be asked by the Jacobins.

Silsbee shaped a course for Réunion. He did not have enough stores aboard for the homeward passage to Salem. He reached the roadstead of St. Denis at Réunion the next day and anchored. The island was also supposed to be under revolutionary rule, and he was careful when he went ashore. He wrote in his journal:

"On landing at St. Denis, I called on the Governor of the island (whose residence was immediately contiguous to the wharf, and who was one of the old Royalists), as was usual, though not obligatory; and immediately after leaving him, devoted myself to the procurement of such provisions as I could find, and the addition of a few bags of coffee to the cargo; which business was not accomplished until towards night,—when, just as I was stepping from the wharf into my boat, with a determination to be at sea before morning, the Governor ordered me to his presence; which order I obeyed from necessity, and with strong apprehension that some restraint was to be imposed upon me."

It is very revealing of the New England character that Silsbee under such circumstances dared to appear in the little public market of the port to bargain for a few sacks of coffee. He could have bought his provisions through a merchant and stayed safely aboard ship ready to sail at the first sign of trouble. What he did was an expression of the great Yankee drive of "business first" that made men like him famous in the outports of the world. He continues with his journal:

"On meeting the Governor, he asked,—'How long do you contemplate staying at Bourbon?*' My answer was, 'No longer than is necessary to complete my business.' He added,—'Can't you leave here tonight?' I replied, 'I can do so if you wish it.' He then said to me, 'As you had the politeness to call on me this morning, and as I should be sorry to see you injured, hearken to my advice, and leave here to-night, if practicable.' I thanked the Governor for his advice,

* The former name for Réunion.

and was on my way towards my boat, when he called me back and said, 'Let no one know what I have said to you.' "

The scene between the two men is extraordinary. The veteran French officer, gaunt with repeated bouts of fever, but erect, proud, very probably with his gilt-tasseled sword at his hip, staring across the candlelight at the lanky, sea-tanned young American, as fireflies thudded against the teakwood window shutters, mosquitoes whined and moths died and clotted around the candle flames.

Silsbee came directly from a revolutionary background; his people had been greatly helped in their war of liberation by men the Governor hated. Yet the old Frenchman respected and liked Silsbee and risked his own life to give Silsbee due warning. Silsbee must have used some graceful phrases in his Salem-accented French as he thanked the Governor and said goodnight.

The journal kept by Silsbee continued:

"I was in my boat and on board the ship as soon as possible after leaving the Governor. There was a brig-of-war at anchor in the roads, a little to windward of our ship. Towards midnight I caused the anchor to be hove up without noise, and let the ship drift to leeward (the wind and current being favorable), without making sail, until from the darkness of the night we had lost sight of the brig; when we made all sail directly from the land. At daylight in the morning, the brig was out, and in pursuit of us; but, in the course of the day, gave up the chase.

"I never knew the cause of the Governor's advice, but *attributed* it to an apprehension, on his part, that my stopping at Bourbon might be supposed by the population to be for the purpose of taking off the French admiral St. Felix [the same old Royalist Silsbee had met earlier], who had rendered himself obnoxious to them, and was known to be then secreted somewhere on the island; and that this suspicion might compel him (the Governor) to cause the detention and perhaps the seizure of my ship, if I remained there until the next day."

The irony of implicating the Salem crew in the possible escape of the scurvy-ridden Royalist admiral was not lost on Silsbee. He kept the brig moving under all canvas from the island. *Benjamin* struck soundings in sixty-five fathoms of water on Agulhas Bank on May 4, rounded the Cape of Good Hope the next day, and May 30 went to anchor off Ascension Island.

The crew for the first time released themselves fully to the impulses of their youth. They had gone through a considerable series of ordeals, and now were joyous in anticipation of their return home.

They caught turtles on the Ascension beaches, shot wild goats in the thickets on the steep slopes, rambled the island from end to end. Then, their sea legs stretched, they loaded fresh water, vegetables, fruit and firewood aboard and sailed June 1 for Salem.

It was a fine passage all the way. Silsbee sent the brig to the anchor July 10 in Salem harbor. The crew had been gone for nineteen months. They had made for Mr. Derby a profit that amounted to four if not five times the sum of his investment. He was very proud of them. He referred to them publicly as his "boys."

But when Silsbee wanted to take Cleveland with him as chief mate aboard *Benjamin* on her next voyage to India Derby would not approve the apointment. Derby gave the job to his nephew; Cleveland could sail as second mate.

Cleveland refused. For a great part of the last voyage he had served as second mate aboard *Benjamin,* and he was quite well qualified to perform chief mate's duties. He spent some months on the beach in Salem before he found another ship. She, too, was a Derby vessel, belonged to Elias Hasket Derby's son. Cleveland was glad to get her. Derby displeasure was hard to avoid in Salem once it was centered upon a man.

A great, vigorous tradition had been established here by Derby, despite its obvious faults of nepotism. The men he chose and trained renewed a pattern that combined superlative seamanship with exceptionally keen business acumen. He used, after all, methods that were not original and stemmed directly back to the Plymouth and London merchants who had sent Hawkins, Drake, Cavendish and the rest of the illustrious Elizabethan mariners off on their voyaging. Before them had been the Spanish, the Portuguese, the French and the

Dutch; and in the Mediterranean the ancient Greek merchant princes had dispatched crews in the same manner.

The Derby tradition was to endure through the clipper ship era. It took the name of "Yankee enterprise" and was respected, condemned and envied in the ports of the world. Admirers said that that was the way to move a ship and keep her laden in cargo. Critics described the trading practices as too sharp and close to the border of illegality. But nobody denied the Yankee shipmasters their skill at sea. That was supreme.

CHAPTER SEVENTEEN

SUMATRA AND THE CHINA-SIDE

There were three men who ruled Salem shipping in the last years of the eighteenth century and whose influence continued for generations. The two magnates, besides Elias Hasket Derby, were Joseph Peabody and William Gray. Unlike Derby, they had gone to sea as boys, and Peabody had served as a mate in Revolutionary War privateers while still in his teens. He built, owned and loaded on his own account and sent all over the world a fleet of 83 ships, and Gray was equally as active and reported to be wealthier than either Peabody or Derby.

The remarkable Crowninshield family was also very prominent in the port's business after 1800. George Crowninshield was the family head and had gone to sea until he was 55, an almost venerable age for the period. His six sons were all seagoing. One of them died at fourteen of the fever in Guadeloupe while serving as captain's clerk. The other five became masters of vessels before they were old enough to vote. Captain Jacob Crowninshield brought the first elephant to Salem.

The beast ecstatically thrilled or abysmally frightened hundreds of children. It heaved its East Indian mahout from its back, nearly killed the man. Then it ate hay and bread, became so tame as to take morsels of bread from spectators' pockets, and it drank porter, pulling the cork from the bottle with its trunk and spilling the liquor down its gullet with a good deal of skill. Captain Jacob was able to sell the beast for $10,000 right on the wharf that was named for his family.

Other Salem and nearby Massachusetts Bay families that grew wealthy at this time were the Pickmans, the Perkinses, the Cabots, the Boylstons, the Thorndikes and the Forresters. The severe financial depression that had gripped New England at the end of the Revolution was almost forgotten, especially by the younger men. The sea promised them many things.

James Howland II, of New Bedford, was given a ship on his eighteenth birthday by his father. He took her to sea with his bride and a full cargo for a honeymoon voyage to the Baltic the same year. John Boit, Jr., of Boston, was nineteen when he was appointed master of the 89-ton sloop *Union*. He took her out of Newport, Rhode Island, on August 1, 1794, for a round-the-world voyage that he completed successfully.

New England boys engaged in the shipping trade knew the values of ginseng and ginger, gum arabic, goatskins, pepper, senna, spices, teas, coffee of various kinds and grades, indigo, hemp, tin, jute, ivory, copal, amber, sandalwood, silks, nankeens and Indian madras. They were able to deal correctly, with no loss to their employers, in half a dozen Oriental currencies, including "Spanish" silver dollars.

Ships in the East Indies trade lay tiered three-deep at the Salem wharves. During the years from 1800 to 1810, which included the disastrous Jefferson embargo, there were more than 1,000 foreign entries of ships, and the trade for the port was $7 million. There were in 1812 alone 126 Salem ships in the deepwater trade, and of that number 58 were East Indiamen. Ships that were setting out for new markets loaded day and night. They slipped their cables after sundown and sailed secretly, only to be pursued at sea for months by rivals.

Boston was busy, and Newburyport, New Bedford, Nantucket, the Maine ports, Providence, all the shipping towns as far south as Baltimore. But little, tight Salem, with a maximum population of 10,000, continued to hold a major share of the foreign trade. Warehouses along the Salem wharves were full of teas and silks from China, pepper from Sumatra, coffee from Arabia, tallow from Madagascar, hemp from Luzon, cotton from Bombay, palm oil from the west coast of Africa, figs, raisins and almonds from the Mediterranean, wine from Portugal and the Madeiras, salt from Cádiz, ivory and gum copal from Zanzibar, sperm oil from the South Seas, whale oil from the Arctic and Antarctic, and hides, wool and rubber from South America.

Most of the ships that handled this trade were built on the North River, and in and around Medford, on the Merrimac. Ever since *Blessing of the Bay* "Medford-built" had meant the best in ship construction. But the North River yards also had an excellent reputation. They turned out an average of twenty-three vessels a year between 1799 and 1804, and in 1801 they completed thirty.

The shipwrights worked for a dollar a day and from dawn to dark. They tramped across the salt hay meadows to work or came by canoe or skiff during the months when the narrow river was free of ice. Twice a day, at eleven in the morning and at four in the afternoon, the foremen bawled out across the clatter of the yards, "Grog-o!" The estimated grog ration was a quart of rum for each ton a new ship weighed. For launchings, special, more liberal estimates were used and often forgotten.

The ships that the Salem merchants put in the East Indies trade were purposely kept small. Safety was their principal maxim, and out of his fleet of thirty-five ships, over a period of fourteen years, Derby lost only one at sea. Joseph Peabody's most famous ship, the brig *George,* made twenty-one East Indian voyages and paid more than $600,000 in duty at the Salem customs house. *George* was 110 feet long, with a 27-foot beam, and considered by her crews to be better built than any structure ashore, and she proved this by remaining in commission for twenty-two years.

Peabody was popular with sailors because of the quality of his vessels and the pay and conditions he offered. The monthly wage of an able-bodied sailor was $18, with the privilege of taking home in trade all he could cram into his sea chest. During the period Peabody was active more than 7,000 men signed ships' articles in his countinghouse.

The average dimensions of the Salem deepwater vessels were about 100 feet in length, with a beam around 28 feet and a tonnage of slightly over 300 when loaded. These small, shallow-draft vessels were designed to sail among the uncharted reefs of the Pacific and the islands of Malaya. There was also to be considered that Salem harbor was so shallow that any vessel that drew more than twelve feet was forced to discharge into lighters; and in Boston at low tide Long Wharf had only twelve feet of water.

The sight the Salem fleet presented along the wild northwest coasts of Sumatra was memorable. The vessels went armed because pirates and local treachery, even in the quietest outports, were common. The crews, regularly trained as gunners and to repel boarders with cutlass, pike, pistol and musket, stood at battle stations whenever any number of natives were near a ship.

The carriage-mounted cannon were made of iron and painted black. But the small swivel pieces on the bulwarks were brass, and took the sunlight, which glanced also from the men's bare, sweaty shoulders, the cutlass blades and the varnished straw hats worn by the mates and the captain.

Native proas passed close to the ship, the yellow-skinned little men, dapper even in loose cotton trousers and turbans, staring as though idly up at the open gunports. They talked in a language that to the Salem crew resembled the chirping of birds. Birds were in the jungle ashore; macaws, parrots, parakeets and egrets could be identified, and they jabbered in constant chorus.

The air smelled of the jungle, mold, wet and rot, yet carried also the tang of the pepper that had brought the ship here.

The strange men in the proas had gone on downriver. The Salem captain relaxed and ordered his boats away, to be rowed in to the little palm-log wharf. The pepper would be loaded there after long hours of barter talk with the *dato,* the head man for the region. But

not all of the crew would work the boats. Half, by the captain's direct order, still stood at battle stations. Caution was what got a ship back to Salem.

Captain Jonathan Carnes was the first to return to Salem with a cargo of pepper. He was in the Sumatran port of Benkulen in 1793 when he heard rumors of wild pepper to be procured on the northwest coasts of the island. He said nothing of this, aware of how much the information was worth, and went home and got hold of a fast, shallow-draft schooner. Then he cleared from Salem without making any declaration of his ports of call.

The parts of the Sumatran coast he searched to find his pepper cargo were a real test of a navigator's skill. They were uncharted; they were littered with coral reefs that with one glancing blow would tear the bottom out of a wooden-built ship; the natives were not to be trusted as pilots. And there was no friendly port within several hundred miles where a ship might put in for careenage and necessary repairs.

But Captain Carnes picked up his cargo. He made the return voyage laden to the hatch coamings and sold the pepper instantly in Salem. The entire cost of the voyage, including the purchase price of the cargo, was $18,000, and Carnes made a 700 per cent profit.

Salem became pepper-crazy. Merchants dispatched dozens of ships to Sumatra in search of the spice. The vessels reached Benkulen all right, but the masters had no knowledge of the northwest coasts and how to reach the cargoes they sought. Months were spent in frustrated waiting in the hot, monsoon-troubled Sumatran roadstead. Then, gradually, the secret was released. Salem and Boston shipmasters began to call regularly at Anabalu, Tally-Pow, Susu, Labuan-Haji, Muckie and Mingin.

Twenty-one American vessels, ten out of Salem and eight out of Boston, lay off the northwest coasts between March 1 and May 14, 1803, and loaded entire pepper cargoes. The dealing with the *datos* was slow, and the sacks of black, sun-dried berries were packed by coolies on carrying poles from many miles inland. The captains had plenty of time to correct and to add to the details of their Sumatran charts. There were as yet no standard charts issued, and each shipmaster designed his own.

Salem became for the space of several years the world center of the pepper trade. The figure for pepper exported from American ports had been 492 pounds in 1791; by 1805 it had reached 7,559,-244 pounds, and this was nearly the total crop from the Sumatran northwest coasts. The trade was so prosperous that in the 500-ton *Eliza,* extremely large for her time, Captain James Cook brought home in a single voyage more than a million pounds of pepper cargo.

Some of the Salem shipmasters had already turned from the pepper trade or filled out their cargoes in distant corners of the Pacific. Boston merchants had taken over most of the Canton trade, and the Salem men concerned themselves with new forms of profitable enterprise. They came home from the Gaspar Straits with loads of tin picked up at Banka Island. This stuff was worked locally and then peddled throughout New England to housewives in need of inexpensive pots and pans.

Back in the Pacific again the Salem men ranged inshore at Fiji, and without charts, greatly daring, they worked close enough to the coast to put boat crews ashore. The crews waded in over the coral heads, hauling the boats by hand in the surf and keeping a careful scrutiny of the beach. The natives here were cannibals, and big and brawny, with shark fins thrust through their noses and war clubs that could kill with a single blow. They had no liking for visitors except as a source of change in their menu, and were known to have feasted on several.

While certain assigned men from the boat crews, armed with cutlasses and muskets, stood guard, the rest moved quickly to gather birds' nests from the rocks at the edge of the surf. These were for the Canton trade, and so were the green-gray, slimy cucumbers pried from the coral formations. The Salem men thought the items wretched to eat, even for the mysterious Chinese. But they reminded themselves that Fijians liked human flesh, and it was time to boil the sea cucumbers and get back aboard ship.

Most boat crews from the Salem ships never had the satisfaction of seeing a Fijian cannibal, war club in hand. They sailed to other South Pacific islands where the natives were more reasonable, and could be hired to dive for mother-of-pearl and tortoise shell. When the ships had taken in all available Pacific cargo they touched at Canton before heading home.

The shipmasters and their clerks contested there with the hong merchants for tea, silks, cottons and chinaware in exchange for the birds' nests, sea cucumbers, tortoise and mother-of-pearl. Then they squared away down the Pearl River into the North China Sea on the long and weary series of courses to Salem. It was often two or three years since they had seen their families.

The merchant fleet owned in Massachusetts and Maine had nearly doubled between 1794 and 1802; and by 1810 it had increased another 50 per cent, reaching the figure of 500,000 tons. These were the great days of Salem and were never to be equaled. Boys were kept busy reporting ship arrivals and were paid as a usual wage a Spanish dollar for the task, which delighted many of them.

They went to Juniper Point on foot or to Great Misery Island by skiff. Off to the eastward, the North Shore stretched with Cape Ann in the distance and the loom of Baker's Island this side of it. Across the harbor, obscuring South Channel, was the rocky pasture land of the backside of Marblehead. With the wind out of the south and the tide on half flood, the boys knew, a ship would wind in around Peach Point, inside Kettle Bottom, the Endeavors, the Triangles and the Aqua Vitaes. Her topsails would first be seen over Naugus Head.

The boys waited, nervously pacing as they stared out to sea and told themselves just what they would do if they were the master of an East Indian homeward-bounder. Then there was the wind-curved white flash of the main topsail against the horizon. The boys delayed only long enough to identify the vessel and started for town. They wanted to be on the wharf, right at the center of things, when she arrived.

She came into the harbor with her ensign at the peak to show that all hands were well. Her gunner let go a fifteen-gun salute for Fort

William, and it was meticulously returned. It took her no more than ten minutes after that to gather in her sails, go through the difficult maneuver of a flying mooring and be fully secure.

The boys stood awestruck. Here was life as it should be lived. Here was the future, and the ultimate, all they could ever wish to attain. Just to be one of those men with the sun-bleached hair and the mahogany-brown faces, and back from places named Susu, Banka and Whampoa.

Boys had a good life in the Salem of that time. They were the favored, the closely regarded, and given much more consideration than their sisters. It was made evident to them from very early youth that they were the crews, the mates and masters and shipowners of the next generation. With them grown to manhood, Salem would continue to prosper.

This attitude was given outright emphasis during the annual parade of the East India Marine Society. The Salem town seal carried as its motto *"Divitis Indiae usque ad ultimum sinum."* Schoolmasters translated it as meaning, "To the uttermost gulf of teeming Ind." The members of the Marine Society celebrated their bonds with the Orient by a daylong ceremony, all very solemnly performed.

The society had been organized in 1799 "to assist the widows and children of deceased members; to collect such facts and observations as tended to the improvement and security of navigation, and to form a museum of natural and artificial curiosities, particularly such as are to be found beyond the Cape of Good Hope or Cape Horn." The by-laws stated that "any person shall be eligible as a member of the society who shall have actually navigated the seas near the Cape of Good Hope or Cape Horn, either as master or commander or as factor or supercargo in any vessel belonging to Salem."

The parade formed promptly each year in front of the massive stone building of the society. This was located on Essex Street and looked out over Derby Wharf. Ships and the bay were in the background as the celebrants took their places. They were led through the town by a member dressed in the splendid silk clothing of a Chinese mandarin; he also wore over his face a Chinese mask. Following him came a Salem boy chosen by the Marine Society for singular honor. He rode in a sumptuously equipped palanquin, carried by Negro servants who worked for local families in the town, the gleaming, red lacquer and gilt litter with its embroidered silk drapes borne on the shoulders of men dressed as natives of India.

The boy was dressed in the robes of a maharaja, and on the front of the turban wound around his head was a large ruby; he had a curved, gold-crusted dagger in his belt and pointed scarlet boots on his feet. Behind him, in great solemnity, keeping martial stride, moved the main body of the members of the society. Each man carried some valuable piece of Oriental ware, a silk screen, a vase, a bowl, a jade or an ivory statuette. They looked around them proudly in the winding streets on the way to Washington Square. They virtually owned Salem; this was their town.

Large wealth was gathered in Salem. When Elias Hasket Derby died in 1799 the estate he left his sons was estimated at a million and a half dollars. The Thorndike family of Beverly, and the Forresters, were supposed to possess about the same amount. But William Gray topped them with his three and a half million, which the Essex Street gossips said could readily be much more.

During the early years Salem merchants had maintained their homes in traditional style right across the street from their counting-houses and wharves. The prosperity that came to them at the end of the eighteenth century induced them to move back from the water-front into more spacious areas, and their wives were greatly pleased.

They left the narrow and cramped structures whose upper stories projected out over the street and whose windows, glazed with bottle glass, were small, low and let in little light. The old houses were somber; the big, hand-rifted clapboards had turned almost black with age. There were no trees, no grass, just cobblestones, the wharves and warehouses, and at night there was often a miasmatic fog from off the Bay.

Essex and Chestnut Streets became popular, and Washington Square. Immense elm trees grew here, and there was space for back and front yards and gardens and stables. A number of the new homes were built by Samuel McIntire. He designed them in Flemish-laid brick, instead of the old style of white clapboard. They were generally three stories high, with four rooms on each floor, and a hip roof. An elegant elliptical porch graced the house fronts, and was supported by Ionic columns. The front door was arched, and had a delicate fanlight and side lights.

McIntire designed his interiors in the Adams style. He suggested that the rooms be decorated in British wallpaper of rich textures, and he used ornamental molding from floors to ceilings, advocated that the floors be fully carpeted.

Some of the early and almost primitive pieces made of cherry wood and maple in the colonial style were put away in back rooms. The new style was less severe, and approached the opulent: mahogany that was ornately worked, and polished until it gleamed, sandalwood and camphorwood and teak from the Orient, Chinese screens and table covers and bowls and vases. There was throughout the distinct influence of the Orient.

The Salem wealthy lived to a fair degree like the potentates they had consciously honored during the parade. Their witch-burning Puritan ancestors would have been more than a little shocked at such display. This for them would have smacked of the unseemly and the immoral.

The wives and daughters of the wealthy of the town were also under the Oriental influence. Their dresses were made of Chinese silks or fine Indian cottons. They wore white camel's hair shawls whose borders were worked in a broad palm leaf design, green, blue or red. When they went to routs and cotillions at Hamilton Hall they adorned themselves with red cornelian necklaces, and pearl teardrop earrings. Pieces of cobweb muslin were in their bodices; gold bangles made in Calcutta or Madras were at their wrists.

But their men, although prospering as never before, were not happy. All of the astute Massachusetts Bay merchants contemplated a very dubious future. The trouble had begun as far back as 1783, when in London an Order in Council barred the importation of meat, fish, cheese and butter from the United States to British possessions in the West Indies. The British had further strangled slowly the trade built up by Americans with the French possessions in the Indian Ocean. Voyages like that made by Nathaniel Silsbee to Mauritius and Réunion were no longer profitable or possible. The Royal Navy sat in Table Bay in force and cruised the Indian Ocean, and since 1803 the French and British had again been at war.

The expanded Sumatran, Chinese and Pacific trade served as an answer to a denial of the other markets, and had brought in wealth. But the ship losses suffered recently from both French and British privateers were severe.

American neutrality suffered extreme strain. Great Britain and then France placed added restraints upon the neutral ship-carrying trade. They declared blockades and by this sought to deprive each other of the means of war. The overwhelming superiority of British sea power, though, made its effect keenly felt upon American seamen. Hundreds of them were being taken off American-flag ships under the charge that they were British deserters.

The wounds of the Revolution were not yet healed, the Massachusetts Bay merchants realized. The Royal Navy, especially the officer cadre, still smarted with the old defeats and proposed to provoke the new nation into any sort of rash retaliation to highhanded treatment at sea.

Then, on June 22, 1807, off the Virginia capes and outside the three-mile territorial limit, the United States Navy frigate *Chesapeake* was hailed by the Royal Navy frigate *Leopard*. The captain of *Leopard* used his brass speaking trumpet to tell the American ship to heave to and receive a boarding party. He said that four of the crew aboard *Chesapeake* were British deserters, and must surrender themselves.

Commodore James Barron was in command of *Chesapeake*. He refused the order. *Leopard* tacked at once, presented her broadside and delivered a crippling salvo into the American ship. Three men were killed and eighteen wounded. Commodore Barron could do nothing but give his assent to another British request; his ship could not be fought. The four alleged deserters were taken away by a British boarding party, and making very slow headway, *Chesapeake* returned to the port of Norfolk, Virginia.

News of the action created immediate and intense anti-British feeling. President Jefferson issued a proclamation on October 17, 1807, that ordered all British warships out of American waters. But the British reply to this was a proclamation that demanded the impressment of seamen by almost any method. There was no settlement of the indemnity for the *Chesapeake* case until 1811, just before war was finally declared.

Meantime, Jefferson decided to use economic pressure as a weapon against the British. He never at any time, despite his famous political wisdom, had any clear knowledge of the uses of sea power. He sent a message to Congress on December 18 recommending an embargo. The bill was passed in the Senate by 22–6, and in the House by 82–44, and was supported mainly by the South and West. The embargo became law December 22.

The South and West, pro-Jefferson because of his agrarian policies, which suited their particular needs, and because the embargo would cause them much less discomfort than in the North and East, continued to live in relative prosperity. It was the New England states that were sorely affected.

The Embargo Act stopped nearly all legal seaborne commerce with foreign nations. It forbade all United States ships to leave for foreign ports. United States ships in the coastwise trade were required to post bond double the value of the craft and cargo as a guarantee that the goods would be reloaded at a United States port. Although importation in foreign bottoms was not prohibited, it was almost outlawed by the provision that foreign vessels could not carry goods out of an American port.

New England shipowners had counted on an annual return of $50 a ship ton before the embargo. The original embargo act and the further acts of January 9 and March 12, 1808, meant for them total economic disaster. The restrictions lasted for fourteen months, and were only lifted by Jefferson on March 3, 1809, his last day in office.

There were soup kitchens in the streets of Salem. Master mariners and mechanics, pump makers and blockmakers and shipwrights and sailmakers and rope loft workers ate there side by side. Some men went into the Canadian smuggling trade in violation of the law. The rest attended town meetings that attacked the embargo as pro-French, and anti-British, and asked for its appeal.

Resolutions were drawn up by the Massachusetts legislature in January and February, 1809, that characterized the embargo as unjust and arbitrary. Governor Jonathan Trumbull addressed the Connecticut legislature February 23, 1809, and said that whenever Congress exceeded its constitutional power, state legislatures were in duty bound "to interpose their protecting shield between the rights and liberties of the people and the assumed power of the general government."

New England governors refused to furnish militia officers requested by collectors for the enforcement of the embargo. The spirit of revolt was further indicated when Thomas Pickering, an outstanding citizen, proposed a New England convention to nullify the embargo.

But for fourteen months the ships lay unmoved in their home ports. The Salem men who were unwilling to enter the Canadian smuggling trade sat on the stringpieces of the town wharves. They hand-lined for cunners and kept away from their sons, who according to local custom did a good share of the cooking at home.

It seemed to be a very long time since there had been on the table a boiled chicken stuffed with bay scallops. Nor was there any talk of a picnic out on one of the islands in the harbor, with a big iron cauldron full of chowder bubbling over a driftwood fire. The clams were to be found, of course, and the bacon and the potatoes and the rest. Mainly, it was the incentive that was lacking.

The Essex Lodge of Free Masons had in Salem 634 members. There were among them 246 master mariners and 293 mariners. Out of the master mariners fifty were lost at sea, and forty-two died in foreign ports. They were regarded as brave and self-sufficient men. But during the Jefferson embargo they had begun to lose the faith in the future that had always sustained them.

CHAPTER EIGHTEEN

HULL HER!

Perhaps the strangest fact about the War of 1812, and certainly the saddest, was that on either side it was not really wanted. Still, in many ways it could not be avoided. Trade war lurched forth into open, bloody conflict. The United States had become a very serious menace to Great Britain as an economic competitor, and Britain was both too proud and too sorely pressed to change her warlike attitude while peace was yet possible.

Impressment of American seamen had been for a long time a galling form of British naval superiority. Any innocent merchant vessel flying the American flag was liable to seizure at any moment, and when overhauled by a British cruiser short of men was sure to be stripped of most of her crew. Hundreds of British seamen had gone into service aboard American ships to escape the press gangs at home, the severe floggings, the general brutality and deprivation of life in the Royal Navy. When the officer in charge of a Royal Navy boarding party asked for some of them back it was standard practice for American captains to state that all of their men were native United States citizens, or at least naturalized.

This sort of harassment, and an occasional scuffle when the reluctant sailors were removed, and the rare use of weapons, led to a great deal of talk about freedom of the seas. What was actually

256

meant, though, was that Americans should have the right to ship cargoes to foreign ports and back without British interference. Impressment was a major issue among American seamen and shipowners and merchants, but much more so were the restrictions that stifled trade.

Then, during the time of heightened tension and bad feeling, a grave incident occurred, and men were killed in an encounter very much like that between the United States frigate *Chesapeake* and the British frigate *Leopard*. Captain John Rodgers, in command of the United States 44-gun frigate *President,* was on patrol off Sandy Hook on May 16, 1811. His immediate orders were to protect American shipping and, specifically, to reclaim from the Royal Navy 38-gun frigate *Guerriere* an American-born seaman who had been impressed from an American brig.

But Rodgers did not find *Guerriere*. He hailed instead the British 20-gun corvette *Little Belt*. When she refused to answer his challenge Rodgers gave the fire order to the broadside battery on target, and *Little Belt* suffered nine killed and twenty-three wounded. It was a reversal of the *Chesapeake–Leopard* affair; it was also the ultimate step leading to war.

The American government was still willing to settle the matter in amicable fashion. It so informed the British minister, Augustus John Foster. There was, though, no relaxation of the American demands for the revocation of the Orders in Council that restricted trade.

President James Madison, who had succeeded Jefferson, declared war June 19, 1812, against Great Britain. His message to Congress asking for a state of war listed four major grounds: impressment of American seamen, violation of United States neutral rights and territorial waters, the blockade of United States ports, and the refusal to revoke the Orders in Council.

The war was far from popular, and the wide division of the Congressional vote showed right at the outset a great amount of sectional disaffection. The House had supported the declaration 79–49, and in the Senate decision had been delayed by Federalist Party and "Old Republican" opposition. When the Senate finally voted the tally was

19–13, and again indicative of the divergence of feeling. The New England states, with the exception of inland Vermont, and other maritime and commercial states, such as New York, New Jersey and Delaware, voted for peace. The vote of the Southern and Western states assured the declaration of war.

New England bitterly protested the war, and sentiment there almost reached the point of public demands for secession from the Union. Alexander Hamilton's and John Adams's theories of a powerful, centralized government had found a lot of support in the region, and New England merchants were vigorous supporters of the Federalist Party. The so-called Essex Junto had a large share of the direction of this opposition.

It was a group composed of Massachusetts merchants and shipowners, most of whose families were intermarried. Their principal spokesman was George Cabot. Other members were Stephen Higginson, of Salem, and Jonathan Jackson and John Lowell, of Newburyport. They had conducted for years an extremely profitable business with British bankers and established close relationships, using a system of letters of credit. But patriotism was not at all prominent in any of the Junto's negotiations.

A number of the sons of members, although active in family business and profiting handsomely from their British banking connections, dealt also in the French privateer trade. They sold, very privately, seized British ships, arranged the transactions in the French West Indies and Mauritius and Réunion. Some of the second generation who belonged to the Junto were so trusted by the French that in 1794 they were permitted to witness the guillotine execution of Maximilien Robespierre on the Place de la Concorde in Paris.

The entire Junto predicted national bankruptcy if the war should continue. They already suffered from what they described as the grievous errors of the Jefferson regime, and what President Madison had done since, and now they were determined to save their fortunes. A proclamation issued in Boston on June 26, 1812, by Caleb Strong, the Governor of Massachusetts, declared a public fast in view of the war "against the nation from which we are descended."

This was the kind of pro-British sentiment that back in the days of the Revolution would have moved a crowd to dump the Governor in the bay. But on the same date of his utterance the Massachusetts House of Representatives issued an "Address to the People" which made out the war to be against the public interest and asserted that "there be no volunteers except for defensive war."

The Connecticut General Assembly condemned the war on August 25, and on July 2 the governor of that state had refused to supply militia for the use of the Federal government. Similar action was taken on August 5 by Governor Strong in Massachusetts, and in New Hampshire, also on August 5, a memorial was publicly delivered that protested against "hasty, rash and ruinous measures" and contained poorly veiled threats of disunion. For the Federalists, the war was being fought to help the French, and at great cost and harm to the United States. They began almost at once well-organized enterprises that supplied beef, flour and other provisions to the British armies in Canada and to enemy vessels off the Atlantic Coast. New York merchants soon followed with efforts of their own, surreptitiously peddling provisions to the British blockading squadron off Sandy Hook.

President Madison was a Virginian, a lawyer, a framer of the Constitution and a philosopher. The strategy of offensive sea warfare was unknown to him. He recognized, though, that such aid to the enemy must stop, and he sent a special message to Congress on December 9, 1813, that recommended an embargo. The measure passed 85–57 in the House and 20–14 in the Senate; it became law December 17, 1813.

But appeals were made to him, pointing out that Nantucket was about to starve, could not survive under the embargo. Madison allowed the measure to be modified on January 25, already given to believe that commercial restrictions would not win the war. He gave his concentration instead to the restoration of the badly depleted United States Navy.

Before the declaration of war he had listened with great attention to the plans and loud-sounding prophecies of the United States Army generals. They were not to win a single major battle, and the grandiose plan to seize Canada by invasion collapsed because of high-ranking stupidity, ineptitude and what in some instances may have been sheer cowardice.

President Madison suspected some of the sorry truth behind the façade of oratory offered him by the generals. He learned his lesson quickly as news of the first Army defeats reached him. It was a very perilous moment for the new nation. Madison realized that he, as the former Secretary of the Navy, had been gravely mistaken in the adoption of the gunboat theory of shore protection. Through the use of "floating forts," the theory ran, the expense of an operative Navy would be reduced and the British would be prevented from attacking American ports by sea.

But the British Navy was the most powerful in the world. Since 1792 each major European nation had been defeated in turn by British fleets. Sir Samuel Hood had scored a tremendous victory over the Russians in the Baltic; the Danes had received crippling losses off Copenhagen, and the Dutch the same at Camperdown; and at Trafalgar the French and Spanish had been crushed by Lord Horatio Nelson.

There were more than eight hundred vessels in commission in the British Navy. The American Navy had at the time of the declaration of war only eighteen ships in fit condition to put to sea. Many of the ships held "in ordinary" on a reserve basis were decayed, decrepit and almost useless. Most of the Navy shipbuilding yards had become storage depots, and a large part of the ships in commission badly needed repair. The odds against the American Navy, the President came to understand, were more than 40–1, and that was a generous estimate.

President Madison could find only one factor that might save the country from almost immediate naval catastrophe. The American Navy had a splendid officer cadre, quite probably superior to the British. The officers were veterans of the undeclared French War and of the savage actions fought against the corsairs along the Barbary Coast. A great many had come to the Navy from the merchant marine and had sailed all over the world in every capacity. The petty officers and the seamen had similar training. They had been going to sea, and had lived on it, since they were able to pick up an oar and trim a sheet. They had handled firearms of nearly every kind ashore and afloat. Their combat experience was broad; they had fought picaroons in the West Indies, Malay and Chinese pirates in the Orient, Tripolitanian corsairs and French and British privateers.

They were an independent-minded lot and often prone to mutinous talk, especially if members of a privateer crew, where discipline was not as strictly maintained as aboard a Navy ship. But they were smarter than their British cousins, capable of action on their own initiative when officers were not present to command them, and much more willing to fight than the British, who had been impressed, and were driven relentlessly by sadistic, class-conscious officers.

Commodore John Rodgers was the senior seagoing United States Navy officer at the outbreak of war. He was a veteran of the French War and of the Tripolitanian fighting and the victor in the *Chesapeake–Little Belt* incident. His command was the New York squadron. He had his ships at sea an hour after the declaration of hostilities and considerably relieved the President's feeling of anxiety.

Commodore William Bainbridge, another veteran Navy officer, was on leave and serving as master of a merchant vessel at the time of the *Chesapeake–Little Belt* incident. When he heard of it his ship was in St. Petersburg,* Russia. He turned her over at once to the mate and started for Finland and fast transportation home. He was convinced that war was now inescapable, and he sought naval assignment.

Although he was hurt in an accident during his journey across Finland, he found fast passage home and arrived to be told by Navy colleagues about the "floating fort" theory. He went to see Madison in company with Captain Charles Stewart and was informed further by the President that it was the Navy Department plan to strip seven of the remaining frigates and make them into harbor duty gunboats.

* Present-day Leningrad.

Bainbridge was a man with a very active record. He had been captured during the French War and again by the Tripolitanian pirates, and he still felt the effects of the injury suffered in Finland. Yet he made a strong and eloquent appeal to the President, and was joined in it by Captain Stewart. When they left Madison agreed to offensive sea action and assured them that he understood the need for naval operation on the frontier lakes and an immediate, vigorous shipbuilding campaign. Bainbridge had been given command of the frigate *Constitution* and took her almost at once to sea.

Among the other veteran Navy officers who held command during the first, crucial months of the war were Commodore David Porter, Captain Isaac Hull, Captain James Lawrence and Captain Jacob Jones. Command of the frigate *Essex* was given to Porter. He was Boston-bred, a pensive and handsome, long-faced man who was the foster father of David Farragut and also raised seagoing sons of his own. It was his inflexible habit never to swear at the men of his crew, although he was famous in the service as a strict disciplinarian. The *Essex* crew bore the reputation of being the best cutlass-hands in the Navy, and were very proud of that and of their commander.

Hull was a Connecticut man. He had seen a great deal of action against the French and the Mediterranean corsairs, at which time the brand-new frigate *Constitution* had been assigned to him. He fought her with such skill that he came to be called by his brother officers "above single [the best] ship captain of the war." This was the sort of praise reserved for John Paul Jones; in the small, sorely beset United States Navy of 1812 it was meant with the utmost of sincerity.

Lawrence was from Salem. He was tall, powerfully built and tough. He sought glory in battle in the tradition of John Paul Jones, and was soon to find it. His command was the war sloop *Hornet*.

Another Jones, Captain Jacob Jones of Maryland, had served aboard the frigate *United States* in the French War. With the rank of Master-Commandant, he took the war sloop *Wasp* to sea.

Joshua Barney of Baltimore was a Revolutionary War veteran with a record as outstanding as his reputation for being quiet and good-natured in peace but absolutely violent in battle. He had served with Esek Hopkins when the Continental Navy raid was made against Nassau, in the Bahamas. Then he was captured by the British, spent five months in the foul prison ship *Jersey,* was exchanged, recaptured and once more exchanged.

But in 1812 there was at first no naval vessel for him to command. So he took out the *Rossie,* a small and fast Baltimore privateer. She was a clipper-lined schooner of the type becoming steadily more popular. Her bottom was freshly copper-sheathed; she carried ten 12-pounder carronades, 3 long guns and a crew of 125 men. Barney was now in his fifties, but still possessed of his great sense of daring.

He cleared from the Chesapeake twenty-four days after war was declared. Ninety days later, he was back, having seized four ships, eight brigs, three schooners and three sloops. The approximate worth of these prizes was put at $1.5 million. There had been hard fighting for several of them, in particular the privateer *Jeannie,* taken on August 9, when the action had lasted two hours; and the British government packet *Princess Amelie,* taken in an engagement of similar length, fought September 15 in the moonlight.

He straightened out his debts with his share of the prize money—he had never been much of a money-maker ashore—and then arranged for the disposition of the 217 men from the prize crews. Word of his exploit had reached Washington, and he was recalled to Navy duty. He was glad to go; the Navy was where he belonged. Still, there were plenty of men who preferred service in the privateers, and as the war progressed they flocked into the ports to sign articles for it.

The government had expressed right along the conviction that privateers would carry the war at sea, and the huge profits made during the Revolution were still remembered. Baltimore became again a center for the trade, as well as New York and Bristol, Rhode Island. Boston was also active, along with a number of the Maine ports, and vessels were outfitted, manned and sent to sea from

Charleston and Savannah. They took a swift toll of British shipping.

Lloyd's announced in London at the end of the first seven months of the war that five hundred British merchant ships had been captured by American privateers. This had sent prices alarmingly high. Flour cost $58 a barrel on the London market; beef cost $38 and pork $36 a barrel; wood planking was being sold for $72 a thousand feet. Insurance rates were mounting rapidly; to send cargo to Halifax the shipper paid 35.5 per cent of the value of the goods. Economic ruin lay ahead if the American privateers were not stopped.

The British Navy responded by tightening the blockade of the American coast with steady pressure. It became increasingly difficult for the privateers to send prizes back to American ports and to make their own way home. The British had a formidable cordon of cruiser squadrons aligned all the way from Halifax to south of Savannah.

The British commander-in-chief of the American station was Admiral Sir John Borlase Warren. He had the usual Royal Navy officer's contempt for anything un-English, and believed the Americans to be very poor seamen. It was his conviction that the war would be finished within a few months. His pride was keenly hurt when he was forced to send dispatches to London asking for reinforcements, "lest Trade be inevitably ruined." His blockade system was quite effective, though, and he had serving under him a number of highly skilled, brave and intelligent officers.

Rear Admiral Sir Thomas Masterman Hardy was in command of the task force sent to harass the New England coast. Big, bluff, bald and a consummate seaman, he had been Nelson's flag officer at Trafalgar. He had been struck in the foot by a splinter aboard *Victory,* and Nelson had been shot down at his side and died in his arms. Hardy knew how to conduct a blockade and went quickly and thoroughly about the closing of the ports assigned to him.

Two of the outstanding Royal Navy ship commanders serving on American blockade duty were Captain James R. Dacres and Captain Phillip B. V. Broke. They were both hard-bitten veterans.

Dacres was a man with a long nose, deeply sunken eyes and a

cocky manner toward his enemies. He boasted publicly that his frigate *Guerriere* could beat any American frigate in "a few minutes *tête-à-tête.*"

Broke was more the Byronic type, tall, lean and handsome. He was a great martinet and a devout believer in all of Nelson's theories of sea warfare. He had commanded the frigate *Shannon* for seven years and put his crew through daily gunnery practice with live ammunition. The expenditure of so much powder while not in action had led staff officers in the Admiralty to order him to the Halifax station as a crackpot theoretician. They were, as they soon learned to their surprise and pleasure, badly mistaken about him.

Royal Navy ships like *Guerriere* and *Shannon* had been cruising American territorial waters for months when Commodore Rodgers took his United States Navy squadron out of New York harbor. He waited for darkness, cleared the channel on the night of June 21 and stood away to the southward. His objective was not the British cruisers, but a convoy loaded in silver and bound from Jamaica to England. He had with him, in addition to his flagship, the 44-gun frigate *President,* the *United States,* and *Congress, Hornet* and *Argus.*

Masthead lookouts sighted on June 23 the sails of a British frigate which Rodgers and his officers mistook for the escort attached to the silver convoy. Rodgers ordered *President* to overhaul and spread all canvas. The enemy vessel was the *Belvidera* and not as fast as the American frigate. *President* was about to close with her when the American's long-barreled chase gun exploded while being served.

The blast was terrific, and sent whipping across the main and quarter-decks an awful hail of split metal and wood fragmentation. Sixteen men were killed, and Rodgers received a broken leg. *President* gave up the chase at once; *Belvidera,* which was unattached and on cruising duty, headed for Halifax to report that American naval units were at sea.

When Rodgers's squadron had left New York, the United States light frigate *Essex* was still in shipyard for repairs. Commodore David Porter hurried the rest of the work and ran her offshore without enemy interference. Then, on August 3, enemy sail was sighted. The commodore played a common privateer trick; he masked his gunports with tarpaulins and gave his ship the appearance of a merchantman.

The British ship was the 16-gun sloop-of-war *Alert*. Her captain allowed her to come within broadside range of *Essex* before he recognized his error. *Essex* mounted thirty-two pieces, and the tarpaulins were pulled inboard fast, the gunports triced up and the big, black weapons run out and served in broadside.

One broadside was enough. *Alert* surrendered, crippled. She was the first British warship to be taken in the war by the United States Navy.

H.M.S. *Belvidera* had duly reported at Halifax, though, and a British squadron under Captain Broke was already in New York coastal waters at the time *Alert* was captured. Master-Commandant Hull, aboard the United States 44-gun frigate *Constitution,* ran into the full formation on July 17 along the flat and sandy New Jersey coast near present-day Atlantic City. The chance for combat pleased Hull; he had headed for sea at the outbreak of war without waiting for orders from the Navy Department. But now the odds were very much against him.

He was confronted by the massive ship of the line *Africa* with her 64 guns, and the frigates *Guerriere, Shannon, Belvidera* and *Aeolus.* They fanned out to seaward of him at Broke's order and maintained a line to keep him between them and the beach. There was very little wind, and that came only in intermittent puffs. *Constitution* was a slow ship, one of the slowest of her class in the American Navy. *Shannon* was fast, and Broke was aboard her, sent her along under all light canvas to overhaul *Constitution*. He was so eager that he several times told his bow-chase gunners to fire although the American ship was still considerably out of range.

But the gap was closing. *Shannon* had begun to overhaul, if only for a few yards with each breath of breeze. Isaac Hull looked astern and to seaward at the Royal Navy display, then ordered his carpenter to chop the taffrail out of *Constitution*. That was to give scope to

the pair of 24-pound cannon Hull mounted there, and he had another pair of 24-pounders manhandled into the main cabin on the
deck below, their muzzles thrust through the fancifully decorated
stern windows. He could match the bow-chase fire from *Shannon*
for some while this way, yet it did not protect him from the rest of
the British when they came up into range.

Now the wind had completely gone. The water was a glassy, un-
ruffled turquoise. Sandpipers could be heard on the beach, and gulls
as they dived. Up aloft, the sails barely whispered against the gear;
the wheel ropes creaked a bit as the quartermaster impatiently spun
the spokes, asking for wind; a powder monkey cursed in a voice
squeaky with strain.

Hull talked with his first lieutenant, Charles Morris. A privateer
at a crucial moment like this might jettison some of her guns to
lighten ship and increase headway. But *Constitution* needed all of
hers. There was 2,300 gallons of fresh water that could be dumped,
and Hull ordered that done. The men rigged the pumps and formed
bucket lines; they laboriously passed the wooden buckets aloft and
wet down the sails that Hull insisted should be held fully spread. The
wetting tightened the texture of the canvas, and would help when
there was wind.

Lieutenant Morris had gone below to the chart table. He returned
with a chart for this coast. It showed that where *Constitution* now
lay becalmed there was twenty-five fathoms of water with a firm sand
bottom. Hull studied the chart and nodded and gave the order for a
kedge anchor to be run out ahead of the ship.

The light anchor was put in the ship's launch, a manila hawser
attached to it. The launch crew rowed to the length of the hawser,
heaved mightily and let the anchor go over the side of the boat. Then
they rowed back to the ship, taking in the hawser slack with the rest
of their shipmates once they were aboard.

All hands were needed to walk the capstan around to haul *Constitution* forward to the anchor. Men took off their varnished hats
and already sweat-sopped jumpers and pitched them into the scuppers. Nobody sang; only a few cursed. It was too hot, and there was

too much work. *Constitution* started to move. She was coming up on the anchor. *Shannon,* back astern with her sails drooping, was stationary, and so were the rest of the British.

The hawser was passed dripping down into the launch and a new crew sent to carry it forward for another heave-ahead. The men who still stood at the capstan pawls leaned blear-eyed with sweat, heads down under the powerful sun. They understood clearly what was before them—hours more of this, until at last wind came.

Broke, aboard *Shannon,* had his long glass trained on the American ship. His usually keen mind had been slow to grasp the skill of Hull's maneuver. Now he ordered all canvas furled aboard his ship so that no untoward gust might impede her motion, and he sent crews away in every boat that could carry a kedge anchor. Then he made a signal, and the rest of the squadron took the same action.

It went on for sixty hours. Men fell stumbling in exhaustion from the capstan pawls, crawled the deck weeping, their hands cramped clawlike from the pressure they had exerted. Hull sent several boats out with extra anchors and hawsers; *Belvidera* was using a pair of exceptionally long cables, with an anchor at the end of each, and she moved steadily through the water.

All of the British crews were engaged. Their bosuns' mates used the cat-o'-nine-tails on the men who failed to haul hard enough. They kept the weapons with the stubby green baize handles inside their hats. The nine iron-tipped thongs generally "started" any man tardy in his duty. But in the breathless calm on the Jersey coast, along toward the end of the second day, men fainted, bloody-backed and worthless.

Then, on July 19, there was wind. It was just a bit at first, light airs that flicked the sea and touched the upper topsails and the jibs, made them tremble, slightly curve. Hull was ready. He still carried all sail bent on, and as the breeze increased he gave a series of helm orders.

He conned his ship forward to the boats that carried the hawsers and kedge anchors. He let the anchors and hawsers go, and performed the very precise maneuver of bringing the boats aboard on the run. Their crews stood erect and caught at the davit falls as the ship veered toward them. They hooked on the falls, and their shipmates hauled them and the boats aboard.

The British still kept stubbornly in pursuit and spread out to catch *Constitution* between them. There were dark, ominous clouds along the horizon that dusk that spoke of possibly violent squalls. Hull tried another maneuver. He furled canvas, remembering the Royal Navy habit of taking in sail whenever wind threatened a ship. Then he and Lieutenant Morris and the rest of his officers stared anxiously astern as *Constitution* began to lose headway.

The estimate of British prudence had been right, though. Ship after ship, *Shannon* first, the British were furling sail.

Hull sent the *Constitution* topmen aloft as fast as they could climb the ratlines. He bent on every sail the ship would carry, and through the glistening silver walls and the rainbows of the rain squalls shaped a course for New York. He made port safely next day, all hands but the watch on deck stretched on deck, deep in sleep.

Hull was at sea soon again with *Constitution* and cruised North alone into Canadian waters. He met nothing worthy of pursuit and was headed for Boston and still about 750 miles out when on August 19 his lookouts reported sail. Hull identified it. This was *Guerriere,* Captain Dacres in command.

Both ships closed as soon as identity was established. Dacres was just as eager for combat as Hull. But Hull let the 38-gun frigate fire first. He yawed *Constitution* off target, and the British long-range shot plunged into the gleaming sea with huge, geyser-like splashes. Hull sailed his intercept course once more, keeping away from fore-and-aft raking fire. He sought the right moment when he could luff his ship across the enemy's bows and rake her. He found it, and as *Constitution* swerved around on the other tack and swung squarely ahead of *Guerriere,* he leaped joyously into the air and yelled, "Fire!"

He was a plump man, and the leap split his tight white breeches along the rear seam. That meant nothing to him, though, as he watched *Guerriere* take her punishment from the American gunners.

When they had fired, and as they hauled, swabbed and reloaded, they yelled, "Hull her, sir! Hull her!"

Hull gave the orders; gun muzzles were depressed, and the next broadside riddled the British vessel between her waterline and her bulwarks. She was badly hurt, yet Dacres could still sail her. He brought *Guerriere* around and hooked her long bowsprit into the American ship's rigging. The vessels were locked together. Both were ready with boarding parties, and almost simultaneously the same order was bawled, "Boarders away!"

Men advanced out along the fouled bowsprit or crawled the foot-ropes or the rigging to get aboard the enemy vessel. They carried cutlasses, pistols, tomahawk-shaped boarding axes and dirks. Their faces were smeared masks of sweat-trickled gunpowder. Their eyes were bloodshot with exertion, fear, rage and hate. Veins throbbed distended in their throats; muscles knotted and flexed and tautened as the weapons were used.

Enemy screamed at enemy, most of the words incoherent and repetitive, a release for hysteria. The wounded and the dead fell without much sound, in surprise, caught up until the last instant within the spell of battle fever. Above them in the upper rigging of both ships Marine sharpshooters in full uniform, shellacked shakos, white-crossed belts and knee-high gaiters, maintained steady musket fire. The targets were easy, the range only a few yards, and a musket ball split a man's skull wide.

But the ships, responding to the wind, wrenched apart. Hull called his boarders back in time, sent the gunners to the pieces. They delivered a broadside that took the foremast out of *Guerriere*. The wounded ship listed deeply and nearly capsized as the vast tangle of wood, rope and canvas went over the side. Her mainmast had begun to topple, described eccentric arcs across the sky, groaned, trembled in its length, snapped stays and shrouds and went with a gigantic crash and a whoop of tumbling canvas.

Hull had stood off so that his ship would not be fouled by enemy gear. Now he closed, to deliver another rake. Captain Dacres stared across at him and knew that the British ship could not continue the battle. It had lasted for fifty-five minutes, and *Guerriere* was an al-most total wreck. Dacres called for the British ensign to be lowered in signal of surrender.

He crossed slowly in his boat to *Constitution* to deliver his sword and personal word of surrender. Bodies, some beheaded, some mu-tilated beyond any sort of recognition, bumped the boatsides. The coxswain steered past smashed spars, festoons of cordage and weird, small islands of half-submerged sail canvas where air bubbles clucked and twitched at the cloth.

Dacres climbed stiffly aboard *Constitution*. He went aft past silent men whose hatred was in their eyes. Then he was on the quarter-deck and bowed to Hull, extended his sword on his outspread hands. Hull grinned at that. He told Dacres that he did not want the sword. He pointed to the very fine half-moon that Dacres wore. "But," he told the Royal Navy officer, "I'll trouble you, sir, for that hat."

Hull started for Boston with *Guerriere* in tow. She was too far gone, and would not answer to the towline because of the water she took. Hull brought her crew aboard *Constitution,* then blew her up and proceeded into port.

There were many interested spectators along the Boston wharves when he moored *Constitution*. She had suffered fourteen casualties and the British seventy-eight. It was the first major defeat for the Royal Navy in fourteen years. The men in the crowd who had been vociferous in criticism of "Mr. Madison's war" and had declared that victory was impossible for the United States left the waterfront with-out looking back and with nothing to say.

American successes continued at sea, and British morale lowered rapidly with the news. Both United States Navy and privateer vessels were busy, but the Navy scored the more significant victories, and this gave great and much-needed impetus to the domestic war effort.

The United States 18-gun sloop *Wasp,* under the command of Captain Jacob Jones, met while on cruise off the Chesapeake capes on October 18, 1812, a large British convoy. It was being escorted by the Royal Navy 18-gun brig *Frolic,* which instantly opened fire.

The British gunners fired their pieces while the vessel poised on the upward-moving crest of the wave. The Americans fired on the downward dip and plunged their fire. The solid iron shot went with a long, deepening whine aboard *Frolic,* over the bulwarks where men crouched in a futile attempt to find cover. The brig was ripped apart fore and aft. She was smashed, gutted beyond any repair or ability to fight. When she surrendered there were only four living men on her decks.

But—and this was not given wide publicity by the Navy Department at home—some weeks later *Wasp* met H.M.S. *Poictiers,* a 78-gun ship of the line. *Wasp* could not escape. She was savagely beaten into a mass of corpse-strewn wreckage, and then surrendered.

The Americans still kept the upper hand, though, and Captain Stephen Decatur emphasized it again while cruising alone on October 25, 1812, off the Canary Islands. He commanded the 44-gun frigate *United States.* Captain Samuel Carden of the Royal Navy chose to stand up to him in the 38-gun frigate *Macedonian.* She was a crack ship, and for a while Captain Carden thought that he had come on the light frigate *Essex* and would not have much trouble. Decatur soon made him lose the ideas about *Essex* and easy victory.

Decatur sailed off from the British ship. He luffed *United States* under light canvas and evaded the enemy fire. His gunners were superior, also his weapons. They put a number of salvoes solidly aboard *Macedonian.* Her scuppers were awash with blood, the decks cluttered with dead and dying men and dismantled guns when, two hours later, Carden decided that he must surrender.

He came over to board *United States* and present himself to Decatur, his manner shaken and dull, his eyes vague with battle shock. Still, he was gripped by a fear greater than that he had felt during action. "What will they do to me?" he asked Decatur.

Decatur knew that the man spoke about his superiors in the Royal Navy and what his future would be once the news of the loss of *Macedonian* was received in London. But Decatur did not expend much time in sympathy. He sent a boarding party to inspect the British ship, and after she was sufficiently repaired, sailed her into

Newport, Rhode Island, as a prize. The British casualties had been 104, the American twelve. Decatur had scored an outstanding victory.

Constitution was back at sea again in the fall of 1812 with a new captain, Commodore William Bainbridge. She was accompanied by the United States 18-gun sloop *Hornet* under command of Captain James Lawrence, and cruised off Brazil after British prizes. They cornered in the harbor of Baía a British sloop that Bainbridge left to Lawrence. He returned to offshore waters alone, and on December 29, 1812, found a target very much to his liking.

She was the British 38-gun *Java,* a former French Navy ship and famous as a fast sailor. She was commanded by Captain Henry Lambert, a veteran with a long battle record. Lambert brought his ship around and sent her without hesitation after *Constitution*.

It was again superb American gunnery that was decisive. Long-range fire early in the battle battered the mizzenmast out of *Java*. Her sailing ability was limited after that, and Bainbridge closed to finish her. *Constitution* raked *Java* with broadsides, but the British gunners raked her furiously in turn at nearly bore-sight range.

A British shot smashed the American ship's wheel, and Bainbridge, standing near it, was severely wounded by a bolt driven into his thigh. He clung to the rigging to keep erect and watched while *Java* rammed her bowsprit over *Constitution's* quarter in the famous, desperate maneuver.

British sailors swarmed along the bowsprit and leaped down to meet the *Constitution* men cutlass to cutlass. But the handystroke fighting did not last long. Marine sharpshooters in the main top of *Constitution* had taken care of Captain Lambert, killed him where he stood aboard his own ship. Battle ardor went out of the *Java* boarders. They retreated, and then the ships swung clear from each other, and Bainbridge clung to the rigging and intently watched *Java*. She was about to lose her mainmast.

It crashed, and *Java* lay like a hulk. Her senior surviving officer came to the rail and called over to Bainbridge the words of surrender. Her flag dropped from the peak, and Bainbridge was aware that his long period of bad luck was finally finished. He sent an inspection party to *Java*. She had received, the inspection officer reported, 122 casualties. *Constitution* had suffered thirty-four, and *Java* could be sailed as a prize.

Bainbridge brought her into Boston under jury rig. That caused a further setback for the Federalist faction and created profound gloom in London. There was more of the same sort of disastrous news to come.

Hornet, while cruising separately, had been chased from her possible prize in Baía by a heavily armed British man-of-war. She rounded the Brazilian capes and took advantage of the Gulf Stream current, lost her pursuer. She was off the low and rain-soaked Guianan coast on February 24, 1813, when she met the British 20-gun brig *Peacock*. Lawrence, a man with perpetual eagerness for battle, called his crew to stations and closed with the enemy ship.

His gunners fired two broadsides into *Peacock*. Those were so shrewdly served they finished her. Lawrence sent over a rescue party as soon as he recognized her condition. *Peacock* was about to sink at any instant.

Lawrence picked up his speaking trumpet and hailed the men of the rescue party. They must hurry. The British brig was settling, wallowing, low in the water. Groans came from her hull timbers, and her hatch tops reared with the thrust of air compressed in her holds. She was going, and again Lawrence hailed her, to warn his men and her survivors. Now she was gone.

Some men sprang from her rail at the last instant, tumbled into *Hornet's* boat. But not all of them made it. She went with nine of her crew, two Americans of the rescue party and her dead captain. Her descent left a roil of surface disturbance which slowly subsided. Then the yellow weed of the Gulf Stream moved in even flow, and the sea was empty there.

The men aboard *Hornet* rested motionless. They had not meant this. They felt strangely frustrated; they possessed none of the exhilaration of victory. War had suddenly become terrible.

Lawrence gave his sailing orders in a low voice. He told his navigator to lay off a course for home. He was unwilling to cruise any further without specific Navy Department instructions. For the time being, battle ardor had deserted him.

Hornet had trouble with the British blockading squadrons before she reached port. She was lucky to get home, Lawrence and his crew were informed ashore. The British blockade had already caught many ships, kept more out to sea and in foreign ports where they waited for a chance to slip through the huge, well-planned cordon.

The British had officially established the blockade December 26, 1812. For the first few months, it only affected Chesapeake Bay and Delaware River waters and shut off the commerce there. Then a Royal Navy task force under Rear Admiral Sir George Cockburn raided the upper Chesapeake, took possession of the area. From early 1813 until the end of the war the British used it as a naval station and depot. The scope of the blockade was also widened, and stretched from the Chesapeake to include Charleston, Port Royal, Savannah and the ports on the Gulf of Mexico.

There had been since November 16, 1812, an unofficial yet quite effective blockade of New York and the Long Island ports. British political thinking meant to take advantage of the disaffection expressed in the New England states. So the New England ports as far south as New London were left open to neutral trade, although offshore British cruisers often seized any vessels considered to be suitable prizes.

It was not until much later in the war, on April 25, 1814, when American determination to win the war was shown to be unbroken, that the blockade of New England was made fully effective. Long before then the merchants of the region were on the point of bankruptcy; trade had been stifled, and the scarcity of goods that had stimulated domestic manufacturing brought about widespread speculation and price inflation. High prices severely hurt the farmers, and loss of customs revenues denied the government a large source of income. The national economy was threatened with collapse, and the prophecies of the Essex Junto were justified in every grim detail.

James Lawrence was conscious of all of this when he received a taunting challenge from Captain Broke of H.M.S. *Shannon*. Lawrence was in Boston, had been advanced in command from *Hornet* to the 38-gun frigate *Chesapeake*. Broke cruised outside Boston harbor in *Shannon,* and he wrote Lawrence:

"Only by repeated triumphs can your little navy console your country for loss of trade."

Lawrence mustered immediately his new and unwieldy crew and took *Chesapeake* to sea after *Shannon*.

They met on June 1, 1813, thirty miles offshore. Lawrence was too much of a sailor to fail to recognize that he sent *Chesapeake* into great danger. His crew of 379 men was larger than *Shannon's* 330, but the Americans were raw, had never worked or fought together before and hardly understood the basic parts of their complex duties. Broke had held the same crew for seven years, drilled them daily with intensive concentration. There was a single and very obvious maneuver that *Chesapeake* must take—instantaneous boarding attack so that her weight of numbers might be used.

Lawrence felt misgivings, even profound doubt. But he was committed; he was a captain of the United States Navy. There was the honor of the service to be considered, and his pride. He drove *Chesapeake* bow-on at *Shannon*.

Broke brought the British frigate broadside-to in an easily executed change of tacks and raked *Chesapeake* with awful effect. Then he raked her again, and again, and over aboard *Chesapeake* men who were new to battle groped with fear-stiff hands at two-ton guns. Most of them did not live long, fired only one or two badly aimed broadsides.

Chesapeake lay disabled, unable to move or fight her guns. Broke realized that this was his moment. He gave a great, wild yell which was not at all typical of a Royal Navy officer; it was an order that sent the *Shannon* boarding party away, and he led them.

Broke, flush-faced beneath the tousle of his gray, short-cut hair, was unmistakable. His high, white stock, his epaulettes and sword sash and nankeen breeches and tasseled half boots marked him. He went aboard *Chesapeake* with his sword sweeping and slashing, and her crew fell away and let him and fifty of his men advance along the main deck.

Lawrence rallied the *Chesapeake* people. He came from the quarter-deck to lead them, big and wide-shouldered and full of fight, a man to inspire confidence. The British were checked where he chose to stand; they drew back from him. It was a snap shot for the Marine perched in *Shannon's* rigging. The musket ball struck Lawrence in the lungs, and he went down hunched, coughing blood.

When he was carried below to the surgeon he was dying. He was aware of that and spoke as clearly as possible. He said to the officer who accompanied him, "Don't give up the ship!"

The *Chesapeake* men, told his words, fought for another ten minutes or so. But then they lost heart for combat. They lowered their weapons and stood in attitudes of surrender. Thirty-two of them were casualties of this melee, and the ship's total casualties amounted to 146 men.

Broke was ready to accept surrender when it was offered by *Chesapeake's* senior officer. These untrained Americans had fought much better than Broke had thought. His own losses amounted to 83 men. He inspected *Chesapeake* and saw that Lawrence's body received correct attention, then went back to his own ship.

The prize crew he put aboard *Chesapeake* managed to get her into Halifax with the help of *Shannon*. Dispatches telling of the victory were sent at once to London. Here was a bit of news to dispel the gloom at Lloyd's.

The news when it reached New England brought seven shipmasters from Salem. They sailed to Halifax under a flag of truce and took Lawrence's body home. Salem was prepared to receive it at India Wharf. The funeral cortege moved with deliberate, solemn slowness to the town cemetery. It went through shadow between the close-set house walls in the narrow waterfront streets. Then the cortege entered dappled sunlight where the great elms lined Essex Street.

It had been the decision of the Navy Department to pay all due honor. High-ranking officers had been sent to march in attendance.

Sunlight caught their somber faces and the eyes that gazed straight ahead, ignoring the crowds, the lovely gardens, the fine houses. They seemed unaware of the sunlight, even of the incessant, deep-tongued tolling of the church bells.

They were Captains Hull, Bainbridge, Creighton, Stewart, Blakely and Parker; and Lieutenants Ballard, Hoffman, Reilly, Wilkinson and Norris. Behind them came the members of the Masonic societies, then the clergy, and Captain Lawrence's relatives and the shipmasters who had accompanied the body from Halifax.

Salem was silent except for the tolling of the bells. The street, dusty with summer heat, gave no sound. Little girls and boys and dogs rested still, contained by awe. They followed the cortege with their glances, but did not move. There was something forbidding about the men in uniform; they kept Captain Lawrence apart, for themselves, and for the past. So they carried his body to the cemetery and the grave.

Lawrence's last words became in the very trying year of 1813 a slogan for the United States Navy. When he was sent from gunboat duty at Newport to the extremely important Great Lakes theater of operations, twenty-eight-year-old Captain Oliver Perry had them inscribed on the flag of his new ship. She was a 20-gun brig, built like her sister ship *Niagara* and the rest of his small command on Lake Erie. Perry named her *Lawrence* after he had arrived from Newport at Presque Isle on May 27 and held an inspection of the flotilla. It was made up of the two brigs and a schooner and three gunboats still on the shipyard ways.

Their construction was the work of a remarkable New York shipbuilder, Noah Brown, and everything that went into them except the timber came from New York or Georgetown, on the Potomac. Ship's gear was supplied by New York and the guns by the Georgetown Foundry. Canvas-covered powder wagons bounced over the hazardously rough trails from Philadelphia to Pittsburgh to Presque Isle, and Perry knew that to outfit vessels for combat under such circumstances was more than a minor miracle.

But Perry was pressed for time. British invasion from Canada menaced all of the Northwest frontier. When the British for strategical reasons evacuated Forts Niagara and Erie on May 27 he was profoundly grateful. He was enabled to move five American vessels that had been held in the navy yard at Black Rock at the eastern end of Lake Erie.

The British blockading squadron was temporarily off station. Perry hurried to float the heavier vessels of his flotilla over the bar into deep water and afterward anchored them off Put-in-Bay. This was north of the mouth of the Sandusky River, and he was there at the urgent request of General William Henry Harrison, who commanded a force of United States militia that badly needed help against the British.

Perry's opponent in the operation was Commodore Robert H. Barclay of the Royal Navy. The Commodore was a Trafalgar veteran, and bore the reputation of being a tough man in battle. He sailed to meet Perry on September 9 with six ships that had a total of 65 guns. Perry commanded ten ships with a total of 55 guns. But his guns were heavier, and also his vessels, although the ships because of the circumstances of their construction were roughly finished and rigged.

The battle lasted for more than three hours, and was one of the bloodiest of the war. *Lawrence* was riddled in the broadside-to-broadside fighting. Her casualties had reached the almost incredible figure of 80 per cent before Perry was convinced that he should abandon her. He left her in a small boat, carrying the blue flag with its bold white slogan of "Don't Give Up The Ship."

The sight of Perry standing upright between the thwarts infuriated the gunners and sharpshooters aboard the British 17-gun sloop *Queen Charlotte*. They fired repeatedly at him, but he transferred safely to *Niagara*. He took command of *Niagara,* sent her captain to bring up the American schooners which had held back and renewed the battle.

Perry's crews were Rhode Island men, a company of Negroes who had been promised freedom for their service and a sprinkling of

Kentucky frontier settlers. The Kentucky men were more expert with their long-barreled rifles than the Royal Navy sharpshooters. Commodore Barclay had lost an arm at Trafalgar; the second was smashed by an American rifle ball, and Barclay believed that further conflict was not worth while. He surrendered, in great pain, to Perry, had an aide turn over his sword.

This was September 10, and Perry sent his famous message to General Harrison: "We have met the enemy and they are ours."

General Harrison was encamped with his troops at Seneca, on the Sandusky River. He was quick to realize that the victory Perry had won placed Lake Erie once more under United States control. It restored also the threat of American invasion of Canada, and the British must now evacuate Malden and Detroit, fall back to a defensive line along the Niagara frontier.

Harrison marched his 4,500 troops down the Sandusky to Lake Erie. He talked there with Perry and learned that at the time Perry had transferred from *Lawrence* only one gun had been left in commission aboard the flagship. Harrison warmly shook Perry's hand. Then he went on with his troops across the lake, invaded Canada.

It was to be the final American offensive action of the war. The country was very near the point of economic prostration, and New England was already bankrupt, the Federal government practically without funds from lack of taxes and usual revenues. The British, sensing this, started large-scale attacks along the coast.

Constitution slipped to sea from Boston early in 1814 and for three months stayed out on cruise. She was able to work her way back in again, but after that the British maintained the blockade with almost completely paralyzing effect. Counting *Constitution,* futile at her mooring in Boston, all of the powerful American frigates were held in port, *Congress* at Portsmouth, *United States* at New London and *President* at New York.

It seemed to be glorious news when on April 27, 1814, *Peacock,* one of the three sloops-of-war built in American yards, scored a victory off the east coast of Florida. The fast 22-gun vessel had slipped from New York and caught up with His Majesty's brig *Épervier* and took her in a running fight. *Épervier* was a Royal Navy pay ship. Captain Lewis Warrington in command of *Peacock* took £25,000 in gold bullion from her strong room. He transferred it to his vessel and sailed her past the British on blockade duty at the mouth of the Savannah River and up the winding reaches to the South Carolina port. There he put it in the right hands, dropped down the river, evaded the cruisers on a misty night and ran out to go raiding in the Bay of Biscay.

But one ship, no matter how well handled or lucky, could not win the war. The year of 1814 offered a very bleak prospect for Americans. The British had finally defeated Napoleon and sent him to Elba. Their armies and the main part of the Royal Navy units were ready to seize the American cities that remained free from assault, crush the little nation into submission.

It was with such knowledge that Master-Commandant Johnston Blakely kept *Wasp* at sea. She was another of the new 22-gun sloops, a sister ship to *Peacock* and the last of her class to be built. During a severe April gale Blakely had taken her out from Portsmouth and laid a course at once for the British Isles. *Wasp* captured fourteen prizes in a row before she met H.M.S. *Reindeer* on June 28, 1814.

Reindeer was an 18-gun brig under the effective command of Captain William Manners. The ships sighted each other right after dawn and maneuvered in light airs until after three o'clock in the afternoon, when *Reindeer,* holding the weather gauge, came down on *Wasp* and engaged.

The men aboard *Wasp* had long hours to pass while they waited for the first broadside to relieve the frightful pressure upon their nerves. They were able to ponder exactly why they were here and what the result of this action might mean to them and to their country.

Nearly all of them were New Englanders. They had learned in early boyhood the hard facts of seagoing, taught by their fathers and grandfathers. Although they were young—their average age was twenty-three—they had few illusions left about the odds in this war. They realized just as well as Blakely and the rest of the *Wasp's* officers that the American Navy could never defeat the Royal Navy. It was certain to be defeated because of ship size, inferior numbers, manpower and armament. But vessels like *Wasp*, cruising independently, taking great, constant chances of capture or annihilation, could wreak profound harm upon the sea trade that was so vital to Great Britain.

Great Britain was being hurt where she felt the pain the most, right in her pocketbook. And she would not pay the price indefinitely. Her merchants would force peace talk in Parliament after they had brought enough inside influence to bear on the Admiralty.

The crew of *Wasp* went into action with great eagerness. Their minds were made up and clear of doubt. They did not welcome battle, but they wished to get done with it, finish the war and, most secret dream of all, return home to peace.

They were met by a crack crew aboard *Reindeer,* a crew proud of the fact that practically all of them came from Plymouth, which had sent so many ships' crews and colonists to the New World in the very early days. The war had come full, cruel circle. Here cousin fought not too distant cousin for a cause neither was willing to relinquish without decisive battle.

Reindeer opened fire with her stubby 12-pound carronades, guns that created terrible damage at short range. *Wasp* could not bring her guns to bear while on the original battle course she steered, took the British broadsides without reply. Blakely trimmed sail, though, and *Wasp* gathered headway and came over on the other tack. He was finally in broadside position; *Wasp's* main battery gunners fired in unison.

The American broadside cut through *Reindeer* like an immense iron flail. It was delivered in line with her gunports. They were battered out of her, and with them her heavy guns. The gun crews were killed, wounded or stood gaping-mouthed, with no weapons to serve. Captain Manners recognized the degree of her damage; he had little time left. Before headway was lost to her he hauled *Reindeer* around and rammed her bowsprit over *Wasp's* quarter, locked the ships together.

It was handystrokes after that for nineteen minutes. The British boarded *Wasp* with the cutlass as their weapon. They were repelled by men who fought with knives, cutlasses, pistols, belaying pins, handspikes and anything that could be lifted and was hard. Sharpshooters were busy in the fighting tops. American fire drubbed the quarter deck of *Reindeer* with concerted volleys; the Marines took Captain Manners as a target, and they found him. He was killed by several bullets that penetrated his brain.

The officer who was second in command aboard *Reindeer* surrendered soon after Manners was killed. There was no sense in further action. *Reindeer* had lost twenty-five dead and forty-two wounded. The casualties aboard *Wasp* were much less: five dead and twenty-one wounded, most of the latter during the handystrokes. It had been one of the bloodiest cutlass fights of the war.

Wasp separated immediately from *Reindeer*. With this scored against him in London, a good part of the Home Fleet would be out after him, Master-Commandant Blakely knew. He sailed the sloop south and repaired her damage as best he could at sea, drilled her taut, shore-hungry crew for hours on end. Then she met on September 1 in the open Atlantic a Royal Navy brig sent to search for her. The brig was named *Avon,* and *Wasp* took her and sank her.

Three weeks later she put into Madeira. A pair of British merchant ships were in the harbor. *Wasp* made prizes of them and left port, headed out into the South Atlantic. She was not seen again, or reported, and must have been lost with all hands.

The war dragged dreadfully on along the American coast. The handsome Connecticut towns, Essex, New London and Fairfield among them, which had been burned in the Revolution were once more destroyed, and Stonington was battered in an unsuccessful sea attack. A British expeditionary force went up the Chesapeake to seize Washington and landed an army. The force was delayed on the way to the capital by a battle fought at a town called Bladensburg. Here Captain Joshua Barney again distinguished himself when he covered the American retreat with 400 sailors and Marines who manned shore battery cannon. They fought until they were taken at bayonet point. Barney was wounded, and it was the third time that he had been captured by the British.

The British, moving on, seized and burned Washington, but failed to take Baltimore. Determined defense at Fort McHenry defeated them. The troops were returned to their transports and left the Chesapeake. It was almost the end of the land assaults. The futile and tragic attack upon New Orleans on January 8, 1815, two weeks after the armistice had been signed, was the last.

Great Britain had been halted by the slow, steady drain of pounds, shillings and pence. Her merchant ship losses were enormous. She had taken from her by American seizure or destruction a total of 1,334 vessels. Her blockade of the American coast had been very effective, but American seamen had thoroughly blockaded Britain.

There had been throughout the war 513 American ships registered as privateers. They had played a great part in the victory. *Yankee,* sailing out of Bristol, Rhode Island, was reported to have taken forty prizes worth $3 million; and right behind her were *Grand Turk* of Wiscasset, Maine, and *Scourge* of New York, and *Rattlesnake* of Philadelphia, and *Neufchatel, Lion* and *Chasseur* of Baltimore.

The Navy had also gathered a very valuable bag of British ships. Captain David Porter in the 32-gun frigate *Essex* had ranged the South Atlantic, then the Pacific as far as the Marquesas. He had captured or burned or sunk a total of more than forty cargo ships or whalers when *Essex* was taken on March 28, 1814, in a severe fight outside Valparaiso, Chile.

Men like Porter, men like those in *Wasp,* in *Constitution,* in the privateers, lonely, desperate, proud, had finally been vindicated in their theory of sea warfare. It was not the best, they had recognized some time ago. But under the circumstances it was the only one they could use against the British. And with some luck and a fair amount of seamanship they had fought Johnny Bull to a standstill. Now they would go home and settle down to peacetime sailing, if their wives did not insist they swallow the anchor.

The issues had still been unclear when the peace was signed. Nothing seemed to have been gained by either side, and a great deal lost, including many fine men and ships. But it was the last time Americans would fight British. It could never happen again; there was too much respect between them. The survivors understood and told their wives and families. That, after all, meant both sides had won a real victory.

CHAPTER NINETEEN

THE END OF AN ERA

The return to peace brought expanded trade with the Continent and the Orient and new accomplishments for America as a seagoing nation. New England whalers began to explore the Pacific grounds, and a fleet of Stonington sealers worked the Antarctic waters south of Cape Horn and the Juan Fernández island group off Chile. The spice trade had lasted only a few years, but tea and fine porcelain ware and silk and nankeen from China took its place as homeward-bound cargo. Fast new ships, of a relatively flat-bottomed design so that they could clear the bars at the entrance of the Mississippi River, ran out of New York to New Orleans in general cargo, then to Europe with baled cotton for the English and French mills.

These vessels were called packets, and they maintained regular runs during the 1830's and '40's. Passenger traffic was also expanding, with a good part of the Atlantic trade held by British shipping companies. American yards were steadily turning out vessels of a more advanced design that was soon to emerge as the clipper ship.

Slavers continued in operation; they ran more or less surreptitiously to the Guinea coast in that most evil of all trades. They were mainly owned by Rhode Island and New York men, and the brutally foul practices of the trade are so well-known that they need not be repeated here. But it should be known that a tragic and ironic phase of slave-running was the fact that it gave very remunerative employment to several excellent Baltimore naval architects.

When slave-running was finally stopped in the United States in the years prior to the Civil War, these men gave up American citizenship in order to retain their lucrative connections with the slavers. They moved, some of them, to Cuba, and others to Brazil. They "went foreign," in the current sailors' phrase, and stayed that way long after slavery had passed.

The booming, almost fantastically profitable, China-side trade inspired in 1843 the first clipper ship of extremely radical design. She was *Rainbow,* and she ran out to Canton from New York in 92 days, and back in 88, with the world's speed record and great reward for her owners, Howland and Aspinwall. Then, in 1849, the California gold rush started, and clippers were in absolute ascendancy.

The clipper ship story has been told many times. It marked the peak of American seamanship and maritime supremacy. The type, as built in American yards by Donald McKay and John Willis Griffiths and other leading naval architects, was the fastest and most beautiful sailing vessel ever to take to the water. With the clipper ship American merchants were able to beat the British to the best markets with top quality Chinese tea. A ship like McKay's superlative beauty, *Flying Cloud,* could make her cost in a voyage or two.

But for all their speed and ability, American clipper ships had one serious handicap. Built out of soft pine, designed to carry enormous spreads of canvas, and driven fiercely by their masters, they soon broke up, unable to take the strain.

At the same time, another development threatened America's role as a seagoing power. With the opening up of the interior in the decades following the War of 1812 young men began to turn their backs on the sea and move west to seek their fortune on the fabulous plains, among the great, coiling rivers and the mountains, beyond which lay gold. The United States was no longer a small coastal nation, hemmed in on the west by forest and mountain barriers, dependent on the sea for survival and profit. Now it was a vast land of endless opportunity.

Foreign-born crews were brought into the American ships. Mates, harassed and overworked, often with sailors who only understood a part of the orders given, began to go armed. They carried brass knuckles and pistols, had quick recourse to belaying pins. American-born seamen would not accept such treatment; they left the ships and failed to come back.

Whaling had gradually lost its sources of profit as the beasts were slaughtered indiscriminately and driven into remote regions of the oceans. Nantucket could no longer be considered a whaling port, nor New Bedford, Salem, Sag Harbor. Ships deteriorated as profits shrank, and to serve aboard a whaler was no more a mark of distinction for an ambitious young man. He packed his gear, not for sea, but for the long hike West. When in the Civil War whaling ships filled with rock ballast were sunk in an attempt to block Southern ports and the rest were captured and burned by Confederate raiders in the far Pacific, the trade was all but finished, and after the discovery of oil in 1859, never afterward flourished.

The death knell for the American merchant marine was sounded as early as 1838, and it was the role of the Boston merchants, men with nine and ten generations of sea experience behind them, to ignore what was certainly manifest destiny for them and their children's children if they were to continue to make their living from maritime trade. In 1838 several shipping companies in the United Kingdom introduced steam as a means of propulsion and durable iron plate as hull material.

Samuel Cunard, with the mail subsidy support of the British government, started a line of steamers in 1840 that plied between Halifax, Boston and Liverpool on a regularly scheduled triangular run. The Boston mercantile brahmins first scoffed at Cunard and his "tea kettles," then accepted him because, demonstrably, he would bring money into the port. They gave several champagne-enlivened banquets for Cunard. They went further, and when Boston harbor froze solid in a severe cold period, paid for a channel to be cleared so that one of Cunard's steamers could sail and maintain schedule.

Then they went again to their usual affairs, and all but forgot about

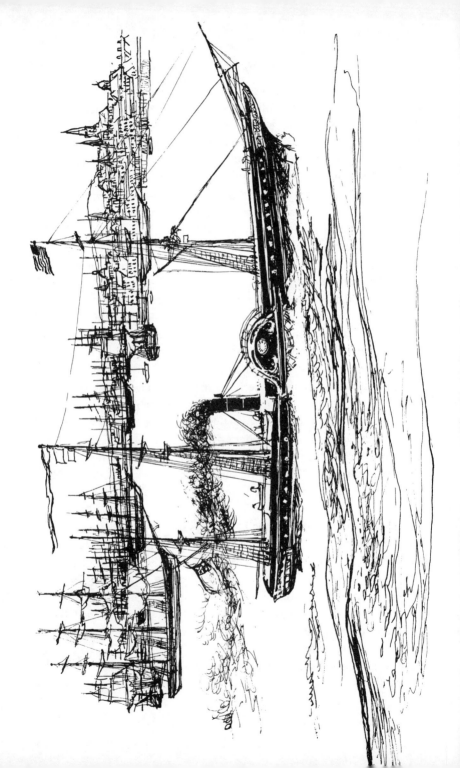

Cunard. They were engrossed with McKay's plans for the next extreme clipper, which bolstered their pride and their sense of national superiority. A ship like McKay's matchless creation, *Flying Cloud,* could soon repay her owners. The merchants told themselves that the British, still their keen opponents in sea trade, had no comparable vessels. The McKay ships were the finest vessels ever on the sea, and what if they were expensive to operate? They could be made to carry more canvas and the hulls take further extreme design. The dream was almost blinding in its brilliance. It hid the fact that because of their short lives most of the clippers did not pay, despite their speed. To his credit McKay, toward the end of his career, started to create plans for iron-hulled ships, but he was too late. The realization that after more than two hundred years America had lost her place as a leading maritime power was long and hard in coming.

Yet the heritage left by the early New Englanders and the sea-minded men whom they influenced during their time of dominance was a splendid one. It demanded fine seamanship, initiative, unorthodox tactics in emergency and considerable courage, and it showed to advantage in war and peace in later American history. The exploits of the American Navy in the Civil War, Spanish American War, World War I and particularly World War II are legendary. The great achievements of the American Merchant Marine during World War II, when American flagships were sent upon courses that traversed every ocean and against determined enemies, was in the great tradition of the early mariners who set out from the new continent in small ships and conquered the sea under sail.

SUGGESTED READING

Abbott, Charles, Rt. Hon., *A Treatise of the Law, Relative to Merchant Ships and Seamen*

Adams, James Truslow, *The Founding of New England*

Albion, Robert G., *The Rise of the Port of New York*

Andrews, Charles M., *The Colonial Period of American History* (4 vols.)

Anthony, Irvin, *Down to the Sea in Ships*

———, *Ralegh and His World*

Barrett, Amos, Capt., *An Account of the Battle of Concord*

Beck, Horace P., *The American as a Sea-fighter in Colonial Times*

Bengsston, Frans G., *The Long Ship*

Blanchard, Fessenden S., *Ghost Towns of New England*

Brooks, Van Wyck, *The Flowering of New England*

Bryant, Samuel W., *The Sea and the States*

Carmer, Carl, *The Hudson*

Chambers, Robert, *The Man They Hanged*

Chapelle, Howard Irving, *The Baltimore Clipper; The History of the American Sailing Navy; The History of American Sailing Ships*

Chatterton, E. Keble, *Sailing Ships*

Cleveland, Richard J., *Voyages and Commercial Enterprises of the Sons of New England*

Coffin, Robert P. Tristram, *Kennebec, Cradle of Americans*

Coggeshall, George, *History of the American Privateers and Letters of Marque*

Collections of the Massachusetts Historical Society, Vol. I, 3rd Series

Collections and Proceedings of the Maine Historical Society, Series I, Vol. I, p. 302; Series I, Vol. III, pp. 314, 355, 356, 358, 362, 373, 377, 381, 399, 402, 409, 413, 420, 433-34; Series I, Vol. V, 370n., Vol. VI, p. 191

Cranwell, John Phillips, and William Bowers Crane, *Men of Marque*

Cruikshank, E. A., Brig. Gen., *The Life of Sir Henry Morgan*

Curtiss, John S., *The Sloops of the Hudson*

Dana, Richard Henry, Jr., *The Seaman's Friend*

Earle, Alice Morse, *Child Life in Colonial Days*

Ellis, George E., *The Puritan Age and Rule in the Colony of the Massachusetts Bay, 1629–1685*

Exquemelin, Alexandre Olivier, *History of the Buccaneers of America*

Fiske, Amos K., *The West Indies*

Fitzpatrick, John C., *The Spirit of the Revolution*

Funck-Brentano, Frantz L., *L'Ile de la Tortue*

Gerson, Noel B., *Port Royal*

Haring, C. H., *The Buccaneers in the West Indies in the 17th Century*

Harlow, Vincent T., *Barbadoes 1625–1685*

Hart, Albert Bushnell, editor, *Commonwealth History of Massachusetts* (5 vols.)

Hawthorne, Nathaniel, *Yarn of a Yankee Privateer*

Hill, Ralph Nading, *Yankee Kingdom*

Howe, George, *Mount Hope*

——, *Salt Rivers of the Massachusetts Shore*

Long Island Forum, article, "John Lyon Gardiner," Part II, July, 1960

Loomis, Alfred F., *Ranging the Maine Coast*

Martin, Joseph Plumb, *Private Yankee Doodle,* edited by George F. Scheer

Masefield, John, *On the Spanish Maine*

Mitchell, Edwin Valentine, *Anchor to Windward*

Morison, Samuel Eliot, *Builders of the Bay Colony*

——, *John Paul Jones*

——, *The Intellectual Life of Colonial New England*

——, *The Maritime History of Massachusetts*

Morris, Richard B., *Encyclopedia of American History*

Mowrer, Lillian T., *The Indomitable John Scott*

Nickalls, John L., *The Journal of George Fox*

Osgood, Herbert S., *The American Colonies in the 18th Century*

Outhwaite, Leonard, *The Atlantic*

Overton, Jacqueline, *Long Island's Story*

Paine, Ralph D., *The Ships and Sailors of Old Salem*

Payne, Robert, *The Island*

Phillips, James Duncan, *Salem in the Seventeenth Century*

Phillips, Paul Chrisler, *The Fur Trade* (20 vols.)

Platt, Rutherford, *Wilderness*

Roberts, Kenneth, *Northwest Passage*

Roscoe, Theodore, and Freeman, Fred, *Picture History of the U.S. Navy*

Roosevelt, Theodore, *The Naval War of 1812*

Rowse, A. L., *The Elizabethans and America*

————, *The English Past*

Russell, Phillips, *John Paul Jones*

Sawtelle, William Otis, *Maine's Historical Trails and Waterways*

Semmes, Raphael, "Captains and Mariners of Early Maryland"; "Ships and Shipping," pamphlets printed for the State Street Trust Co., Boston, Mass.

Southey, Thomas, *Chronological History of the West Indies*

Spears, John R., *The Story of the American Merchant Marine*

————, *The Story of New England Whalers*

Tebbell, John, editor of *The Battle for North America,* from the works of Francis Parkman

Wedgwood, C. V., *The King's Peace*

Wilgus, A. Curtis, *The Development of Hispanic America*

INDEX